Archaeology beyond Postmodernity

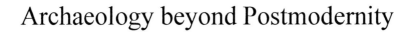

Archaeology in Society Series

Series Editors
Ian Hodder, Stanford University
Robert W. Preucel, University of Pennsylvania

In recent decades, archaeology has expanded beyond a narrow focus on economics and environmental adaptation to address issues of ideology, power, and meaning. These trends, sometimes termed "postprocessual," deal with both the interpretation of the past and the complex and politically charged interrelationships of past and present. Today, archaeology is responding to and incorporating aspects of the debates on identity, meaning, and politics currently being explored in varying fields: social anthropology, sociology, geography, history, linguistics, and psychology. There is a growing realization that ancient studies and material culture can be aligned within the contemporary construction of identities under the rubrics of nationalism, ethnoscapes, and globalization. This international series will help connect the contemporary practice of archaeology with these trends in research and, in the process, demonstrate the relevance of archaeology to related fields and society in general.

Volumes in This Series

Archaeology beyond Postmodernity

A Science of the Social

Andrew M. Martin

ALTAMIRA
PRESS
A division of
ROWMAN & LITTLEFIELD PUBLISHERS, INC.
Lanham • New York • Toronto • Plymouth, UK

Published by AltaMira Press
A division of The Rowman & Littlefield Publishing Group, Inc.
A wholly owned subsidary of The Rowman & Littlefield Publishing Group, Inc.
4501 Forbes Boulevard, Suite 200, Lanham, Maryland 20706
www.rowman.com

10 Thornbury Road, Plymouth PL6 7PP, United Kingdom

British Library Cataloguing in Publication Information Available

Library of Congress Cataloging-in-Publication Data

Martin, Andrew M., 1973–
Archaeology beyond postmodernity : a science of the social / Andrew M. Martin.
pages cm. — (Archaeology in society series)
Includes bibliographical references and index.
ISBN 978-0-7591-2357-1 (cloth : alk. paper) — ISBN 978-0-7591-2358-8 (electronic)
1. Archaeology—Philosophy. 2. Archaeology—Methodology. 3. Social archaeology—Methodology.
4. Interdisciplinary approach to knowledge. 5. Archaeology and history. I. Title.
CC72.M38 2013
930.1—dc23
2013011636

∞™ The paper used in this publication meets the minimum requirements of American
National Standard for Information Sciences Permanence of Paper for Printed Library
Materials, ANSI/NISO Z39.48-1992.

Printed in the United States of America

To Adèle

Contents

Acknowledgments

The extent of my gratitude for all the support that has enabled me to research and write this book cannot be easily expressed in a short section. I am very grateful to those at Cambridge University who encouraged me to write it, including Robin Boast, Ian Hodder, John Robb, and Colin Renfrew, all of whom provided much support during my postdoctorate research there. I must thank the Wiltshire Museum for employing me to catalog and photograph their immense Bronze Age collections, a job that I still cannot believe they paid me for. I am also grateful to Bournemouth University for giving me a research fellowship that provided the resources to finish the book and enabled me to participate in one of the most actively engaged departments that study the Early Bronze Age. Tim Darvill's encouragement, insights, and help in reading sections of the book were invaluable, as were down-to-earth discussions with John Gale and others during and after burial mound excavations.

Many others have helped to read sections of the book and have offered valuable advice. Thanks to Bruno Latour for his comments and suggestions, to physicist Herb Sterling for reading through the sections on scientific method, to Kate Ness for reviewing the archaeological chapters, to John Robb for reading the theory sections, and to Ian Hodder and Bob Pruecel for their many suggestions. Many thanks to the Wiltshire Museum, the Prehistoric Society, the Illinois Archaeological Survey, the Gilcrease Museum, and the Center for American Archaeology for permission to publish images from their collections and journals, and to Springer and Oxbow Books for allowing me to republish sections of previous articles for chapters 6 and 7. Finally, I would never have been able to write this book without the constant encouragement and loving support of my wife, Adèle.

Introduction

It is often a pleasant surprise when we realize that archaeology is not an island cut off from other disciplines, but that our friends and colleagues in the next department down the hall are actually having the same debates we are having. It used to be that this realization was limited to an accidental passing conversation. However, today it is quite clear from any search on the internet that many core problems in archaeology are shared by most if not all of the social sciences. The most striking realization is that a common thread runs through many of these debates. Most debates often boil down to the question "how can we say anything about human actions in the past with assurance?"

It is clear that this question has spawned thousands of debates across the social sciences. On the one hand, realists argue that we should reason only from what we can observe (modernist analytical philosophy), and therefore we should stick to science and scientifically proven materialist theories rather than social theories to understand human actions. On the other hand, idealists argue that human actions are the result of human consciousness or power-play (postmodern continental philosophy), and therefore we can only really reason from psychological or social theories. However, this postmodern negation of the ability to reason from what we observe is merely the result of taking a modernist line of reasoning (that created a division between nature and society) to its extreme. By creating more divisions—between cultures, subcultures, and even individuals, postmodernists have reasoned that not only are we different from nature, but we are also different from each other. Therefore we can never hope to understand actions scientifically and can only provide an eclectic range of possible analogies and social theories to explain them.

Yet, such extreme positions are problematic because they rarely allow a solution to debates to be found. Phenomenology, Heidegger's notion of *Being*, and cognitive science are just a few solutions that have attempted to reconcile the two positions, but while coming close, none have actually managed to overcome the dichotomy altogether.

The most recent solution for many in the social sciences and within archaeology has been to combine social theory with scientific techniques. Over the past fifteen years social archaeologists have embraced an armory of scientific applications for their analyses. In addition to the increased use of radiocarbon and other dating methods, numerous scientific analyses have been devised: artifact analyses to identify materials and their sources, bone analyses to identify the material biographies of individuals, environmental analyses to reconstruct past landscapes, and geophysical analyses to identify buried features and to understand their surroundings. Yet in order to reconstruct past human activities, the pieces of secure data gained from these analyses must still be linked together with a social theory—an effort that comes with all its attendant postmodern assumptions that deny the scientific validity of the reconstruction.

Combining such assumptions with scientific results has therefore not been wildly successful, and it seems like the same problems and divisions between modern analytical philosophy and postmodern social theory remain and cause contention. At the end of 2010, the American Anthropological Association (AAA), an organization that represents archaeology as well as anthropology in the United States, removed all references to "science" from its mission statement and replaced them with "public understanding," causing an enormous outcry from scientists. Apart from the AAA apparently denying the validity of anthropological and archaeological science, anthropology and archaeology departments in the United States and United Kingdom have continued to split over the issue of science, creating bad blood between colleagues. The need to end this warfare and find a solution has never been more important, especially for anthropology, but also for our own discipline of archaeology.

Anthropology, for instance, has found itself increasingly limited in terms of what it can say given its postmodern stance. The postmodern or poststructuralist notion that our interpretations are situated and that we can comprehend other cultures only through a dense fog of cultural filters between "us" and "them" has meant that anthropological practice has been on shaky ground for quite some time. While anthropologists have usually put up with this critique, in recent years numerous native people have entered graduate and postgraduate education in anthropology and can now publish their own (less filtered) explanations of their societies. This has left many Anglo-American anthropologists with less and less of a justification for practicing their profession. While archaeologists have not encountered problems on this scale, largely due to the inability of the dead to protest our interpretation of them, many archaeologists studying the archaeology of a current indigenous people have also had a tough time justifying their interpretations. In both cases, it is clear that a serious problem exists in the ability of Western academics to justify their interpretation of other cultures.

The very real threat of oblivion for much of anthropology has forced many to reconsider their perspectives and actively seek alternative approaches that can provide a more secure basis for interpretations. Although archaeologists do not have the same threat to their existence, funding for archaeological research has increasingly required a more scientific approach to interpretations, while social theories and ethnographic analogies have become less and less popular for use in interpretation

(Thomas 2004, 241; Holbraad 2009). This has already led many to seek different approaches to archaeology, but not so far as to readdress postmodern assumptions. Yet, in a similar way to anthropology, a reevaluation of such assumptions may be necessary in archaeology as well.

The theme of the 2009 annual meeting of the American Anthropology Association, entitled "The End/s of Anthropology," was to salvage the approaches that had enduring value, propose projects that anthropology could safely study, and redefine cultural relativism, among other assumptions (Jackson and Thomas 2008). Coming from the AAA, this third objective was surprising since cultural relativism is one of anthropology's central tenets (ibid.), but it was a measure of the desperation of a field in search of legitimacy. Along with the acknowledgment that relativism has eroded the legitimacy of anthropology—and as a result, anthropologists' role as cultural critics of foreign policy (ibid.)—many have also realized that cultural relativism has also legitimized several destructive elements in our society (Brown 2008; Boudon 2004; Li 2006).

For instance, cultural relativist critique is now used by global warming skeptics, creationists, and conspiracy theorists to deny facts established by science, facts which help and may save lives. In political wrangling over global warming, Republicans now coach lobbyists to "make the lack of scientific certainty a primary issue," using poststructuralist arguments to undermine global warming science (Luntz 2003, 137 in Latour 2004b). The eminent professor and social constructivist Steve Fuller has now written several books and actually testified in court in support of teaching Intelligent Design in schools, using poststructuralism to claim that science is a cultural imposition. And in an oft-quoted essay by philosopher of science Bruno Latour, entitled "Why Has Critique Run out of Steam?" Latour writes, "What has become of critique when my neighbor in the little Bourbonnais village where I have my house looks down on me as someone hopelessly naïve because I believe that the United States had been struck by terrorist attacks?" (Latour 2004b, 228).

The AAA's objectives—to salvage anthropological approaches, to find projects that can be safely studied, and to re-evaluate cultural relativism—have been a constant presence in Latour's work for several decades. This may be why Latour is one of the most influential philosophers in anthropology today. While many others have provided anthropology with needed energy and ideas in the last ten years (Philippe Descola, Eduardo Viveiros de Castro, Martin Holbraad, Tim Ingold, et al.), Latour's ideas are imprinted on many of these new approaches, illustrating his impact on a range of emerging solutions.

Latour has the advantage of having had a head start on most of anthropology since he identified problems with postmodernism as early as the 1970s. This was the result of being one of the first to try to apply social theories to individuals who could actively object—in his case, people working in science. Latour writes, in a talk to anthropologists:

> My contribution to anthropology can be summed up by a sentence
> written exactly thirty years ago. . . . "To apply ethnographic methods to
> scientific practice." . . .
>
> Everything I learnt during two years' [anthropological] fieldwork
> in Abidjan seemed pretty useless after two days in the Roger Guillemin
> laboratory at the Salk Institute [in California], not to mention the use-
> lessness of my five years of epistemology courses. . . . I must admit I
> still haven't got over this event. You can't go very far with ritual–
> myth–symbol in a laboratory. . . .
>
> But anyway, one of two things: either the Californian researchers
> managed to extract themselves from the narrow prison of their cultures
> in order to access nature, and that would explain why ideas imported
> from Africa to study cultures in the plural could not work. Or . . . or . . .
>
> And I hesitate to continue with this second branch of the alternative
> in front of such an inner sanctum of anthropologists, the reasons given
> for the existence of cultures in the plural were not, after all, all that
> powerful. . . . If anthropological explanations, once they are applied to
> the exact sciences, give such an impression of incongruity, weakness,
> even of foolishness, it is perhaps because the occasion to become aware
> of the weakness is lacking under tropical conditions, but hits you full in
> the face in the Californian air-conditioned rooms. (Latour 2007, 14)

In the same way, one can be sure that *if* anthropologists have had a
hard time becoming aware of the weakness of their social theories, despite their informants objecting to them right in front of them, archaeologists (left to themselves) will have an even harder time becoming aware
of the weakness of their social theories. Therefore, anthropologists of
science have done us a great favor as well.

More importantly, anthropologists of science awakened a newfound
respect for science in social theorists. It was apparent that science did a
much better job at describing the world than anthropologists did. As a
result, Latour and his newly formed discipline, science studies, have investigated for over thirty years the process of scientific practice in order
to understand how social science can become more scientific. Tired with
the way social scientists superficially mimicked scientific techniques—
applying statistical tests without understanding and adapting to the differences in data—they strove to pare down scientific practice to its essential processes. Their translation of scientific techniques into social scientific techniques has developed over the years as scientific practice has become better understood, but it was clear from a very early stage that
science was a very different process from that which it claimed to be, or
from that which the social sciences thought it was and tried to mimic.

For example, during the laboratory analysis that Latour studied at the
Salk Institute in San Diego, a substance was being defined through tests
(Latour and Woolgar 1979). The characterization of this substance (the
TRH growth hormone) involved finding funding, setting up a laboratory
with instruments and staff, selecting hundreds of elements to test the

substance with, observing its reactions to elements through instruments, reducing the observations to symbols and equations of relationships, and combining the symbols with other known relationships to create formulas that were then published in a scientific journal.

The traditional (realist) view of this process would be that man is merely a facilitator for the expression of the natural world—a transparency through which the natural world is seen. The sociological (idealist) view of this process would be that man views the natural world through the filters of his culture, his upbringing, his sex, ethnicity, age, etc. As a result, the published formulas are either seen as "natural" and solid facts (if they are proven true and not falsified) from a realist point of view, or as "cultural" and contingent fictions, viewed from a sociological perspective. However, in both cases the actual process through which they were developed is less important because it is seen as merely the means to the "natural" or "cultural" end-product. Both these philosophies of knowledge are problematic because if characterizations of things are seen as "natural" or "cultural" and the process behind them is largely ignored, then characterizations end up being badly misrepresented.

For realists, by reifying or "black-boxing" scientific formulas as '"natural" after their acceptance, and by ignoring their process of development, it is almost impossible to describe the local character of particular entities except in universal terms. It also makes it difficult to continue augmenting understandings, unless they cease to work and need reevaluating. Yet, a change in any one element in the supporting network of facts, or the addition of a relationship, has the potential to change the characterization of the object. As countless developments in scientific knowledge prove, characterizations of objects often change with new information or tests. Without the knowledge of what exactly has gone into their development, and by claiming characterizations as "natural," it is difficult for them to be easily updated. Preserving the history of objects makes it easier for the process of information accumulation, reduction, and combination that went into characterizing objects to continue long after those characterizations or explanations have been published, instead of being stopped prematurely to meet publication deadlines.

For idealists, by calling scientific formulas "cultural," and ignoring their process of development, problems also arise when trying to explain objects. By neglecting the selection of elements to test the object, the instruments used to understand them, the many tests, the referenced material and established theories needed to substantiate claims, idealists fail to explain how formulas gain the power to explain and predict the natural world. They also have a difficult time explaining scientific change.

However, Latour realized that the same problems exist when these different philosophies of knowledge are applied to understand the social world. If social objects or actions are perceived as either "natural" or "cultural," the local processes through which they came to be expressed are also ignored as superfluous. This means that the reasons why social objects and practices change and the reasons why they are so powerful are also often missed.

In addition to highlighting problems with basic anthropological approaches and traditional assumptions, which I've touched on above, the anthropology of science (and Latour in particular) has had an even more significant impact on social-scientific methodology. This is because the social sciences have based their methodologies largely upon traditional understandings of scientific method. Any significant development in the understanding of scientific method, therefore, has a huge impact on the methodology of social scientists.

The problem with social-scientific methodology, Latour writes, is that it often imitates a superficial view of the natural sciences. "It is the attempt at imitating a false view of the natural sciences that bogs down the social ones" (Latour 2005, 137). By largely ignoring the *process* of scientific practice—in seeing it as merely a means to a "natural" end—much has been missed in the understanding of scientific methodology. In order to understand scientific practice better, Latour and his colleagues in science studies have focused purely on the processes of characterization and development of scientific and technological formulas. By understanding how scientists and instruments translate observations and relationships into expressions, these scientific methods were able to be rendered into sociological techniques. The methods they used to follow this process were merely translations of the methods and instruments they studied, but instead of translations based upon philosophies of knowledge that largely misrepresented characterizations, these methods followed the actual practice of science.

The essence of these methods is to follow the actions and reactions of the object under study as it is subjected to various tests. As vast amounts of information from tests are accumulated, that information must be reduced, and reduced again, through increasingly compressed descriptions that detail the relationships between the object and various phenomena juxtaposed with it (including the relationships previously established for those phenomena). This enables a lot of information to be observed in a small space and thus allows the observer to come to conclusions (or formulas) about the object. The use of instruments to assess reactions, compress information, and present it in compact descriptive forms merely provides other ways to observe this vast amount of descriptive information in a small space.

While this is a very abstract portrayal of scientific practice (and is described later in more detail), it illustrates the difference between Latour and other descriptions of science. Rather than seeing scientific practice as the formulation of a theory or hypothesis that is then tested (Popper [1934] 1959), Latour characterizes scientific practice as the constant testing of objects through the juxtaposition of associations and the reduction of information about their relationships. This also helps to explain why hypotheses usually continue to be modified with additional information and not thrown out if they are "falsified." As a type of descriptive activity, it becomes one that the social sciences can engage in as well, as long as, as in science, the rigid rules of engagement are followed. These are outlined later on, but they essentially limit all description to what the object (or subject) "does" or does not "do" under certain conditions. This is Latour's definition of objectivity—to allow the object (or subject) to "object."

Latour's focus on the process of characterization also helps to understand the relational nature of objects. If formulas are the objects of science, then objects are seen as comprising numerous relationships in a network that led to their existence. Objects start to appear like asterisks with multiple lines connecting them to specific historical events, places, other materials, other objects, theories, people, etc.—all of which were necessary for the object's characterization.

RAMIFICATIONS FOR ARCHAEOLOGY

Inevitably the insights gained by Latour and his colleagues have had a direct impact on social-scientific practice, and for our purposes, on archaeological practice. Several archaeologists have embraced this new understanding of scientific practice as a way to enhance the practice of archaeology and have offered new media and techniques to implement this alternative understanding in archaeological fieldwork (Pearson and Shanks 2001; Witmore 2004, 2006; Webmoor 2007). Others have advocated Latour's interpretive methodology (Actor-Network Theory) for interpretation (Olsen 2003, 2010; Knappett 2005; Knappett and Malafouris 2008; Dolwick 2009; Hodder 2012). Yet few have actually applied it or provided an explanation of how it might be applied to study the archaeological record.

The reason for this lack of applications might be that while Latour's ideas have met with great enthusiasm in archaeology, they run contrary to many assumptions of modernism and postmodernism and therefore have also met with great confusion. Because our discipline is fundamentally dependent upon theories, and new theories function chiefly to supplement existing theories, Latour's philosophy has been adopted and added to theories and methodologies that are based upon a dichotomy between nature and society—precisely the dichotomy that Latour rejects. Such a fusion has the result of creating contradictions.

Supplementation may be fine for theories that are built on similar premises, but grafting Latour's philosophy onto social theories of Pierre Bourdieu, Anthony Giddens, or Martin Heidegger can only produce a problematic approach that would never have been reached through logical reasoning (Latour 1993, 2005; Latour et al. 2011). Because Latour is critical of traditional descriptions of science (like many postmodernists), he is often assumed to be postmodernist too, and his ideas have consequently been used to adorn those of postmodernists. But considering that Latour focuses most of his criticism on these and other postmodernist theorists (Latour 1993, 55–67; 1999, 7–10; 2004b), while praising the way that scientists actually practice science, it is safe to say that he would be much more comfortable on the side of science in any debate between science and postmodernism.

From this misunderstanding stem most of the problems with the application of Latour's ideas in the social sciences and in archaeology. Over time, Actor-Network Theory (ANT), a theory loosely based on Latour's philosophy, has taken on a life of its own, infused with postmodern ideas. In the social sciences it has generally been used as a postmodern theory such as Giddens' Structuration Theory or Bourdieu's habitus—as an alternative description of the form that objects take. After ANT grew very different from Latour's philosophy in its usage, Latour disowned the theory in 1997 and tried to rehabilitate it in 2005, after ANT continued to be misused and misrepresented as his own (Latour 2005). The problem with it was that his term "actor" was seen as a human or non-human *micro* entity, and his term "network" as a *macro* entity. Actor-network "theory" was then conceived as a way to oscillate between micro and macro scales, an enterprise central to postmodernism but one that Latour had purposely abandoned in the 1970s (Latour 1996; 2005). Yet Latour's "actors" and "networks" are essentially the same thing, neither micro nor macro entities—since both are local and comprised of supporting networks—and his philosophy is certainly not a theory. Because of the internet, networks are now generally seen as macro entities, or "nets" that connect objects to other related things. But Latour's original meaning of the word "network" was the series of local supports that are essential to the very existence of an object and help to make that object appear solid (Latour 1998b).

For this reason, instead of talking about actor-network *theory*—a theory that subsequently has several problems with it—I have tried to explain what Latour's *philosophy* might mean for archaeology, and what an interpretive methodology based upon it would look like. A philosophy or methodology does not try to explain or create a framework for description (like a theory), but instead provides a vehicle to help the researcher experience phenomena themselves and come to a unique explanation of them (ibid.). Latour's philosophy is not without its problems as well, and I have tried to address these problems and provide solutions throughout the book. The most common criticisms of Latour, though, are based on misunderstandings of his work (which can easily happen due to his Gallic way of expressing things). At one time or other he has been falsely accused of being a relativist by scientists (Sokal 1997) or of giving social agency to matter by social scientists (Schaffer 1991; Pickering 1995). Yet giving objects a background of multiple relations and a variety of influences is not relativist, nor does it mean giving intentionality to objects, it merely means that objects are given much more representation.

This increased representation has several interesting ramifications. Firstly, it is clear that the reductive description of everything in terms of either "nature" or "society" has molded many assumptions and techniques in archaeological theory that need to be revisited. For example, the belief that human objects and actions are "natural" or "social," and therefore need natural or social theories to interpret them, has hugely distorted the explanation of those objects and actions. By providing a less reductive definition of objects, Latour allows a more accurate description of them. Secondly, Latour's understanding of objects as completely supported by networks of associations, rather than self-supported "social" or "natural" entities, has the potential to help us understand how objects have power in society and how they change in meaning. Thirdly, the understanding of object networks has the potential to help explain the formation, composition, and change of groups of people and gives a more nuanced understanding of cultural groups or ethnicities. Fourthly, Latour's translation of natural scientific methods into a methodology for the social sciences presents archaeology with a valuable methodology for objectively studying human actions and objects without resorting to theories. The following book is an attempt to detail these ramifications and apply this methodology to two case studies—one from North America and one from Great Britain.

Chapter 1 describes the history behind the modernist dichotomy between nature and society and how this dichotomy was maintained. It also explains how the division has been perpetuated through postmodernism, and especially poststructuralism, despite avowed attempts to eradicate the split. Instead of reevaluating both the natural and cultural categories that emerged from such a division, poststructuralist sociologists have sought to remove the divide by claiming much of science and all other human activities to be purely cultural enterprises (Bloor [1976] 1991; Barnes 1974; Collins and Pinch 2005). Poststructuralist anthropologists and sociologists such as Marilyn Strathern (1992), Sarah Franklin (1997), and Donna Haraway (1985) have further argued that nature is so "assisted" by people and integrated with society that much of nature should be redefined as culture (Inglis and Bone 2006, 279)!

These accounts allow somewhat of a crossover between categories, but they leave a huge amount of untouched nature or pure science out of cultural reach and therefore maintain the distinction between nature and society. Redefining large parts of science as cultural in this way is nothing more than an attempted *coup*, and a pretty feeble one considering the huge technological advances in science. What is really needed is a redefinition of society—one that corresponds with the actual culture of science that scientists can agree with and explains the great achievements that science has wrought.

Chapter 2 examines the archaeological practice of using theories to interpret—a practice that has emanated from the problematic separation of nature from culture. While the definition of society as a separate entity from nature has long been lamented as causing enormous problems for archaeological practice and interpretation (Sian Jones 1997; Andy Jones 2002, 2007; Julian Thomas 2004), solutions have almost always been sought by bridging this divide—by combining traditional conceptions of society with traditional conceptions of nature—not through redefining them in their entirety. Yet, solutions do not come from scientists adopting sociological theories (Jones 2002, 2007; Boivin 2008) or, for that matter, from social archaeologists adopting scientific theories (Kuznar 2008). By combining these divergent concepts, problematic conceptions of both society and nature are combined, creating even more difficulties for theory and interpretation (Latour 1993, 9).

Chapter 3, therefore, lays out a more inclusive definition of objects. Since the 1990s many in the philosophy of science have argued that no theoretical juggling act that attempts to bridge the divide between nature and society will make up for the fact that no division exists (Latour 1993; Pickering 1995). Instead of trying to mend philosophical, social, and scientific theories that were based upon this false dichotomy, they have investigated what a new integrated and holistic definition of objects would mean for philosophy, and for social and scientific theory. To illustrate this definition, the third chapter first lays out Latour's understanding of how objects are created and changed, using examples from laboratory studies. This non-modern definition of objects is then compared with pre-modern conceptions of objects and object creation—which it closely parallels—using first- and third-person accounts by Native Americans and other scholars of indigenous knowledge. These examples provide new ways to perceive and approach the material record of a culture.

Chapter 4 tackles the problematic archaeological techniques that derive from the notional separation of nature from society, with a particular focus on the typological method. After examining the assumptions about society that led to the use of typology, the fourth chapter first illustrates the influence of typology on various archaeological theories and methodologies, including the perception of ethnicity and cultural groups. The assumptions behind typology are challenged and a new perception of cultural groups is then laid out, derived from Latour's understanding of groups. It is argued that without adapting typology to take in this new understanding of groups, typology will continue to perpetuate erroneous assumptions about society that are encoded into it.

Chapter 5 details the methodology used to trace networks of information encrypted into objects. This lays out the techniques of anthropologists of science, including contributions from Charles Sanders Peirce, and attempts to adapt them to the study of archaeology. By adopting an adapted version of typology, together with a method almost universally used by sociologists of science (that of studying resistance and conflict), a new methodology is presented for the study of cultural material. With these new techniques, studies have more likelihood of accessing object information and are no longer hamstrung by the modernist (and post-modernist) belief that cultures are merely self-referential (Latour 1999, 9; 2005, 146).

Chapters 6 and 7 apply an alternative concept of society to two detailed archaeological case studies—one on the Early Bronze Age burial mounds of Wessex in Great Britain and one on the Hopewell burial mounds of the Lower Illinois Valley in North America. In these two case studies, the techniques used by anthropologists of science to examine information and relationships encrypted into objects and structures are used to trace networks of information behind burial practices. These examinations provide fruitful insights into prehistoric life and objects from a valuable resource—burial practices—one that has been vastly misunderstood because of the modernist nature/culture dichotomy and therefore largely underutilized.

As many in the social sciences have come to accept that "nature" and "society" are problematic concepts, Latour's reevaluation of these concepts and his practical approaches have provided many in the social sciences with a starting point to address problems in their own disciplines and to create alternative techniques that avoid the problems created by the modernist dichotomy. In addition to anthropology, Latour's illustrations of how objects, practices, laws, and formulas are created have become increasingly relevant to many diverse fields, including sociology (Law 2004), cybernetics (Meynen 1992), law (Ewick and Silbey 1998), economics (Callon 1998; Thévenot and Boltanski 2006), and philosophy (Harman 2009). In the same way, we can benefit from Latour's evaluations and revisions and greatly improve our own theory and methodologies.

ONE

Entangled by Modernism

The eclectic nature of archaeological theory is often claimed to be one of its greatest strengths. Since there has never been a unified theory that can explain all aspects of human life, numerous theories have been promoted that deal with various aspects of existence, which are utilized depending upon the evidence at hand. Controversies between archaeologists tend to result from overlaps in the application of these theories and especially between those who advocate functionalist theories and those who advocate ideational theories for the same data. Yet, the very viability of theories has rarely been questioned. This is the question that lurks in the dark places of every archaeologist's subconsciousness.

Occasionally this question does emerge, but it is usually dealt with in two ways. Either theories are claimed as absolute, universal truths, or they are seen as contingent but necessary evils. Yet all see theories as a bastion between imposing our own subjective beliefs and not being able to understand the archaeological record at all. The ideal, of course, would be to interpret the archaeological record purely from the data obtained from the ground. However, such an attempt has long proved unattainable without a framework to identify which data is relevant from the vast amount of data available, and to provide possible interpretations of that data.

In 1986, Ian Hodder, writing about "Contextual Archaeology" in *Reading the Past*—a new method that attempted to form interpretations from the ground up—also confronted this dilemma. Hodder understood the historical contingency of the archaeological record and wanted to follow the contextual data precisely to come to contingent conclusions, but like many others before him (Binford 1982, 160; Childe 1949, 24; Taylor 1948, 143), he came up against the difficulty of choosing which dimensions of variation were relevant and which were not (Hodder 1986, 135).

As Lewis Binford often argued, without a framework to work within, it is virtually impossible to piece together an explanation from millions of pieces of disparate data. Binford writes, "We may talk of color, size, shape, number of items, association, co-variation, and all manner of other properties of the archaeological record. . . . Things are not so simple when we face the task of describing the past. . . . [T]he past is gone, mute and only recognizable as such through inference. We cannot use a 'direct' strategy of describing the past. All our experience is in the present. . . . Quite literally, our descriptions of the past are constructions" (Binford 1982, 160). For this reason, Binford strove to develop middle range theories from anthropological studies and experimental archaeology that could be "tested" on the archaeological data. These functionalist frameworks provided the relevant dimensions of variation that Binford needed. In other words, they highlighted the types of data to look for in the disparate data of the archaeological record. These middle range theories then provided hypotheses to test against that data.

In his second edition of *Reading the Past*, Hodder took a different path, arguing that "social theories" were crucial to identify the relevant dimensions of variation (Hodder 1991, 139). Yet Peter Kosso (1991) has argued that the only differences between Binford's and Hodder's solutions were the type of theories they adopted (Kosso 1991; also Binford 1982, 162). Hodder took the side of culture in opposition to Binford's concentration on nature as the sole agency behind action. Instead of functionalist, economic, or ecological theories, theories were selected from structuralism, poststructuralism, and Marxism, which saw action as derived from mental structures. The battle lines between processualism and post-processualism were formed largely along this fault line. But the theories that were selected and deemed correct by different camps in archaeology (as in the rest of social science) depended upon which theories were intuitively sensed as right, not from any actual objective reasoning (Latour 2004b, 241). These theories were then claimed as true (as opposed to the other camp's), forming the frameworks that determined which dimensions of variation were sought and outlining which explanations were valid.

However, the process through which these theories were created and universalized is not something that is found in many archaeological textbooks. Nevertheless, it is an important process to ponder before the choice to use theories is made. All archaeological theories come from somewhere—usually from an anthropological or sociological study of a contemporary culture. The process by which such studies and their explanations of local information become universal theories usually involves ignoring local ethnographic information, or the historical and contextual circumstances that influenced actions and led to their explanation, and then generalizing those actions and explanations as universal.

This process was first advocated by Emile Durkheim, the father of modern sociology, and has been followed faithfully by the social sciences ever since. Central to Durkheim's philosophy is the notion that nature is distinctly separate from society. This allowed him to carve out a niche for sociology as the science of society. Durkheim saw society as possessing its own universal laws (similar to natural laws) that determined human actions. The social sciences consequently saw their role as investigating these purported laws behind human activity. While structuralists sought cultural laws that determined human actions, functionalists sought natural laws. Unfortunately, by seeing actions as reflections of universal laws, the historical and contextual circumstances that actually influenced actions were generally seen as unimportant. The belief that nature has little influence on culture has compounded this assumption. Yet nature gives cultural actions contextual relevance and fluidity (Cajete 2000), without which cultural actions would be static and only meaningful in relation to themselves (Latour 1993, 2005). Consequently, once cultural actions are seen as purely cultural, they are seen as static and are easily universalized into laws.

When *post*structuralists questioned the validity of these "universal" laws or "social theories," it was because each culture or subculture was seen to be a separate incommensurable world, not primarily because such laws were seen to be merely local explanations of particular spatial/temporal contexts. By reasoning out from the modernist division between nature and culture and exacerbating it, they divided the world into many natures and many cultures. Thus it was argued that we can never really "know" another culture through science, nor through social science, since both observe the world through the lens of a particular culture (Latour 1999, 10). For this reason, rather than rejecting social theories, their truth didn't matter. Since theories were seen as closer to the truth than unalloyed attempts to understand the past—which would have involved imposing our own (largely unconscious) twentieth-century worldviews on "the Other"—they continued to be used, as long as they were considered together with many other theories and were offered as mere suggestions with caveats.

Nevertheless, many in anthropology, archaeology, and other social sciences have long disagreed with such relativist conclusions (Jarvie 1984, 1993; Arkes 1986; Aya 1996; Boudon 2004; Cook 1999; Li 2006; Fleming 2006; Johnson 2011; Jones 2002). Cultural relativism may have taken over our theoretical apparatus through reasoning out from the modernist nature/culture division, but that does not mean that there are not deep reservations about it. The main argument for cultural relativism was that it encouraged tolerance and internal understanding, but Michael Brown (2008) writes that instead of encouraging tolerance, cultural relativism has exaggerated differences between cultures and undermined any attempt to transcend those differences or understand them. The evidence against such incommensurability is also overwhelming. For instance, there is enough recognition among non-Western people of the value of

Western scientific logic (when conversant with it) to argue for some level of cognitive similarity between cultures (ibid.). Ernst Gellner (1985, 86) has written that "no anthropologist, to my knowledge, has come back from a field trip with the following report: their concepts are so alien that it is impossible to describe their land tenure, their kinship system, their ritual." But although many agree that cultural relativism has done much harm and has many empirical problems, few have successfully attempted to overthrow it philosophically (Brown 2008, 371).

Instead, the postmodern reaction to a sense that all is not well with this arbitrary separation of nature from society, and each culture from one another, has been to mix science and natural theories with social science and social theories (A. Jones 2002, 2007; Boivin 2008; Kuznar 2008). The result has been an eclectic approach to interpretation, treating theories like tools in a tool bag that can be selected depending upon the circumstances (Pierce 2011, 85). However, this does not avoid the problem that theories are constructed from, and applied to, local contingent actions with a history behind them.

This chapter attempts to trace how the use of theories in archaeology stemmed from the basic separation between nature and society, which has structured our ontology and made it very difficult to understand premodern cultures. But rather than eroding the last vestige of any hope in understanding the past, the discovery that nature and society have always been intertwined enables most of our practices of archaeology to continue and offers a new hope for empirical interpretation.

What is needed is not a modernist concept of society, nor a postmodern patch to fix a flawed conception, but an altogether new concept of society that takes into account the total integration of society and nature. This non-modern or pre-modern concept of society as nature/culture has long been crying out for attention from the fringes of the modernist world, but it needs articulation in Western terms, a philosophy to understand how it structures action, and a methodology to follow how it has molded the past in individual ways, in order to overcome the poststructuralist deadlock. Otherwise, we end up with merely more ethnographically defined templates to impose on the past. Fortunately, several other disciplines have long recognized the need for such an articulation and for related methodologies to describe human action. The trail has been blazed for us. All we need to do is to follow it and take up the mantle of developing some foundations along it.

THE TRAILHEAD

Occasionally evidence stands out that cannot be explained by theories, and which forces us to rethink our categories. I was fortunate (or unfortunate) enough to have been confronted with such an occasion while conducting research on the Hopewell burial mounds of Illinois in the mid-1990s. At the time, a huge range of theoretical approaches were fashionable to explain ceremonial and burial sites. Structuralist, Marxist, phenomenological, and structuration theories were the interpretive approaches of choice. I set out from Cambridge University with a research grant and an armory of these approaches to interpret Hopewell burial mounds in the backwoods area of West-Central Illinois. I aimed to come back when I had enough information to successfully apply them.

Arriving in the Lower Illinois River Valley in winter (about six hours' drive south of Chicago across flat rain-drenched plains) was like entering an American heart of darkness. The pre-Columbian culture that had existed there from 50 BC to 200 AD was probably a lot more civilized than it is there today. In the Hopewell period, over five hundred burial mounds had been built on the high cliffs above the Illinois River with large ceremonial mounds in giant plazas on the valley floor. All that exists there today are a few run-down hamlets surrounded by rusting trailers. In the 1970s there had once been a thriving archaeological community in the valley with a center based in one of the hamlets, Kampsville. However, when I arrived only five people remained, and as an archaeologist from Cambridge University using Marxist theories, I was not particularly welcome. However, I was kindly given the village priest's old house, and over the course of a year I proceeded to compile a database of all data from unpublished excavation reports of burial mounds that I could find in the center's dilapidated library.

The data from the excavations was very good—several entire mound cemeteries had been excavated comprising about fifty excavated burial mounds—many excavated by eminent archaeologists from the University of Chicago. This provided a unique opportunity to study variation within and among cemeteries. But the variation that I encountered became increasingly confusing. This should not have been surprising considering that the mounds had confused several generations of archaeologists, leading to the conclusion that the mounds were "contexts where random variability may occur" (Buikstra et al. 1998, 92). But naïvely I continued to try to untangle them.

After entering all the data available into an SPSS database, I started running cross tabulations to identify any significant patterns in their structure, burial, or artifact associations. These tests were first conducted at a regional level, but as with other archaeologists studying the region, the results were largely inconclusive, showing a fairly complete range of contexts and associations for every variable analyzed. Judging there to be spatial inconsistencies, I attempted to analyze the data at the level of cemeteries. Again there was a large range of different contexts and associations for each variable. Considering that the mounds had probably changed over time, I tried to seriate the mounds at each cemetery chronologically, using a topographical dating method proposed by Lower Illinois Valley archaeologists (Bullington 1988 and Charles 1985). While several general trends were observed, many associations and configurations appeared to go against these sequences, presenting another confusing array of differing representations.

One day, after finally deciding to reduce the level of analysis even further—to a comparison of burials within a single mound—I noticed that the mound, and several others like it, contained more than one episode of construction. By separating mounds into their component parts I realized that several of the mounds had been disturbed by the insertion of a secondary tomb directly into the top of them. This sometimes occurred before the first mound was even finished and often involved the destruction of the earlier tomb by fire along with evidence of violence, including numerous decapitations (Martin 2005). In each of these occasions the secondary mound and burial practices contrasted distinctly with the primary mound. This, I realized, had caused enormous taxonomic confusion for previous archaeologists studying the valley.

The existence of two very different types of burial practice and structure not only at the same place, but also from the same time, involved in the destruction of each other, was not something that I could find an explanation for in the theories and approaches I had been given. Violence done to monuments does not feature very prominently in processual or post-processual theory and is usually considered part of a process of augmentation (Last 1998), appropriation (Mann 2005; Bradley 1993), or erasure (Horning 2004) of historical monuments by one group much later on, rather than something that happens between groups at the same time. The assumption of cultural monogamy for entire areas or regions was clearly the reason why processual archaeologists had not understood the Illinois burial record, but I also found that the same assumption was held by post-processualists studying other times and places. Both were happy to conflate very different monuments and practices from the same time and place.

Archaeologists almost all know of instances where sacred monuments of other cultures were built over by Christian churches—such as the church built over Knowton Henge, the Cordoba cathedral built over a Muslim mosque, or the Montmartre church built over a Celtic shrine in Paris. Many can even point to alterations of sacred sites by other cultures—such as the Viking ship burial placed over a Christian cemetery on the Isle of Man (Tarlow 1997), the placement of a late Neolithic settlement over the sacred cave at Escoural in Portugal (Lillios 2008, 239), or the placement of stone circles on top of wooden henges in the Beaker period. But these instances are almost always interpreted as an appropriation or erasure of much earlier sites (and their power) by later monolithic cultures, rather than a suppression or redefinition of contemporary ideas.

Once back in England, I tried to understand why the existence of conflicting ideas in one place was so difficult to explain theoretically. As I dug deeper, I found others asking the same question (Matthews 1995; Jones 1997). The more I dug, the more I found other archaeologists who were battling similar conflations of burial monuments in the same time and place (Martin 2011). While these conflations are rarely problematic in archaeology, except when we confront obvious clashes between different burial or ceremonial practices (Thorpe and Richards 1984), the fact that such conflict exists, but cannot be explained theoretically, clearly indicates that something is amiss with our archaeological conception of culture.

Eventually I found that Bruno Latour had confronted this problem in sociology, and his explanation provided a useful way of understanding it in archaeology. As Latour argues (explained further in chapter 4), the reduction of anything to the "natural" or "social" category, instead of to a network of both, effectively results in its being seen as monolithic (Latour 2005). When cultural objects are seen as monolithic, this gives the impression that the cultures that they come from are also monolithic. Conceived as social mechanisms for risk management (Service 1972; Sahlins 1976), bodies of cultural ideas (Bradley 1984), or sources of social control (Thomas 1991), cultures have largely been monocultural entities to archaeologists (Jones 1997), whether seen as invisible guiding habituses, governing elites, or ethnic groups. Even if society is broken up into various segments to avoid being monolithic—for example, along the lines of gender, class, ethnicity, or the atomistic individual—as long as the society is considered to be an actual entity, then these segments are considered to be mini-subcultures within a broader monolithic whole. Thus the notion of some overarching society or social category prevents us from seeing the patchwork of unique and continuously changing groups that appear for a while, create alliances, conflict with others, and disappear at a very local level. Without conceiving that such a patchwork exists, the idea that a dissenting group could emerge with its own unique set of issues—encrypted into a different practice that creates a controversy with others—is largely beyond our theoretical imagination.

Fortunately several archaeologists have recognized problems with categorizing individuals into stereotypical categories or social groups and have gone some way to remedy this by further breaking up gender, class, and ethnicity into multiple parts, allowing specific individualities to be recomposed with their unique identity depending on the archaeological data (Meskell 1999; Voss 2008; Joyce and Claassen 1997). However, the problem remains that these networks of characteristics, composed of human or cultural elements, are still too weak to explain symbolic violence between them. Yet in today's atmosphere of political and religious strife—flaring up between individuals of differing parties, religions, or sects within countries like Iraq, Syria, or Ireland, or between countries like India and Pakistan, where cultural icons or temples representing religious ideas are constantly attacked—this anomaly in our theoretical apparatus is all the more important to understand and correct.

In order to understand this anomaly better, Latour and Peter Weibel brought together over one hundred artists, writers, theologians, and philosophers for a major project on "Image Wars" that asked why cultural icons and practices caused so much violence. Hundreds of examples were given, from the destruction of religious images by the Puritans to the destruction of the Bamiyan Buddhas in Afghanistan by the Taliban. Yet one of the most striking conclusions that emerged from the project, set out in the seven-hundred-page tome *Iconoclash: Beyond the Image Wars in Science, Religion and Art* (Latour and Weibel 2002), was that Western philosophy has enormous difficulty in explaining such "symbolic" violence.

Latour argues that philosophy has difficulty because both modernism and postmodernism see art objects, religious ceremonies, and structures as purely human expressions rather than representative of networks of natural and human relationships. This in itself is not new—objects, structures, and ceremonies have long been seen by anthropologists as encryptions of indigenous knowledge about the world. However, indigenous knowledge has ultimately been viewed as purely "cultural" and thus impotent in comparison with Western knowledge, which is viewed as "natural" or true. This discrepancy in perception means that although indigenous knowledge is seen as structuring some indigenous actions, because the process of indigenous knowledge creation is considered purely cultural, it is not seen as real or taken seriously. As a result, it is rarely acknowledged as powerful enough to shape significant actions, and instead, general social or functionalist theories, often derived from the West, are used to explain these actions (Latour 2005, 116). It would be like claiming that Western science has no relation to nature—no relevance outside its own system of symbols. Western science would be seen as equally impotent, and information from science could never be seen as powerful enough, of itself, to influence actions.

However, when indigenous or religious groups are actually asked why they do things, it is because of the perceived *reality* of their so-called cultural constructions. For them, their "cultural constructions" explain perfectly well the structure of nature as well as the structure of their culture, and none of them would call these constructions purely "cultural" (Latour 2005, 48). When a Native American explains that using an animal effigy mask in a ritual dance enables the wearer to "touch the world of the sacred and supernatural" (Hill and Hill 1994, 129), they do not mean something else—either conducting a rite of passage, inducing an altered consciousness, or whatever else is fashionable to explain indigenous actions in anthropology. They mean that by using an effigy mask, the wearer is empowered to "touch the world of the sacred and supernatural." Latour argues that we must restrain our Western condescension and start to listen to our informants' reasoning behind their statements rather than translating everything into social theories (Latour 2005, 48). Informants can give us a far better explanation about why they do things than can anthropologists. Only by learning what these explanations tie together can we learn the meaning and power behind them.

The trouble is, Latour argues, to the Western ear these explanations often sound "baroque, and most idiosyncratic" (ibid., 47). As a result, most explanations are thrown out and only those that fit our own conceptions, or can be translated into a social theory, are kept. Because these explanations usually sound "cultural," they are labeled "cultural," with all the postmodern problems, outlined above, that accompany this label. Viewing indigenous explanations from such a Western standpoint is often claimed to be the only standpoint that we can view them from. However, Latour argues that we can and must attempt to view them from the indigenous standpoint (Latour 1987, 189). In order to comprehend and piece together these heterogeneous explanations, the researcher must understand how explanations are constructed and thus what the terminology used by them actually means.

Latour briefly illustrates in his book *Science in Action* how knowledge, both indigenous and Western, is constructed through three examples (ibid., 198–201). Using the example of a young girl who is trying to learn her mother's categories of nature, Latour explains how she first creates a category—"flifli"—for everything that darts away, including sparrows, squirrels, and balls. Gradually she learns the structure of her mother's categories by pointing to different things and being corrected by her mother, testing what her mother holds to by using the natural elements around her. Moreover, she learns the relationships between these elements by discovering what is tied to what and what is not.

Latour then illustrates how knowledge constructions in indigenous societies are also revealed when categories are threatened. While studying the Karam of New Guinea, anthropologist Ralph Bulmer attempted to categorize a cassowary as a bird—since it has two legs, lays eggs, and has wings. But he was immediately confronted by Karam tribal members who then presented a large amount of evidence, both natural and cultural, against his classification. Apart from the cassowary being very large, flightless, and having no feathers, the Karam tribe classified it based upon its genealogy and habitat. What Bulmer learned through testing their classifications was the shape of the Karam culture—what was tied together by it.

In paleontology, the eminent professor John Ostrom also had problems with the classification of a bird. Ostrom claimed that the Archaeopteryx could not be classified as a bird—despite its wings and feathers—because it could not fly. Instead of being a bird, Ostrom claimed that the Archaeopteryx had feathers because it was warm-blooded and needed to retain heat. Since without feathers it looked just like an ordinary dinosaur, it was good evidence that all dinosaurs were warm-blooded. Thus Ostrom and a few others argued in favor of doing away with the classification of "bird" altogether and classifying animals as either dinosaurs or mammals instead.

In all of these cases, people learn or change their knowledge of the world through testing cultural categories with natural information to discover the categories' boundaries (ibid., 201). This process of accumulation of information, reduction of it through categorization, and combination of categories to represent relationships between elements is not dissimilar to the process that Latour identifies in Western science. Yet they are enormously different at the same time. The Western category of birds comes from a dataset of many thousands of species and millions of birds that enables a significant enough correlation between traits to classify them together as birds. The difference that separates these various classifications is not so much their methodology, but the extent of the network of information that is connected to substantiate claims. The difference, Latour argues, is similar to the difference between "a slingshot, a sword and an armored tank, or when comparing a small earth dam on a little brook and a huge concrete one on the Tennessee River" (ibid., 210).

Despite the difference in scale, the similarity in method means that cultural practices can no longer be described as purely "cultural" and must begin to be understood in terms that allow clearer views of those practices. Because of the unusual forms of information encryption and the resulting false portrayals of cultural practices as purely cultural, many valuable insights into cultural processes have been missed. These insights arise only once the processes of each type of knowledge production are closely followed and accurately portrayed. Only then can we understand why objects and ideas hold the power they do to influence actions.

SCIENTIFIC CULTURES

It has long been understood that the ancient cultures of Samaria, Egypt, Greece, and China possessed forms of scientific practice that enabled them to generate general scientific theories and principles. Many of these scientific principles form the basis of our modern science and are still in use today. Historical records from these cultures enable the practice of science to be traced back to as early as 3000 BC, or as far back as historical records go, with accounts demonstrating a complex knowledge of mathematics, geometry, astronomy, and law (Hoyrup 2008). Many astronomical and mathematical principles were well understood by Samarian and Egyptian philosophers and were encrypted into complex architecture and calendars. Their efficient agricultural systems and metallurgy also attest to a complex knowledge of material science. By the time of ancient

Greece, scientific discoveries were attributed to individuals, and due to the continuity between Greece and Rome, we still have accounts of these individuals. To Thales the first surveying equipment, maps, and sundials have been attributed; to Pythagoras—the conception of the world as round and a knowledge of anatomy; to Empedocles—a primitive knowledge of evolution; and to Anaxagoras—a scientific understanding of the sun, moon, winds, water, and the atomic structure of matter—all before 400 BC. Records also exist of China's considerable scientific development in astronomy and mathematics as early as 1000 BC (Needham and Ronan 1985).

It should not be surprising, therefore, to conceive of science as having been part of human activity for much longer than the last three hundred and fifty years of modernism. It is also likely that science extended much further back than written encryptions, which may have merely continued traditions of encrypting scientific knowledge into objects and instruments (Latour and Woolgar 1979, 153; Latour 2005). Indeed, the discovery of the Nebra sky disc—a bronze disc depicting the sun, the moon, the stars, and the solstices, from 1600 BC—indicates that the encryption of scientific knowledge into objects clearly occurred in prehistoric cultures (Meller 2004). Yet, examples of pre-modern scientific abilities are often seen as merely practical knowledge (Samarian and Egyptian) or fortuitous anomalies (ancient Greece)—as opposed to scientific know-how (Olsen 2010, 2).

The reason that modernist historians of science have drawn such a distinction between ancient and modern science lies in the tendency of pre-modern scientists to include so-called religious imagery in their descriptions. To modernists, the failure of ancient scientists to make a distinction between nature and culture laid them open to charges of cultural bias. Indeed, many ancient Greek scientists held important religious posts or went on to start religious cults of their own (Pythagoras and Empedocles). In modern histories of ancient Greek scientists, these religious writings or affiliations are often downplayed by arguing that their best scientific work occurred only when they avoided religious explanations (Williams 1904, 105). The implications of this argument are that Greek scientists were not true scientists except when they made a distinction between nature and culture.

Yet the notion that modernism created a new man—freed from the superstitious notion of an entanglement between nature and society—is hardly viable today. It was buried years ago by countless studies of entanglement in science (Golinski 1998). These studies illustrate that science was never purely a natural activity. However, proving that science is not a purely natural activity does not mean that science is a purely *social activity* instead, as some sociological critics of science would have it (Feyerabend 1975; Bloor 1976; Aikenhead and Ogawa 2007). This is because in this new context *social activity* is no longer a correct descriptive term either, even for society, given the entanglement of nature and society. Science is a highly empirical practice, as anthropological studies have shown (Latour and Woolgar 1979; Latour 1987), but scientific conclusions are not built out of pure earth or air. All of its conclusions are painstakingly built by connecting every new element with solidly built tools, tests, associations, and formulas from the past (each built in the same way themselves) to create a new knowledge. All new knowledge is built on the shoulders of knowledge from the past, and without such careful construction of facts out of these building blocks, conclusions in science would not be considered true. This laborious construction of scientific knowledge is a much more complex activity, involving humans and non-humans, and while it is a vastly distributed activity, not merely involving nature, it is by no means social in the sociological sense.

The interesting corollary conclusion (for archaeology especially) that Latour draws from his anthropological studies of both science and pre-modern cultures is that culture is not social in the sociological sense either, but a much more descriptive enterprise than sociology has given it credit for. As a more descriptive enterprise, therefore, culture becomes much more like the science of Latour's understanding, and therefore can benefit from advances in the understanding of science and scientific processes. Instead of seeing cultural objects as only having meaning in relation to their culture, they can begin to be understood as encryptions of old and new knowledge from culture and nature, opening the door to a more fruitful engagement with objects, and one that allows a more scientific examination of them.

The belief that natural science is a modern invention—a practice separate from cultural activity—has created enormous problems for our understanding of the world, and especially for our understanding of the past. Latour argues that instead of seeing science as a normal activity participated in by pre-modern and modern cultures alike, the separation of science from society has meant that social activities such as ceremony and burial have been defined as purely cultural activities in opposition to science—activities without any relation to the real world. Indeed, even the slightest suggestion of culture as a representation of the natural world is currently being meticulously removed from archaeological theory (Jones 2002, 178; Barrett 2000, 63; Boivin 2008).

Yet these definitions of culture have cut us off from a productive understanding of cultural activity, an understanding that is enriched by an understanding of science. Over the past thirty years, extensive anthropological studies of science have been conducted that have enriched our understanding of what scientific practice is. By following the process of gathering, reduction, and encryption of information to create formulas, and the ways that these formulas are used to control, predict, and protect, studies of science have provided detailed understandings of how objects are created and used and how they come to wield such power.

Many commentators in the philosophy of science have demonstrated the similarity of such processes to the processes of object creation and use in non-industrial societies, illustrating that science as practiced today was as important in the past as it is in our own society (Latour and Woolgar 1979, 153; Latour 1987; Agrawal 1995; Watson-Verran and Turnbull 2005; Montgomery 2000; Turnbull 2000a; Selin 2008). Pre-modern "culture" was a type of science, not a type of culture. While keeping in mind the enormous differences between ancient and modern science, as well as the differences between ancient and modern culture—the result of three hundred and fifty years of both science and culture trying to be modern—these studies argue that many of the core processes learned from anthropological studies of scientific practice can help us to understand premodern cultural practice and its associated artifacts and monuments.

Although archaeology has not ventured to apply such an understanding, due to the modernist "Great Divide" that we have self-imposed between moderns and pre-moderns, the conception that "we have never been modern," argued by Latour, can gradually dissolve this divide. The effect of dissolving such a divide is not to decrease the importance of science, but to elevate the concept of culture to a new understanding of what science actually is.

A BRIEF HISTORY OF MODERNISM

Conceptions of culture and science have undergone significant reevaluations in the past thirty years. In the 1980s and 1990s, there were several attempts to revisit the origins of modernism and the separation between nature and culture that molded conceptions of culture and science. Two particularly far-reaching studies were *The Leviathan and the Air-Pump: Hobbes, Boyle, and the Experimental Life* (1985), by Steven Shapin and Simon Schaffer, and *We Have Never Been Modern* (1993), by Bruno Latour. Both have been hugely influential in the history and philosophy of science, compelling historians of science to question the universality of the modernist division between nature and culture. More recently, other disciplines, including archaeology, have also begun to question this modernist division and to grasp how it molded central assumptions in their fields.

Shapin and Schaffer's book essentially traces the origins of the modernist division between nature and culture, while Latour's book follows its ramifications for the development of science and philosophy. While the philosophical division between nature and culture, or between objects and subjects, can be dated back to Classical Greek philosophy—to Plato and Aristotle—it has not been consistently observed or implemented, and Latour argues it has never actually been followed except in theory (ibid.). However, in the 1660s England made a radical break from the pre-modern world when a theoretical division of the world into nature on one side and culture on the other began to be enforced. Shapin and Schaffer trace this break back to the social and political chaos at that time that ensued from a series of political events.

After the English Civil War (1641–1651), the victorious Oliver Cromwell set about creating a degree of religious freedom that had never before been seen in Britain—by ridding the country of the king and the Church of England. Yet by beheading Charles I and abolishing the Church—the traditional arbitrators of truth—Cromwell left no authorities to distinguish what was true from what was false. This led to a proliferation of multiplè conflicting social, scientific, and religious ideas that strove with one another for supremacy. During Cromwell's Interregnum, enthusiasts, sectaries, and hermeticists constantly threatened the peace, and many feared that these groups might spark another civil war. While Cromwell kept the peace largely by force, when Cromwell died, the ensuing chaos prompted parliament to reinstate the monarchy in 1660, although many felt that the repression of freedom was not the right thing either.

At first the new king, Charles II, declared a "liberty to tender consciences," since it was argued that "passion and uncharitableness" had produced social strife (Shapin and Schaffer 1985, 285). But sectarian risings continued to occur despite his appeal to toleration. It was soon clear that "disputed knowledge produced civil strife," and in 1661 Parliament banned all private meetings of sects and imposed harsh censorship (ibid., 283). The Church of England also resorted to its earlier doctrinal beliefs and cracked down on dissent within the Church, ejecting hundreds of dissenting ministers from their parishes. However, the problem arose of what else was then legitimate to say, apart from church doctrine. The suppression of social and political ideas was harder to enforce without a proper way to distinguish truth from falsity. It was generally agreed that a solution to this problem—how to determine truth—was imperative to bring the huge number of radical ideas under control (ibid.).

One of the solutions, proposed by Thomas Hobbes, was to give power solely to the king, who would rule without division and would lay down fundamental philosophical principles, from which natural philosophers could reason analytically to determine truth. To Hobbes, philosophy was pure and scientific, like geometry, and could determine absolute truth so long as its foundational principles were not undermined (ibid., 338).

In contrast, Robert Boyle, an aristocrat and alchemist, proposed a way to determine truth based upon scientific experiments. This method deferred authority to objects rather than to people, in order to determine truth, by using instruments in controlled experiments witnessed by a group of expert witnesses (akin to a jury). Boyle argued that by deferring authority to objects one avoided the overt interference of social or religious bias, and this allowed for a consensus to be formed, even between individuals of differing religious or social backgrounds. Sound facts could then be used to make sound political or religious decisions. Most importantly, by forcing adversaries to use material evidence in their arguments, they would no longer resort to attacks on each other's personalities—the main source of antagonism between individuals—and would instead argue with their opponent's evidence. However, in order to preserve the appearance of objectivity, it was imperative during the experiments that any overtly political or religious questions were excluded.

While our own modern response to Boyle's solution is to treat it as self-evidently the correct one, it required several important conditions to which Hobbes and other natural philosophers at the time reacted with ridicule. Shapin and Schaffer attempt to understand this reaction from the point of view of Hobbes. Rather than using hindsight to judge his opinion, they attempt to view his arguments against Boyle in light of the historical and material context. Their detailed analysis of Boyle's experimental philosophy has been crucial to understand the origins of modernism and the subsequent separation of nature from culture.

Boyle's experimental philosophy was physically very complicated and had to overcome a good deal of skepticism. It did not help that his air-pump, a vital part of his experimental apparatus, constantly broke down and leaked, thus requiring a huge effort on Boyle's part and numerous academic articles to legitimize it as a tool. In order to legitimize the scientific evidence produced by the pump, no less an authority than the prestigious Royal Society could exercise enough authority for the evidence to be accepted by others. Witnesses to his experiments also had to agree on the legitimacy of his apparatus as well as many other preconditions in order for the experiment to carry any authority. These preconditions included "conventions concerning how a fact is produced, about what may be questioned and what may not, about what is normally expected and what counts as an anomaly, about what is to be regarded as evidence and proof" (Shapin and Schaffer 1985, 225). Even then, it was not easy to convince people with the results of the experiment, and it had to be replicated by others in order to be accepted. But replication could only occur on a machine that worked, and it was only considered working if it could replicate the experiment. Thus an experimenter had to consider the experiment a fact before they experimented (ibid., 226). Hobbes argued, indignantly, that such a way to determine truth was hugely artificial, with the experimenter himself outlining the questions and answers that could be inferred from the experiments, and a select group of fellow collaborators at the Royal Society determining which of them were correct. A group of men, Hobbes argued, however learned, could not possibly arrive at the absolute certainty they desired and were certainly not free from bias. Only natural philosophy could discover truth (ibid., 320).

The other problem Hobbes had with Boyle's "experimental philoso-phy" was Boyle's supposed separation between nature and culture. In order to know the world, Boyle argued, it was essential to separate the world into natural/objective/non-human things that could be studied by scientific instruments, and cultural/subjective/human things that could not be studied objectively by scientific tools. Hobbes fiercely rejected any such separation and saw Boyle's claim that he could achieve such a sep-aration as deceptive. He saw Boyle's vast artificial effort to enroll ma-chines, individuals, the natural world, and religious or political ideas—in order to establish facts—as good evidence for the inseparability of nature, society, and politics. He argued that Boyle could not claim that religion and politics had no role in experiments when the "facts" he claimed to prove were so religiously and politically charged. For example, at first Boyle made no secret of his ambition to prove God's existence through experimentation. His experiment using an air pump to prove that a vacu-um existed—a space containing neither matter nor air—was also often promoted by the Church as proof of incorporeal Spirit, a conclusion in-itially encouraged by Boyle (ibid., 319). Hobbes' attacks merely forced Boyle to hide his ambitions more deeply. It was largely through these political moves to hide his ambitions, while aligning himself and his experimental philosophy with the interests of powerful allies, that Boyle's experimental philosophy was eventually adopted.

By limiting the boundaries of inquiry to questions that could only be settled experimentally (ibid., 45), and by overtly excluding politics and religion in answering them, Boyle effectively wrote our "Modern Consti-tution"—a "constitution" in the sense that it laid out (by implication) a radically new system or body of natural and social principles that gov-erned the way of looking at the universe (Latour 1993, 15). The modern world that emerged from this seventeenth-century break initiated the largest effort in revisionism ever undertaken, amounting to a categoriza-tion of everything as either natural or cultural. This left God with the ability to influence the social and human, but placed everything else under the direction of material laws. Such a separation was not seen as arbitrary, but universal and absolute. While "society" has taken over from "God" as the main influence on humans and culture, this division has remained largely intact.

BRUNO LATOUR

Philosopher of science Bruno Latour may be said to have taken up where Shapin and Schaffer left off. In his book *We Have Never Been Modern*, Latour illustrates the philosophical legacy of modernism and the impact of this theoretical separation of nature from culture on the social sciences (Latour 1993). First, Latour explains the problem at the root of this separation. He argues that, in practice, there is never any separation that occurs in scientific work. The need to control knowledge justified more, not less, use of social and political methods in science, yet it stimulated a presentation style that fudged the actual processes of scientific work in order to disguise such methods. The effort to categorize new scientific works as "natural" in presentations or publications, once a fact has been established, ends up ignoring the huge amount of work, both social and political, that goes into establishing it. This enables scientists to avoid the complications that come about by acknowledging social influences. By going back to modernism's origins—to the very real threat of civil war that a truthful description of scientific work involved—we can understand why this presentation style was so necessary. But we can also see why the modernist classification of "nature" does not adequately account for the facts themselves.

So, how could science be correctly defined? The many different definitions of scientific practice, offered by scientists themselves, illustrate the great difficulty in defining science. Articulating an authoritative definition of science has long been the focus of much heated debate in the sciences and in the social sciences, to little avail. Yet, once it is realized that no separation exists between nature and culture, and once the arguments based upon such a separation are extracted from descriptions of science, most definitions of science have a lot in common. Having spent two years doing anthropological work in a scientific laboratory, Latour presents a definition of scientific practice, based on acute observation of scientists, in his book *Science in Action* (1987). The scientists that he followed also acknowledged the broad accuracy of this description (Latour and Woolgar 1986, 274).

This description of scientific practice does not invalidate Popper's theory of falsification or "hypothetico-deductive method" entirely—the theory that hypotheses are inductively arrived at and deductively tested until a hypothesis is found that can no longer be falsified—but illustrates that Popper's theory does not begin to explain what actually goes on in science (Nordmann 2009, 334). Popper's falsification principle is only part of a more comprehensive explanation of science—one that takes in what happens before and after laboratory work. Instead of hypotheses being "thought up," tested, and rejected, Latour argues that hypotheses essentially enable accumulated observances to be allied, reduced, and combined—with better hypotheses enabling bigger and better alliances, reductions, and combinations (Latour 1987, 215–40; 1999, 24–79). Such an interpretation is in line with Charles Sanders Peirce's understanding of hypotheses as products of abductive reasoning (Peirce 1934). But, in order for hypotheses to be accepted down the road, they also require the building of alliances with other scientists, funding bodies, previously established facts, and civilian or even military uses.

The main obstacles to associating the modern practice of these rudimental processes with the pre-modern practice of science, apart from the misleading assertion that science deals with nature in opposition to society, are the many terms used by scientists to describe what they do (Latour and Woolgar 1979, 153). The creation and use of new terms such as "hypothesis," "proof," and "deduction" give the impression that modern scientific practice is somehow different or new. Alfred Schutz illustrated long ago that these terms are merely new words for commonsense rationality or compatibility with current knowledge (Schutz 1953 in Latour and Woolgar 1979), criteria that are equally important in pre-modern science.

Once these presumptive and linguistic obstacles are removed, there is sufficient room for a comparison of their methods (Latour 1987, 223; Turnbull 2000a), discussed in more detail in chapter 3. But such a comparison does not undermine scientific truths or give pre-modern science more veracity. There is an ocean of difference between the results of modern science and pre-modern science. Yet, instead of the difference between them lying in some objective versus subjective dichotomy, or falsification versus confirmation dichotomy (Popper 1934), Latour argues that the difference can be found in their scope of investigation. The scope of Western science—through its combination of vast amounts of information from a wider field into instruments which allow an even larger amount of information to be studied—makes its conclusions more broadly applicable than those of indigenous cultures, whose investigations are extremely limited in scale. This is not to say, however, that modernist science produces absolute truth—something that even scientists refute—but it does produce truth in so far as it applies to the information that it has accumulated and reduced (Latour 1987, 232).

The crucial difference between Latour's philosophy of knowledge and others—one that has prevented others from positing such a clear understanding of scientific practice, and has led them to neglect the scientific process—is that Latour refuses to let this truth then ascend to a pantheon of universal truths. Traditionally, once a truth is seen to predict the information that it reduced, it is somehow seen to have been there all along—as a universal truth transcending all local data—and is labeled "natural." Thus the process through which it came to be posited is seen as inconsequential and is merely referenced to explain why it is right, not how it came to be. Such an explanation is the equivalent of Whig History—history of science as written by the victors.

Yet, this traditional view of scientific practice certainly appears to be true when facts apply to information that they did not reduce. But Latour argues that this is merely the result of additional work to extend the network established in the laboratory to the outside world. To explain the appearance of universality that exists for some facts, Latour cites the enormous attempts to extend the influence of "facts" created in laboratories by extending the "shop conditions" and creating an environment in the outside world for facts to apply (Latour 1987, 250). This gargantuan effort is largely rendered invisible by encrypting objects and instruments with the information necessary for it. Using an analogy, he writes, "Facts and machines are like trains, electricity, packages of computer bytes or frozen vegetables: they can go everywhere as long as the track along which they travel is not interrupted in the slightest" (ibid.). A good indication of the effort it takes to merely maintain the right conditions so that facts can be applied elsewhere is the amount spent on calibration every year—6 percent of US Gross National Product (three times what is spent on Research and Development), as calculated by the National Bureau of Standards in 1980 (Hunter 1980 in Latour 1987, 251)—actually only a small, but crucial, part of the effort to extend the influence of facts.

To understand the localized nature of modern science is not to question its efficacy, but to illustrate that the difference in results between modern and pre-modern science stems from a difference in scale more than a difference in method. Modern science could be viewed as a ramped-up version of pre-modern science, and as such, it is obviously a much more powerful and useful science, able to predict the mineral construction of distant planets or the precise activity of individual atoms, but it still comprises the same basic principles. By explaining this process, it is not Latour's intention to cast doubt on the reality of substances either, as even many of his supporters have suggested (Law 2004; Harman 2009). Latour is quite clear that "there are substances that have been there all along" (Latour 1999, 170). But it is extremely important that the construction of explanations of those substances is understood and not mistaken for the substances themselves or "nature." Likewise, it is extremely important that the practice of pre-modern or indigenous science and its construction of explanations, misrepresented by anthropology and archaeology as "cultural," be recognized and the misrepresentation corrected.

To give pre-modern science its due, the smaller scale at which indigenous science operates often allows indigenous or native science to present a more fine-tuned portrayal of a local region or phenomenon than one painted in broad strokes. By providing a much more detailed representation of local phenomena, indigenous science has often provided Western science with scientific solutions for many Western needs. The book *American Indian Contributions to the World*, by Emory Keoke and Kay Porterfield (2003), lists over 450 inventions and innovations by Native Americans that are in use today. These include medical cures such as quinine and aspirin, and many others that have been used as a source of inspiration to create new medicines (such as vitamin C—adapted from a Native American cure for scurvy). It has been calculated that over 75 percent of all Western plant-based remedies stem from traditional indigenous medicine (ibid.). Western scientists continue to examine indigenous ideas and inventions that have been ignored, such as remedies for cancer and other diseases, or innovative engineering designs from the Incas and other societies (Ochsendorf and Billington 1999). Many of the same solutions to problems faced by Europeans were also found independently by Native Americans, including similar agricultural technology, surgical and dentistry techniques, oral contraception, antibiotics, anesthetics, and syringes. Most interesting is the level of Native American political science. Indeed, the US Constitution and Friedrich Engels' *Communist Manifesto* reputedly took much of their inspiration from the Iroquois system of government (Keoke and Porterfield 2003).

If "necessity is the mother of invention," then this level of scientific prowess should not be surprising. Many cultures would not have survived their cripplingly hot or cold climates for millennia without developing working solutions through the scientific process of observation, classification, and problem solving (Snively and Corsiglia 2000). The Yupiaq or Eskimo people of Southwest Alaska have survived because they reduced and encrypted knowledge of their harsh environment into their technology and have used it to navigate icy waters, to brave storms, to heal, to hunt, and to warm themselves (Kawagley et al. 1998). In a similar way, the reduction and encryption of astronomical and geographic information into a star compass has enabled the isolated island people of Micronesia to navigate vast distances between islands in the Pacific, to colonize them, and to create support networks for thousands of years (Turnbull 2000b, 137). Thus, if the needs, solution processes, and outcomes are the same in non-modern as well as modern contexts, we cannot claim that there is a distinction between modern and indigenous science, or between theoretical formulas and practical technology.

The real distinction lies in a difference between the modern aversion and pre-modern willingness to admit an integration of nature and culture in the scientific process. It is true, however, that without an imaginary, theoretical division between nature and culture, the West would never have been able to industrialize to the extent it has. By claiming that scientific practice is purely natural and thus has no impact on society, scientists have been able to innovate on an industrial scale with virtual impunity. But the theoretical existence of such a division has never prevented scientists from actually mediating between nature and society in practice, to establish "facts" or machines. Latour writes, "Moderns think they have succeeded in such an expansion only because they have carefully separated Nature and Society (and bracketed God), whereas they have succeeded only because they have mixed together much greater masses of humans and nonhumans, without bracketing anything and without ruling out any combination" (Latour 1993, 41). It is the constant process of mixing natural and cultural elements that enables innovation, and it is difficult to name any fact or technology today that is not thoroughly infused with cultural information. Information about how people best communicate, eat, sleep, wash, travel, work, and play is encrypted into new facts and technology, and little is created that is not useful or explained in terms of human characteristics. By categorizing "established" facts as "natural," however, they avoid the complications that come about when social impacts and influences are acknowledged (moral complications that beset the pre-moderns and prevented rapid industrialization).

Latour argues that the resistance to innovation that exists within pre-modern societies is largely due to the obsessive fear of eroding the social or natural order by creating a dangerous hybrid. This taboo is well illustrated by anthropological accounts of non-modern societies where any innovation is dwelt on endlessly for the problems it might incur for the cosmos—including its potentially destructive effects on social or natural laws (Levi-Strauss 1962, 267; Horton 1967; Descola 1993). By categorizing hybrid innovations as purely "natural" once they had been created, the moderns were able to reassure themselves that innovations had no serious consequences for the social order and that social innovations had no consequences for the natural order. Thus a powerful ideology evolved, allowing what the pre-moderns ruled out and enabling moderns to accelerate innovative combinations without moral complications—curiously not unlike the way that eighteenth-century racist theories of cultural evolution were expediently adopted to justify colonial expansion and subjugation of native peoples.

As Latour urges, however, "as soon as we study in detail the work of production of hybrids and the work of elimination of these same hybrids . . . we then discover that we have never been modern" (Latour 1993, 46). This is because everything produced by science has always been the result of mediations between humans and non-humans. Latour argues that this does not negate the veracity of these productions; it just negates the description of them as purely "natural." The classification of such hybrids as "natural" denies, or at least obscures, the process through which they were actually produced. Latour argues that the recent proliferation of obvious hybrids that defy reduction to either nature or culture, such as social technology or environmental problems, have made it especially difficult to justify a modernist separation by jamming the process of modernist classification. As a result of man-made environmental catastrophes in particular, we in the twenty-first century can no longer claim that society has no effect on nature, or that science has no effect on society.

RAMIFICATIONS FOR SOCIOLOGY

Although the theoretical division of the world into these two realms has enabled great technological advances (by avoiding the perceptual complications that beset the pre-moderns), it has caused huge problems for the description of both science and society. In the social sciences, the assumption that the world is divided into two halves—human activity on one side and the natural world on the other—has structured most descriptive approaches. Human objects and ideas are seen as "mere idols shaped by the requirements of social order, while the [real] rules of society are determined by biology" (Latour 1993, 53). Thus sociologists have traditionally looked for universal social theories that could explain general human behavior, but when it has come to understanding science, sociologists have only ascribed scientific mistakes to social factors (e.g., Kuhn 1962; Lakatos 1970).

In the early 1970s, however, sociologists at the Science Studies Unit at Edinburgh University attempted (rather naïvely) to argue that scientists, and all their findings, were influenced by sociological factors (Barnes 1974; Bloor 1976). Studies were conducted that examined the social conditions attending scientific discoveries in order to draw parallels between them. Such attempts—which Latour argues resulted in comprehensive failure—brought upon sociologists a good deal of ridicule by the scientific community during the so-called Science Wars—"wars" in which scientists consistently attacked "postmodernists" in journals and books during the 1980s and 1990s, accusing them of relativizing and of undermining scientific authority (Gross and Levitt 1994; Sokal 1996). Their criticism was largely fair given that "postmodern" texts on science were being used by creationists in their fight to rid schools of evolution classes, and purportedly by the government to eliminate science funding. Regrettably, the often stinging polemic blinded many to the nuances gained by earlier studies of science and forced scientists to advocate an even more rigid dichotomy between society and nature (Latour 1993, 55; 2005, 100).

While many sociologists have maintained their claim that science is determined by society (Labinger and Collins 2001), Latour saw their failure to apply a characterization of culture to the workings of science as casting doubt on traditional sociological approaches. Latour writes, "the implausibility of this claim was so blatant for the 'hard' [sciences] . . . that we suddenly realized how implausible it was for the 'soft' ones as well. Objects are not the shapeless receptacles of social categories" (Latour 1993, 55). This was the first time that sociologists had tackled a dataset and a group that could forcefully object to their social explanations and make itself heard. Until this time sociologists had mostly studied human behavior at the fringes of society and had attributed action to universal social explanations, often despite the objections from their subjects. The huge backlash by the scientific establishment against these sociologists so dramatically publicized the problems with this approach that Latour claims it forced many sociologists, including himself, to begin reconsidering their traditional sociological assumptions altogether (Latour 2005, 101). Starting with the philosophy of science and creeping slowly through sociology, this failure of the modernist characterization of science began to unravel central assumptions of other social sciences.

RAMIFICATIONS FOR PHILOSOPHY

Latour and others began to realize that this modernist dichotomy had structured far more than just sociological approaches to description. Philosophy, Latour argued, had been especially damaged by adhering to the nature/culture division. Even with the multiplication of obvious hybrids in society, the major philosophies still adhered to the idea that the world is divided into two incommensurable spheres, despite many avowed attempts to reconcile them. Latour explains that starting with Kantianism, "Things-in-themselves become inaccessible while, symmetrically, the transcendental subject becomes infinitely remote from the world" (Latour 1993, 56). Despite successive attempts to rid philosophy of this false division, Latour argues that Western philosophy has unwittingly entrenched and widened it.

The German philosopher Martin Heidegger in his book *Being and Time* (1927) attempted one such settlement of the nature/culture divide through his explanation of the concept of Being. Being was seen to exist in landscape rather than in science or social science. However, by ignoring science, science is left unassailable as the designator of pure nature. Being, Latour argues, is not found by escaping the modern world, but by entering into it. Being is everywhere, in the networks of subjects and objects that define science, social science, and technology (Latour 1993, 90; 2004b, 233).

Phenomenology—the study of our experience of things in the world— was another attempt to reconcile nature and culture. In order to cover the middle ground, phenomenology at first rejected the existence of a pure consciousness and a pure object and talked of the "consciousness of things" (e.g., Husserl [1931] 1960). But this was, as Latour puts it, "nothing more than a slender footbridge spanning a gradually widening abyss" (Latour 1993, 58). Later phenomenologists (e.g., Bachelard 1967) capitulated and accepted the objectivity of the sciences. Postmodernists have continued this separation between nature and culture by seeing scientists as non-human mediums for truth, and in this sense they remained modern, but they were termed postmodern because they disallowed any mediation between the realms to occur (i.e., hybrid production), failing to realize that this was in fact one of the great advantages of modernism (Latour 1993, 61).

Another movement, semiotics, has concentrated on how mediation between nature and culture occurs through language. By translating everything into a sign or sign system, it avoided the problem of having to speak of a pure nature or a pure culture (Saussure [1916] 1974; Barthes

[1985] 1988). As a result, semioticians investigated explanations other than nature or society for how meaning was produced and developed many useful tools for following meaning production. Yet objects and subjects merely became "fictions generated by meaning effects; as for the author, he is no longer anything but the artifact of his own writings" (Latour 1993, 63). While helping to understand the process of mediation, semiotics as a philosophy was finally shipwrecked alongside sociology when applied to the practice of science. Latour writes, "It is hard to reduce the entire cosmos to a grand narrative, the physics of subatomic particles to a text" (Latour 1993, 64). Such a disastrous attempt has compelled many to return to the nature/culture divide and to side with either nature or culture as a basis for discourse, while denying the other side any authority (ibid.). Others have succeeded in giving some weight to both sides while retaining the structuring element of language. The result is usually three purified worlds in one—a natural and technological world, a society of false consciousness, and a world of discourse—that require bridging. Yet some have begun to use Charles Sanders Peirce's semiotics—a semiotics very similar to Latour's which can offer some useful insights (Preucel 2006; discussed in chapter 3).

As methods with which to approach description, these philosophies have provided immensely valuable techniques. Semiotics, in particular, has highlighted the rich, layered texture of humans and nature and has numerous techniques for studying meaning production. However, to avoid the problems with reducing everything to discourse, these insights and techniques can be put to much better use by ruling out the dichotomy between humans and things and seeing discourse as intertwined with things and human action in networks. Nature, discourse, or society are not the cause of phenomena, either separately or together, but are the product of these networks (Latour 1999, 145). This makes it important not to understand how nature, discourse, or society produces meaning but to understand how the networks of interrelationships between elements actually create nature, discourse, and society.

HISTORY OF EXPLANATION

One of the central arguments to come out of Bruno Latour's work, as well as philosopher Gilles Deleuze's, is the recognition that to understand the world, we cannot look outside of the network of local cultural and natural activity and associations that lead to physical reality. Both Latour (1993) and Deleuze (Deleuze and Guattari 1980) illustrate that if objects or actions are placed in either the "natural" or the "social" sphere—and modernism has educated us to do this as soon as things are characterized—all developmental activities from their opposing spheres, which led to their origin or change, are neglected. This leaves huge gaps in our understanding of things—gaps that many sociologists who study local phenomena have recognized, but are unsure of where to look to fill them. Instead of seeking information from a blend of cultural and natural sources at the local level, the gaps are usually filled by resorting to external theories or universal agencies from the same sphere, which exacerbate the problem.

Deleuze calls this approach "hylomorphism." This is the belief that "the order displayed by material systems is due to the form projected in advance of production by an external productive agent, a form which organizes what would supposedly otherwise be chaotic or passive matter" (Bonta and Protevi 2004, 162 in Normark 2010). The external hylomorphic agent can be class, society, economy, ecology, or an individual agent, depending on your slant, but the problem with using such an external agency is that it ignores the local network that actually gave it shape. The human individual or other factors may be part of that network, even the catalysts that directed the flow (Normark 2010), but they were never the originators of anything.

Archaeologists who advocate individualist, social, or cultural agencies to understand culture, in opposition to deterministic ecological models of earlier interpreters, have really only replaced one set of external agencies with another. Instead of seeing natural forces, such as population density or environmental factors, as determining human behavior, they have merely taken the opposite stance of using cultural forces, such as social structure, class struggles, and power consolidation, to explain behavior instead. The idea that people are pawns in a cultural system or power relationship, determined by anthropological or social models of behavior, is not much better than seeing them determined by materialist forces in an ecological system. When the same explanations are used for vastly different cultures, from Central America (Joyce 2000) to Neolithic Britain (Shanks and Tilley 1987b), and different cultures start to sound a lot like each other, the question has to be asked: do these external agencies have any explanatory power or are they just being imposed, bolstered by arbitrarily selected material?

One of the reasons why archaeologists choose to rely on a universal theory of social agency or power politics, rather than seek an explanation from a local blend of cultural *and* natural sources, may be the framework that they rely on. For archaeologists of agency this framework is primarily Pierre Bourdieu's concept of the habitus and Anthony Giddens' Structuration theory, which is a reworking of Bourdieu's concept. According to Bourdieu, individuals are influenced to act by a combination of their social affiliation and the social structure of their society (Bourdieu 1977, 70–72). This social structure, including modes and rules of behavior expressed in domestic and religious beliefs and practices, is imprinted on the consciousness of individuals through living in a society and observing others. It then structures those individuals' actions as they emulate others, thus perpetuating the structure further. Anthony Giddens argues that these principles are not as rigid as Bourdieu claims but are constantly negotiated and changed through intentional class struggles or unintentional consequences of action (Giddens 1984, 14). Yet neither Bourdieu nor Giddens believes that the principles behind social structures have any relationship to physical reality. Bourdieu writes, "Every element receives its complete definition only through its relation with the whole of elements as a difference within a system of differences" (Bourdieu 1990, 7 in Schinkel 2007).

By seeing culture as comprised of symbols that are merely meaningful in relation to other symbols, it is not surprising that archaeologists consider it impossible to ascertain the real reasons why people acted in the past. Neither is it surprising that without an idea of what comprised ancient social structures, social structures from non-industrial cultures have been co-opted, reified as universal theories, and applied to interpret the past.

However, there are distinct problems with this approach, and such an application has its share of side effects. The focus of most discussions about this interpretive method is the extent to which individuals are either determined by social structure or have free will (Dobres and Robb 2000, 10; Dornan 2002, 320). But few archaeologists investigate the contingency of universalized structures and agencies, or whether these agencies exist at all as separate determinative phenomena. Severing specific natural circumstances and social histories from local objects and actions to universalize anthropological analogies and explanations and co-opting these explanations to interpret another culture means that archaeological material is largely "trapped in the ethnographic present" (Brown 1997, 466).

In reality, everything has a history. It is a history of cultural and natural events, people and things that converge to create the conditions and specific rules for local action. They cannot be divorced from that history, nor can they be divorced from the specific natural and material elements that gave them shape. Why then does this divorce appear so acceptable to us? Latour argues that this is largely because of our modernist impulse to classify local objects and practices as natural or cultural entities and ignore the history of their development once they are classified as distinct things. In the same way that scientists believe they have discovered a drug by ignoring its local development once it has been defined and classified as "natural," social scientists often ignore the history of social practices and their local contingency once they are defined as social entities in sociological or anthropological publications. In addition, the lack of time-depth involved in anthropological and sociological studies means that the local historical elements behind practices are often missed and practices are seen as two-dimensional social phenomena. This enables social scientists, like archaeologists, to remove practices from their local associations and apply them universally without fearing that they might be tied to local natural or historical phenomena.

As mentioned earlier, the main advocate of divorcing local social practices from their specific contexts and universalizing them was Emile Durkheim, who helped to form sociology as a separate science by aggressively separating society from nature and limiting sociological study to the social sphere exclusively. Durkheim saw the social sphere as largely an entity in itself that controlled individuals through universal laws. It was these laws that Durkheim believed sociology should attempt to discover (Latour 2002a). Most of our universalized explanations for ritual action come from followers of Durkheim such as Robert Hertz (burial as collective representation), Marcel Mauss (burial creates obligation as a forum for gift giving), Bronislaw Malinowski (burial maintains social stability), and Radcliffe-Brown (burial cements kinship relations). Through generalizing specific ethnographic practices and applying explanations of them to similar forms of practice elsewhere (without a close understanding of the local historic meaning of those similar forms), these sociologists, and many after them, have taken specific local explanations and turned them into general social theories.

RELIGION AS A SEPARATE ENTITY

In the process of divorcing explanations from their local circumstances, explanations for social practices have ended up focusing on purely "social" factors to the exclusion of the "natural" or real world. In explanations of religion and religious practice, for example, Durkheim set the standard by designating religion as an entity separate from the natural world and from empirical truth. Following this line of thought, many other sociologists have created theories of religion that exclude the natural world. Marx saw religion as the expression of material economic realities, arguing that religious doctrines had no relation to the natural world and that religions were merely expressions of social inequality that maintain that inequality. Van Gennep saw society as almost as tangible as an individual and religion as society's way of conducting its members through one stage of life to another. But again, religion had no relation to empirical realities (D. Davies 2005, 359–62). Freud further reduced religion to biological and social drives, also in opposition to empirical observations of nature. Yet together these thinkers formed the basis of most social explanations of religion.

Under the influence of functionalist and subsequent schools of anthropology, the perception of religion continued to be seen as divorced from nature. For Bronislaw Malinowski, religion satisfied the social needs of individuals, while Radcliffe-Brown saw religion as meeting the needs of society. While Claude Levi-Strauss's structuralism interpreted religion as a group of universal mental structures and Clifford Geertz saw religion as a system of symbols relevant to particular cultures, both separated society from nature. Mary Douglas and Victor Turner's emphasis on the performance of ritual and the psychological needs of society again assumed that religion was isolated from the natural world.

The debate among anthropologists in the last decades of the twentieth-century continued to revolve around the role that religion played in society, but with an increasingly postcolonial slant. Postcolonialism consists of the idea that the lens through which we look at other cultures is highly biased by the assumptions and prejudices of our own modern society. Such a "postmodern" slant is extremely useful in identifying possible influences on interpretation and helps us be aware of our limitations. However, postcolonialism itself can be seen as an extension of the modernist separation between culture and nature. The idea behind this type of cultural relativism—that neither cultures nor religions have any common reference points in objective reality—is a natural progression from the isolation of culture from nature. Without any common reference points in nature, cultures are seen to have no relation to one another and therefore are deemed incommensurable (Giddens 1984). Therefore, as a continuation of the same "modernist" line of thinking, Latour argues that postmodernist theory appears not to be the liberation of modernism that it thinks it is (Latour 1999, 7).

TWO

Archaeological Use of Theories

Over the past thirty years, the cultural and religious actions of many prehistoric societies have been interpreted using ethnographic analogies, effectively rendering much prehistoric material into a facsimile of the ethnographic present. The *a priori* assumptions that a separation exists between nature and culture and that cultural and religious actions belong in the cultural sphere have long prompted archaeologists to look for purely social motivations behind cultural and religious practices. The local and natural factors behind these practices have often been overlooked. Looking back over twenty years of his archaeological experience, James Brown states, "it is unsure that archaeology has anything to contribute other than exemplifications of ethnographically documented practices and beliefs" (Brown 1997, 470). Just as social theories did not get very far in explaining scientific facts during the Science Wars, except in a very broad and meaningless way—such as the explanation that Einstein's calculations of relativity stemmed from his turbulent youth (Feuer 1974)—neither do social theories explain much about prehistoric societies. On the contrary, they can actually stifle further explanation by closing discussion on a practice (Latour 2005, 105).

Another consequence of using ethnographic analogies is bad science (Latour 2005, 124). While prehistoric accounts have reams of good objective analyses (of ceramics, bone, lithics, etc.) and objective attempts to weave this data together, the use of ethnographic analogies to explain this data nullifies this objectivity. "Objective" is usefully defined by Latour as giving objects "a chance to *object* to what is said about them" (ibid., 125). The problem with social theories and generalized ethnographic analogies is that they are so amorphous and broad in their applicability that they can incorporate most data thrown at them, while little can contradict them. Karl Popper actually formed his scientific method of

41

falsification in reaction to this observed problem with theories—specifically with Marxism (Chalmers 1999). While originally an ardent Marxist
himself, Popper realized that Marxism or any grand theory could never
go wrong because they were flexible enough to accommodate any instance of human behavior and appear to be compatible with it. But, instead of being powerful, "they could in fact explain nothing because they
could rule out nothing" (ibid., 59). In talking about the commonly used
theory of power and domination (although this could also be said of most
other social theories), Latour states, "it never fails to explain. This is why
it always runs the danger of becoming empirically empty and politically
moot. Leaving open the possibility for failure is important because it is
the only way to maintain the quality of the scientific grasp and the chance
of political relevance" (Latour 2005, 251).

THE BRITISH NEOLITHIC

A test of such theories would be whether, over the past thirty years of
using social theory and ethnographic analogies, these analogies have
ever been refuted on the basis of new material, or whether they have
remained unassailable and have even halted further explanation. In this
next section I take a brief look at interpretation of the British Neolithic—
the archaeological field of origin for most of post-processualist theory. By
following particular analogies and theories applied over the past thirty
years—as an enormous amount of new material has been excavated—the
extent of damage done by them is measured, rather counterintuitively, by
their endurance and level of criticism. Following Popper's (1934) criteria,
the longer they have endured and the less criticism they have received,
the more damaging they have been. The importance of tracing these theories back to their place of origin is essential to highlight their contingency
and arrest their continued adoption by archaeologists in other fields.

Archaeologists of the British Neolithic have been particularly susceptible to the use of external explanations, and much of the archaeological
trend in using anthropological or sociological theories can be traced back
to this group of researchers. The susceptibility of the Neolithic to theories
stems largely from the poverty of data coming down from it. In a similar
way to sociologists who were able to apply social theory to the fringes of
society because objections were never heard, so too are Neolithic archaeologists able to apply social theories to the Neolithic with little contrary
object evidence objecting to them.

Thus several texts on the British Neolithic could be mistaken for
anthropology or sociology textbooks that happen to use archaeological
examples. While a great number of texts provide a rich contextual view of
the period with a genuine attempt to understand the nuances of regional
ritual and domestic life, these texts would be better served if anthropo-

logical analogies or sociological theories were avoided. While some claim that such analogies merely provide a range of possibilities (Whittle 2003, 130) and others provide disclaimers that they are not the last word (Thomas 1999, 128), it is disingenuous to think that others do not see these as interpretations. The argument that we are not preconditioned by them since we have the option to find an analogy that will best fit the evidence (Wylie 1985) is not much of an option given the limited number of analogies for particular practices. Not only do these analogies provide hypotheses and structures for the investigation, type of material to be collected, and frameworks for chapters or entire books, but they are rarely contested once such data is accumulated.

Ancestor Worship and Other Theories

In 2002 James Whitley wrote an article critiquing the use of one such theory, "ancestor worship," in interpretations of the Neolithic. He claimed it was being used to interpret everything that looked ritualistic with very little contextual consideration (for instance: Thomas 1991, 76; Tilley 1994, 40; 1999, 238; Parker Pearson and Ramilisonina 1998, 319; Edmonds 1999, 61 in Whitley 2002). He had begun to see it being "stuck on to Cretan material" in his own field and applied to interpret monuments elsewhere in Europe (Whitley 2002, 120), overpowering any nuanced interpretations offered. Ancestor worship, he claimed, was being accepted as a universal behavior with very little proof.

The theory of ancestor worship originally stemmed from Maurice Bloch's ethnographic study of the Merina of Madagascar (Bloch 1971)—a tribe of agriculturalists who interred their dead in collective tombs within special ancestral villages. Agriculturalists were seen as the first people to start appreciating past actions, since agriculture involved staking a claim to land and seeding and preparing the earth, which took time (Meillassoux 1972, 99). It was a small additional step to see ancestral graves, believed to coincide with early agriculture, as territorial markers used to stake claims to land (Chapman 1981; Goldstein 1981). Conversely, others believed that such graves provided the perception of time and land ownership needed to proceed with agricultural practice (Bradley 1984, 16; 1993, 17). With graves as the arbiters of ownership, it was argued that ancestor worship was only natural.

In the past twenty years the coincidence between agriculture and early Neolithic monuments has increasingly been questioned (Bradley 1993, 11–12; Thomas 1991). Other societies with elaborate monuments are not known to have had agriculture at all (Hopewell and Northwest Coast Cultures). Yet ancestor worship is still used as an interpretation. In addition to this, the great variety of ethnographic views on ancestry—comprising different qualifications for ancestral status, different locales for worship and reasons for worshiping—also mean that labeling rituals as

ancestor worship is speculative at best and far too general to mean anything (Whitley 2002, 122). In fact, Whitley concludes that "it is difficult to
find any theoretical grounds at all for holding on to ancestors in the
British Neolithic" (Whitley 2002, 121). It is not just that ancestor worship
is problematic as an interpretation, but that it can actively mislead interpretation by implying continuity between separate periods. Whitley cites
one interpretation that claimed that a reuse of Breton menhirs in later
Breton tombs merely represented a shift in location for ancestor worship
(Kirk 1993, 209 in Whitley 2002), implying a continuity rather than destruction and reinterpretation (Whitley 2002, 123).

In a similar way, the application of other analogies and social theories
to interpret the Neolithic should be addressed with equal skepticism
since they are likely to be misleading as well. The following interpretations of burial practice, artifacts, and "ritual" architecture are selected
from a range of literature on the Neolithic. Like ancestor worship, these
interpretations have become accepted as a body of orthodoxy with their
anthropological sources cited less and less in later publications, but it is
important to understand that they come from modern anthropological
explanations of local phenomena. The endurance of these interpretations
over the space of twenty or thirty years, with very little critique, indicates
that they have also overpowered contextual data and stymied further
investigation.

Interpretations of burial practice often include the use of Marx's notion (via Giddens) of masking social differentiation to legitimize authority, and Hertz's theory of collective representation in death, to explain a
lack of differentiation between individuals in long barrows (Shanks and
Tilley 1982, 152; Bradley 1984, 20; Thomas 1991, 113; 1999, 136; Tilley
1994, 202). Van Gennep's notion of burial as a rite of passage is frequently
co-opted to explain the series of stages from death to secondary burial in
order to affect this deceit (Bradley 1984; Richards and Thomas 1984, 190;
Thomas 1999, 129), and it is even applied to stages of monument use by
Hodder (1994, 81). Using Bloch (1982, 224), several archaeologists argue
that after incorporation into collective tombs, the bones from these crypts
would have then been widely circulated and used to wield power (Thomas 1991, 113; 1999, 136; Tilley 1994, 200; 1996, 220; Whittle and Wysocki
1998; Bradley 2007, 61). Thus burials are conceived as an expedient resource for legitimizing and maintaining power.

It is safe to say that interpretations of Neolithic artifacts usually use
the theory that objects in ritual contexts represent some kind of symbol or
metaphor for something else (from Levi-Strauss). Since Ian Hodder introduced the concept in the 1970s, most other post-processualists interested
in the Neolithic have used the concept to a greater or lesser extent and
still do. Bourdieu's related idea that artifacts are a means through which
people understand and order the social world and that they create contexts for social interaction and discourse is also used (Bradley 1984; Bar-

rett et al. 1991; Barrett 1994; Thomas 1996, 159). This is often joined with Giddens' (1984) idea that material culture is created for the reproduction of social authority (Bradley 1984, 47; Barrett et al. 1991, 116; Thomas 1996, 178; 1999, 36). As props for social discourse and prestige, artifacts are therefore also merely seen as a resource for legitimizing and maintaining power.

Interpretations of Neolithic architecture are the largest recipients of social theory and ethnographic analogy. Foucault's (1977) theory of panoptic surveillance, which he developed from a study of Victorian prisons, is used by Julian Thomas (1991, 105; 1999, 129) and John Barrett (1994, 72) to explain a technology of discipline in the architecture of Neolithic burial mounds. This is extended to include the phenomenological notions of architecture as embodying social principles of order that are imprinted on users unconsciously through their movement within and around monuments (from Cosgrove 1984) (Richards 1991; 1993, 149; Thomas 1991, 113; Richards and Parker Pearson 1994b, 20; Barrett 1994; Tilley 1996). Examples of social principles again come from ethnographic and social theory, including Turner's (1967) theory of the liminal position of burial in society (Bradley 1984, 28; Thomas 1996, 159; Parker Pearson and Ramilisonina 1998), Heidegger's bridging of natural and cultural features in the landscape (Barrett et al. 1991; Barrett and Ko 2009, 289), and Giddens' definition and legitimization of class differences through inclusion and exclusion (Bradley 1993, 55; Tilley 1994, 9; Barrett 1994, 15; Thomas 1999, 36; Bradley 2007, 105).

Interpretations using these theories or analogies usually begin by first analyzing a range of micro contexts, combining the data and synthesizing information before testing it against analogical concepts. The result is a unique expression of these concepts in a richly contextualized form, but we should not be surprised that the general analogies match the evidence provided so perfectly. Frameworks have a tendency to influence the selection of evidence (Latour 2005, 147; Law 2004).

While these concepts have continued to be used for over thirty years and have rarely been challenged, some development in research has occurred over this period. There has been an increasing focus on the spatial and temporal context of study, starting with Barrett et al. (1991) and becoming gradually finer in focus (Bradley 2007). A resistance to core/periphery interpretations of the Neolithic, that see Wessex or Orkney as central areas and other regions as peripheral imitators, has also been articulated recently (Barclay 2002; A. M. Jones 2011). There has also been an erratic increase in the contingency of symbolic interpretation. It is over these three points that much of the debate between British prehistorians is centered, reflecting differences in the level of reliance upon Bourdieu, Giddens, or Levi-Strauss. Nevertheless, surprisingly little has changed in the content of interpretations of particular practices or monuments since the time that ethnographic analogies or social theories were originally applied to them, despite enormous amounts of research and excavation. This indicates that such analogies have effectively stymied further explanation by capping interpretation with over-generalized theories.

Recently, many of these theories have also been imposed upon barrows of the Early Bronze Age. As with the Neolithic, Richard Bradley and Elise Fraser write that stages of barrow construction represented rites of passage for the dead (from van Gennep) (Bradley and Fraser 2011, 45). Barrows are claimed to have been reopened to gain bones that could then be circulated as powerful relics (from Bloch) and to have contained symbolic materials in construction that acted as metaphors for rites of passage (from Levi-Strauss) (ibid., 44). Such interpretations that attempt to explain all burial mounds in a region as a single entity inevitably focus on similarities and conflate differences. The impression that is left is one of continuity in space and time. This is all the more shocking since for several years Bradley has been the leading member of a major effort by the University of Reading to create an exhaustive corpus of excavation reports on Early Bronze Age burial mounds from all developer and university-funded excavations. The arbitrary way that these theories overrun all of this data illustrates the destructive nature of these theories.

While much can be learned from ethnographic and social analogies—including an understanding of the range of uses, content, and perceptions of objects and monuments and how they transmit that information—the main problem with preconditioning experience with specific explanations of practices (pulled directly from ethnographic sources or social theory) is that contextual reasons for local action end up being overlooked.

The argument often given—that ethnographic analogies are a necessary evil since it is naïve to suppose that we can objectively examine the world without imposing some idea of what it constitutes from our own standpoint (Hodder 1991, 99; Wylie 1985)—is also problematic given their disastrous side effects. In philosophy of science, such an argument has been turned on its head merely by applying the argument to science. What would a natural scientist say if he/she were told that they could not possibly study the natural world without imposing their own standpoint upon it? Latour argues that "all the sciences have been inventing ways to move from one standpoint to the next, from one frame of reference to the next" (Latour 2005, 146). The invention of means to move standpoints has been Latour's contribution to the social sciences and is what we need to do too. Is not accumulating data and marshaling it in various ways changing one's standpoint? Each change of standpoint helps us to align our interpretations more closely with the past, and each time we add new data and connections we get closer to it. Adopting ethnographic analogies takes us further away from this data.

What about political relevance? Applying the notion that all actions are influenced by a desire to legitimate or maintain power, advocated by numerous philosophers from Marx to Nietzsche and Foucault, postmodern social scientists and archaeologists have long used interpretation to champion the oppressed in the past and thereby highlight the afflictions of the oppressed in the present. Latour is often criticized for his refusal to apply such a notion to explain science or society. The Marxist, feminist, and Foucaultian arguments against Latour claim that by allowing matter to take the blame for actions, the ways that things are used in the interests of power are neglected, thereby doing injustice to the victimized (Haraway 1997, 35; Winner 1993, 375; Söderberg 2011; Bloor 1999; Restivo 2011).

Yet Latour does not reject power as a factor, but argues that specific explanations—of which power may be a factor—must be arrived at (composed) rather than imposed (Latour 2005). Composition of interpretations does not mean it is our role to create general theories about power or even to understand how power has operated in specific instances (which would be presupposing its role in events). Our role is to create theories about how objects are created and used in specific times and places. If power is found to be a factor in relations, then of course its specific use should be described. Anything more, though, would actually give disproportionate analytical weight to a particular elite which may unduly empower them by focusing attention on them to the exclusion of others and other factors.

Explanations of Change

Another consequence of using ethnographic, "natural," or "social" theories to explain objects or human practices, rather than relying purely upon local history and context, is that the explanation of change becomes problematic in several ways. The first problem with using universal theories to explain actions is that they then have to be used to explain change too. The lack of temporal depth in most ethnographic studies unfortunately means that anthropological or social theories rarely explain why things change. Thus archaeologists have had to adopt several "fixes" to cope with the problem of variation and change in the archaeological record. One of these "fixes" is the adaptation of ethnographic analogies or social theories—originally developed to explain *static* practices in anthropology—to explain *dynamic* transformations in archaeology.

Thus Bradley (1984) and Thorpe and Richards (1984) adapt the anthropological theory of conspicuous consumption, originally used by Franz Boas to explain the "waste" of prestige goods by American Northwest Coast Indians in potlatch ceremonies (Boas 1897; Veblen 1899; Benedict 1934), to create a universal theory for artifact change. This model sees certain exotic objects as items of status, relating to their rarity, craftsmanship, or the exoticism of their raw materials. Bradley's adaptation argues that when a particular item or assemblage becomes too available and

commonplace in society, a more exotic range of items with a more controlled supply network will be welcomed, thus changing the elite's artifact repertoire (Bradley 1984; Bradley and Edmonds 1993).

A similar explanation is adopted for changes in architecture and burial practice. Barrett (1994, 117) argues that the introduction of round barrows represented a new context for elite ostentation, enabling individuals
to control conspicuous consumption and the communication of symbolism. The change from communal to individual burial in these round barrows is explained through the adaptation of another anthropological theory—using Marx and Hertz's theory of collective representation in reverse—and is interpreted as a denial of the undifferentiated collective
representation of society (Barrett et al. 1991, 139). The subsequent change
from inhumation burial to cremation burial practice in the Early Bronze
Age is also viewed as providing a better context for ostentation and communication. By removing the distraction of the individual from deposits,
Barrett argues that it was then possible to unambiguously communicate
the symbolic meanings of deposits (Barrett 1994, 119; Mizoguchi 1995,
248).

The second problem with using anthropological theories is that, while
explaining general changes, there is a disjuncture between old and new
objects and practices. For example, claiming that prehistoric people
moved from one artifact to another or from one practice to another for
reasons of political expediency gives the impression that new artifacts,
architecture, or practices popped into existence fully formed. Such an
approach fails to explain how they emerged or why they emerged in the
form that they did. The explanation that changes occurred for the reproduction or legitimization of authority is too broad an explanation to explain the similarities and differences in new forms and practices. For
example, the idea that Beaker assemblages were adopted from the conti-
nent, and Beaker burial practices adopted from Scotland, to augment a
southern social organization and ideology that was already in place
(Bradley 2007, 152) does not explain their unique configuration in the
south and the convergence of a new assemblage, burial practice, barrow
structure, and changes in ceremonial monuments (Martin 2011).

This brings us to a third problem with imposing external theories to
explain changes: such theories obscure how change is viewed. By seeing
social and religious activities as the expression of universal behavior,
these activities are seen as a mere surface layer of social behavior on top
of a much more solid social or structural organization that changes more
slowly. Social and religious activities are either seen as merely a medium
for the invisible "habitus" that structures the deeper consciousness and
actions of individuals from behind the scenes (Bourdieu 1984), or as the
medium for social reproduction by social organizations (Giddens 1984).
In each case, deeper social entities are considered more solid than the

activities through which they act: activities that can adapt to circumstances more readily to provide the optimum medium.

Thus by using ethnographic or social analogies and ignoring the specific nature and history of changes, change is viewed as progressive and part of a continuum. From this modernist perspective, the replacement of long barrows by round barrows and the substitution of communal graves for individual Beaker graves in the Early Bronze Age are viewed as a progressive change (Barrett 1994, 140). Bradley even argues that "the adoption of Beaker pottery did not involve a radical change" but instead reflects a continuity in settlement and deployment of pottery. Moreover, changes in burial practice are merely seen as representing superficial changes related to increasing social divisions (Bradley 2007, 152).

This conflation of regional practices and the emphasis on similarities—while de-emphasizing differences in practices, artifacts, and monuments over time—is a fourth problem that theories present. Paul Garwood has recently discussed such a trend in relation to the Late Neolithic and Early Bronze Age. Garwood argues that continuity within and between periods is often sought by prehistorians who desire to formulate or justify general theories. He writes, "it is too easy, in this context, to conflate what was temporally separate, to confuse profoundly different forms of cultural signification, and to represent these as if they all belonged to the same milieu of cultural expression" (Garwood 2007, 31). Profound ideological separations within and between periods evident in radically different burial practices, assemblages, and monuments are thereby downplayed. In talking about monuments spanning the transition to the Beaker period, Bradley writes, "as so often, an unnecessarily rigid typology conceals what was probably a continuum" (Bradley 2007, 81). This offhand rejection of enormous transformations enables him to argue that there were "a whole range of ideas that had been present in Britain and sometimes Ireland from the first introduction of agriculture" (ibid., 83).

Thus according to British prehistorians, the Neolithic elite adopted new artifacts because they were more exotic; new architecture because it was more conspicuous; and new burial practices because they enabled better communication. The general impression that these leave is that change was superficial and welcomed. From the modernist perspective this model is perfectly acceptable. However, from a pre-modern perspective this interpretation would be unthinkable.

PRE-MODERN PERSPECTIVES

As Latour has argued, the reason that modernism has been so successful is because moderns have been educated to believe that nature is firmly separated from culture and society. This allows us to create hybrid products with the firm belief that we are creating purely natural products that could not affect the social order. Conversely, change in the social sphere is perceived as having no impact upon the natural order. By compartmentalizing such changes, change is seen by the "modernist" as positive, as relatively insignificant and non-threatening, allowing for more change to proceed.

To the pre-modern, the natural and social orders are completely integrated, so that natural change results in the modification of the social order and vice versa. Changes are enormously significant to the premodern and any alteration in either demands elaborate contemplation of the implications that alterations might bring. Claude Levi-Strauss described this contemplation, stating, "[T]he native is a logical hoarder. . . . [H]e is forever tying the threads, unceasingly turning over all the aspects of reality, whether physical, social or mental" (Levi-Strauss 1962, 267 in Latour 1993, 42). Others have attributed the homeostasis of indigenous culture to the mental inertia that such a complex contemplation imposes every time a change is suggested (Descola 1993, 405 in Latour 1993, 43). The very job of the cultural anthropologist is to illustrate the complex interconnectedness of indigenous societies in order to understand their sociologic, yet archaeologists continue to believe that cultural change could be related to something as trivial as status. Such a belief in the relative irrelevance of cultural changes, while flying in the face of anthropology, strongly suggests that we have been influenced by our own modernist view of change.

This is not to say that we should necessarily resort to anthropology for our techniques and assumptions. Anthropology itself has not been exempt from modernist assumptions, despite realizing the differences between our perceptions and those of indigenous peoples. There is a crucial difference between seeing the interconnectivity between nature and culture in indigenous societies and believing that this connection really exists (Latour 2005, 116). Without this understanding, cultural anthropologists have only been able to explain indigenous connections culturally, not naturally. Instead of being forced to investigate the natural history of connections, anthropologists have resorted to a range of stock social explanations. Latour writes, "It had become so easy to account for deviation! Society, beliefs, ideology, symbols, the unconscious, madness— everything was so readily available that explanations were becoming obese" (Latour 1993, 93).

OBJECT BIOGRAPHIES

Nevertheless, one valuable contribution from anthropology for understanding object change has been the notion that objects have extensive biographies. Arjun Appadurai's book *The Social Life of Things* (1986) has provided a valuable corrective to the assumption that objects are static entities. Object biographies were conducted as early as the 1960s by processualists such as Michael Schiffer (1972) and Binford (1983) to assess how objects entered the archaeological record (Joy 2009) — Chaîne Opératoire was used to identify the process of object manufacture (Leroi-Gourhan 1964), and use-wear analysis was used to study the changing use of objects (Tringham 1994), but Appadurai's (1986) and Igor Kopytoff's (1986) concept of the changing social meaning of objects was brought to archaeology by Chris Gosden and Yvonne Marshall (1999). They write that the processualist "object here is a passive, inert material to which things happen and things are done. Such analyses do not address the way social interactions involving people and objects create meaning" (ibid.). Their biographical approach sought to follow the interaction between people and things and to show how the meanings of objects change through exchange, performance (ibid.), and appropriation (Gillings and Pollard 1999). Jody Joy (2009) has stressed that the lack of data about different stages of an object's life presents problems for object biographies, but that by presenting histories of objects in idealized form, with information from many objects of a single object type, and by applying all of the above techniques, a general history of an object type can be reconstructed.

Yet, while these are all valuable ways to attain information about objects, they each tend to present objects as commodities, either social, economic, or functional, that change meaning by being passed from one individual to another or from one function to another (ibid.), retaining their meaning in between. This conception of objects and change again derives from the assumption that objects are solid natural or cultural entities, rather than networks of associations. As solid objects they are perceived as being able to maintain their stability for extensive periods of time between different adaptations, rather than changing constantly whenever they are introduced to new associations (Latour 2005, 35; Jones 2012). Stability then becomes seen as the rule rather than the exception and is assumed to be uncomplicated. Thus, biographies of objects tend to view the various "careers" of an object in ten- to two-hundred-year increments, with their meaning still static in between changes. It also means that objects of similar form are seen as sharing meaning and function over time and space and therefore can be used to speak for all similar objects (Joy 2009).

When seen as networks of associations, objects suddenly become extremely susceptible to change. The mere introduction of a new association can completely change their meaning. If the stability of an object's meaning (or the stability of its associations) is desired — and the stability of many objects is crucial for the stability of groups — then that meaning must be protected and maintained at a huge cost in human effort (in the same way that laboratory conditions must be extended and maintained for facts to apply in the outside world today). This means that stability of meaning is actually a rarity and needs to be identified and accounted for in our analyses.

The precariousness of object meanings is another reason why changes to stabilized object meanings are so resisted by pre-moderns, and why such changes need to be identified and accounted for by the researcher as well. Stability is not a natural default position that occurs to any object, nor is change to stabilized objects inconsequential or accidental. This difference in the perception of change has huge consequences for how the archaeological record should be examined. Primarily, it illustrates the importance of identifying and following stabilized objects to understand how meaning is maintained and changed (more on this, and how it helps to avoid using theories, in chapter 5).

COMBINING THEORIES TO BRIDGE THE DIVIDE

Archaeologists have long been aware of the problems that the modernist division between nature and culture creates. Many have claimed that this division is responsible for numerous problems in archaeological practice and interpretation (Sian Jones 1997; Andy Jones 2002, 2007; Thomas 2004). However, solutions to these problems have usually been sought by creating a bridge over this divide (Renfrew 2004; Kuznar 2008; Jones 2002, 2007; Boivin 2008).

Latour argues that instead of solving these problems, attempts to bridge the divide between nature and culture have actually helped to maintain and perpetuate the division. This is because those who purportedly bridge the divide between natural and cultural spheres inevitably end up placing an unequal emphasis on one or other of the spheres (Latour 1993, 67). For example, while Andy Jones has come a long way since 2002, in his book *Archaeological Theory and Scientific Practice* (2002) he roundly criticizes processualists for starting from situated utilitarian premises, and post-processualists for their ideological perception of everything, but ultimately falls back upon Structuration theory as an independent, self-evident theory that can unite the two. The hermeneutic interpretive method is also heralded as a way to mediate between social theories and scientific data when studying the past. Yet these are theories and methods central to post-processualism and are seen to be part of the problem by scientists, not part of the solution. Science, on the other hand, is only seen as useful in providing a few techniques that can be used in a post-processual interpretive framework (ibid.). As a result, this proposal comes across as more of a strategy for the requisition of science rather than a peace offering.

In the science or processualist camp, proposals to bridge the divide are curiously similar. In a series of articles on the Eastern North American Woodlands, Jane Buikstra and Douglas Charles attempt their own reconciliation. They first criticize post-processual theories (Structuration theory in particular) for starting from situated premises, before detailing utilitarian theories as self-evident (Buikstra et al. 1999). As a peace offering they argue that more ideational meanings for artifacts and practices could be tacked onto the back of their functionalist interpretations. Ethnographic analogies are seen by them as a legitimate resource for understanding meanings of artifacts and practices—as long as they do not touch their functionalist interpretations of short- or long-term processes.

Thus it can be seen that each side predictably follows the logic of their convictions, eventually castigating the other for their "impositions" of situated theory, while seeing their own as universal. The adoption of a few elements to embroider their own unchanged framework—assuming that these represent the best from the other's framework—is considered sufficient to create a peaceful settlement. However, such a settlement avoids the vast differences between and among them, something that the diatribes of Hodder, Binford, and Shanks and Tilley in the 1980s at least recognized.

The real problem is the assumption that there are any theories, either processual or post-processual, that are universal. The attitude generally adopted in mediations between processualists and post-processualists is that one has the "truth" while the other is "situated"—an attitude that is lacking in logic. This attitude is similar to one that Latour sees in mediations between positivists and poststructuralists. He sees both as antifetishists who "debunk objects they don't believe in by showing the productive and projective forces of people; then, without ever making the connection, they use objects they do believe in to resort to the causalist or mechanist explanation" (Latour 2004b, 240). While both concede a few self-criticisms, none reject all theories as contingent and agree to start afresh from a new basis. But this is exactly what is required (ibid., 243). Only by accepting that all theories are constructions from local information will peacemakers ever stop imposing theories and be empowered to genuinely re-construct their own interpretive methods.

By understanding that both groups originally developed their theories with only half of the information available (rejecting the other half as irrelevant), the only solution is to build new approaches to interpretation that see objects as an integration of natural and cultural information. However, this does not mean building approaches out of the building blocks of current disciplines either.

CREATING THEORIES TO BRIDGE THE DIVIDE

Recently, several attempts have been made to create theories and approaches that bridge the divide between nature and culture, while maintaining assumptions from disciplinary spheres. A review of such attempts is Nicole Boivin's recent book *Material Cultures, Material Minds* (2008). Boivin first follows phenomenological techniques. Instead of the sort of phenomenology that adds human experience to symbolic and textual accounts (see Tilley 2004), Boivin advocates neurophenomenology, a technique that adds a human element to materialist views of culture—following phenomenologist Merleau-Ponty. The consideration of emotions attached to material objects is argued to be crucial in order to understand objects and the role they play in people's lives. This attachment is then understood by reference to studies of cognition and the brain that see memory and decision making as being enhanced by emotions (Damasio 2003). Taking this approach, Boivin explains emotion as the driving force behind actions and object creation by showing (through cognitive science) how certain actions and objects induce emotions. From this perspective, cultural phenomena such as rock art or religious experiences are interpreted as designed to create altered states of consciousness (Needham 1967; Lewis-Williams 2002; Dornan 2004 in Boivin 2008).

However, attempts to create theories and approaches that combine the extremes of unconscious subjective and unconscious objective determinism fall prey to the same problems that combining theories do. They assume that both phenomenological theories about emotion and cognitive scientific theories about the brain are absolute and universal and that these are the most important factors influencing behavior. Imposing such theories ignores the contingency of these theories and overwhelms the material context and history of objects and actions that actually led to past behavior. Of course, emotions may have been part of the mix, and certain actions or objects most likely produced strong emotions or altered states, but it is unwise to assume which emotions these were, or that because they heightened cultural experiences this was the primary origin and intention of such actions or objects. Such a view sees cultural actions as little more than irrational subjective behavior determined by our material bodies. Instead of eliminating a divide between culture and nature, neurophenomenology appears to bring the weaknesses of both sociological and scientific explanations together—the sociological notion that culture lacks a basis in reality and the scientific notion that culture lacks a basis in thought—maintaining and exacerbating the idea that culture has no rationale grounded in observation (Latour and Yaneva 2008, 83).

The idea that the body is a universal standpoint from which to reason, with universal types of identity, emotions, desires, and mental and material characteristics, is unstable ground once any of these particular characteristics are examined closely. Latour argues that the body is no more universal than cultural theories (Latour 2005). He compares the body's competencies and characteristics to plug-ins, applets, or patches—downloads that allow you to see or do different things on the Web. Latour writes, "if you began to probe the origin of each of your idiosyncrasies, would you not be able to deploy, here again, the same star-like shape [network] that would force you to visit many places, people, times, events that you had largely forgotten? This tone of voice, this unusual expression, this gesture of the hand, this gait, this posture, aren't these traceable as well?" (ibid., 209). Instead of the neo-Darwinian interpretation that we are born with cognitive abilities, a psyche, and emotions, Latour argues that each one of these has a local history that can be traced to books, songs, films, friends, etc. "Every competence, deep down in the silence of your interiority, has first to come from the outside" (ibid., 213). This approach is not so different from Peirce's approach to the self and the mind, which he also argued are comprised purely of external associations (Peirce 1998 [1903] in Colapietro 1989, 102)

The result of Jones' and Boivin's compilation or creation of theories is an approach to material culture that requires a proficient competency in multiple disciplines and an ability to combine multiple conflicting theories. In practice this complex enterprise is rarely possible, let alone desirable. Instead of helping to desegregate the different fields of archaeology and erode the nature/culture divide, directives to seek common ground and combine theories and methods are much more likely to preserve the status quo. By leaving individual practices and theories alone and merely attempting to combine rather than rebuild them, the existence of these approaches is effectively legitimized. The difficulty in mastering other fields and the very real conflict between theories means that most archaeologists will continue practicing their separate approaches unthreatened, as part of a greater whole that somebody else can combine later. As Andrew Fleming has recently said on behalf of most archaeological scientists (quoting Terence Kealey), "we live with the postmodern insights by ignoring them in practice while acknowledging them in theory" (Fleming 2006, 279).

Yet the main problem with combining theories or creating new approaches to culture from both sociology and science is that the assumptions and theories from these disciplines were created from a consideration of only half of the nature/culture equation. In the same way that social theories and analogies assume that culture is derived from a purely cultural system of references, scientific theories of culture assume that culture is derived from a purely natural system of references. The outcome of both assumptions is the same—a strong sensation that an enormous amount of information is missing from local accounts of action, and as a result, the creation of a body of external theories to account for the missing agency. Latour argues that external theories would never have been sought in the first place had it been understood that all agency resides in purely local natural and cultural factors encrypted into objects. Thus the idea that a solution can be found by combining external theories from both sociology and science is fairly ridiculous. Neither psychological, phenomenological, cognitive, anthropological, nor biological theories can provide an interpretation that is built from the bottom up and includes purely local information.

Admittedly, it has been difficult to free ourselves from modernism long enough to see this, let alone adopt an alternative. Julian Thomas argues that without modernism archaeology would not exist at all and therefore an alternative would not even be desirable (Thomas 2004, 210). Yet, as Latour has argued, "we have never been modern." Despite our theoretical understanding of what we do and how we understand ourselves, our practices may have largely remained untouched. This means that most of what we *do* can continue to be practiced and productive, but that part of our practice that has been affected by modernist (and postmodernist) theory should be revisited.

PERSPECTIVISM

Recently, there has been an attempt in anthropology to go beyond theories and ethnographic analogies and to create interpretations based upon alternative ontologies. This is based on a movement in anthropology, led by Eduardo Viveiros de Castro, to promote the alternative ontology of Amazonian Perspectivism as a basis for interpretation of anthropological material across the Americas. By applying Latour's methodology to understand his extensive ethnographic work in the Amazon, Viveiros de Castro (1998, 484) argues that instead of indigenous ideas and practices being the manifestations of universal social or cultural practices, they are instead the result of philosophically complex reasoning from an entirely different ontology than our own. In the same way that our own modern society has been built upon the ontological separation between nature and culture, Viveiros de Castro argues that Amerindian society has been built upon the inseparability between nature and culture. Instead of there being one unchanging nature and many separate changeable cultures (as in our own Western perception of the world), Amazonian Perspectivism sees one Culture/Soul/Mind and many natures, or in other words, one set of qualities that everything shares, and many forms that express different combinations of those qualities (ibid.).

This helps to explain philosophically, rather than analogically, many of the unusual perspectives and accounts by Amerindians. For instance, if forms, whether they are animal, human, plant, or mineral, are different because of their different combinations of qualities, then these forms can change with the attainment of other qualities or through the emphasis of certain qualities. This helps to partly explain the Amerindian idea of fluidity and change in the "natural" environment. It also accounts for Amerindian animal-human shape-shifting and indigenous accounts of animism and totemism. Viveiros de Castro writes that "myths tell how animals lost the qualities inherited or retained by humans. . . . Humans are those who continue as they have always been: animals are ex-humans, not humans ex-animals" (ibid., 472). Therefore, the qualities that both animals and humans share are very human qualities—dispositions and capacities that are expressed by their actions, interactions, and communications and are symbolized by the form of their bodies (ibid., 478)—the only difference being that animals have fewer of our qualities, but also others that we have lost. This is very similar to Latour's understanding of both humans and non-humans as entirely composed of local assemblages of traits, qualities, and elements grouped together or attained and constantly changing (Latour 2005, 212).

For example, both Viveiros de Castro (1998) and Tim Ingold (1998) argue that the act of wearing a mask or animal skin, or carrying a depiction of an animal, is an effort to attain additional qualities or traits that those animals possess. Wearing animal clothing activates the qualities and powers of that animal in the same way that a deep-sea diving suit enables divers to function like a fish (Viveiros de Castro 1998, 482). Thus animal skins and depictions have considerable power.

While some archaeologists have already benefited from these ideas and applied them to understand their own sites (Heckenberger 2005; Conneller 2004; Brown and Walker 2008), several anthropologists and archaeologists have already taken issue with Viveiro de Castro's idea of an Amerindian Perspectivist ontology that stretches across the Americas and purportedly everywhere. Tim Ingold has argued that at least two different types of ontology exist, not one—animism and totemism—that represent separate ontologies with different practices (Ingold 1998), although Viveiros de Castro argues that they both "apprehend the same phenomena [Perspectivism] from different angles" (Viveiros de Castro 1998, 476). Going further than Ingold, Descola claims that Perspectivism is just one of several different ontologies that exist, including animism and totemism (quoted in Latour 2009b). Archaeologists Alberti and Marshall (2009) go even further and argue that individual ontologies should be extracted from each culture—from local ethnographic analogies or mythologies—before being applied to their archaeological material.

While these critiques provide many valuable examples of the differences between modernist and non-modernist thinking, there are problems with their solutions too. Unless the archaeological sites under study are very recent, the effort to derive ontologies from local ethnographic analogies or mythologies to understand them is little better than using universal ethnographic analogies or social theories—the same problems exist. Apart from the obvious problems with imposing a recent model of behavior or sociologic on the past, ontologies are perceived by Alberti and Marshall as similar to social structures or systems of meaning. In the same way that objects are seen to operate within social structures to solve social problems, objects are seen to operate in ontologies to: stabilize meaning (Alberti and Marshall 2009), embody powerful energies (Bray

2009), or attract animals (Haber 2009) — also fulfilling social functions. An invisible force (this time an ontology instead of society) is seen to determine actions and objects. While the people who hold such an animistic ontology may not see a separation between nature and culture, by seeing their animistic objects as merely mental creations with social applications, the archaeologist or anthropologist maintains the split between nature and culture.

Yet a more pressing problem with Amazonian Perspectivism is not that Viveiros de Castro is too universal, but that he is not universal enough. His specificity in detailing the expression of Perspectivism in actions and meanings of objects lays him open to charges of contingency. By treating the specific Amazonian ontology like a universal analogy, he sees it as an explanation for material correlates in other cultures rather than as a philosophy for building local interpretations. While Perspectivism provides a valuable expression of a local Amazonian cultural system and a good example of the application of Latour's methodology to understand it, because he does not explain the process through which animals or objects gain their power, and how they could gain different meanings, Perspectivism has limited applications.

An ontology is a theory about the nature of being, and as Alberti and Bray have asserted, such theories differ enormously from culture to culture. Ontologies vary over time and space largely because of new information that constantly impacts them. All that we can really assume about past ontologies, based upon studies of non-modern societies (and even modernist practices) is that they rarely maintain a division between nature and culture, subjects and objects. Our job as archaeologists is not to guess at another culture's "ontology" and impose it (like a theory) to understand their practices, but to build it up from the objects, associations, and geographical and historical contexts of the time and place we are investigating. Nevertheless, the understanding that objects and practices involve an integration of both nature and culture enables us to better understand the role that objects and practices play in articulating ontologies and provides a valuable basis from which to reconstruct them.

Viveiros de Castro has provided a priceless illustration of how such an integration is expressed in the Amazon, but in order to understand how other local expressions/ontologies are articulated, we must know the process through which these expressions are articulated. This way we can identify the steps taken in the past to articulate them and find ways to follow and understand these particular expressions from the bottom up (Holbraad 2009, 436). Otherwise, the past will continue to be merely colorful "exemplifications of ethnographically documented practices and beliefs" (Brown 1997, 470).

Martin Holbraad has written that "the most pressing line of research in pursuing such an alternative . . . is namely to overhaul archaeological methods in ways that render them sensitive to alternative ontologies of things" (Holbraad 2009, 440). Such an entanglement in modernist thought obviously makes our efforts at changing research and interpretive methods extremely difficult, but fortunately Latour and others in the sociology of science have spent several decades disentangling them for us. The result is an understanding of culture that Latour calls "non-modern," together with an alternative science of the social.

THREE

Object Science

What sets Latour's "science of the social" apart from other attempts to understand society and the past is primarily its premise. Instead of accepting the sociological and anthropological definition of culture as a set of human beliefs and rules reflected by purely cultural symbols, Latour argues that "the very notion of culture is an artifact created by bracketing Nature off. Cultures—different or universal—do not exist, any more than Nature does. There are only nature-cultures" (Latour 1993, 104). From this radically different perspective of culture, Latour has built up an alternative understanding of objects and institutions, as well as the sociological methods to study these new entities. The value of this understanding and its accompanying methods is that it dispenses altogether with two of the main dilemmas in the humanities and social sciences: how to reconcile micro actions with macro structures and how to avoid imposing social theories.

The first dilemma—reconciling micro and macro scales—is avoided by redefining culture as a "bundle of ties" rather than an actual macro entity. Latour argues that cultures are mistaken for actual entities when the process of their becoming, and the associations which are networked to form them, are ignored. This is very similar to the way that theories are universalized when the history of their construction is ignored, as discussed in the first chapter, and it results in the similar impression that society and culture are very powerful forces, when in fact they are merely the overall picture of many local actions. By focusing on the network of local associations that constitute society's character rather than looking for some general power or social influence, the researcher is able to remain on the local level without resorting to a macro level. In fact, Latour argues that any study that desires to understand the true nature of a society, culture, or religion must never look outside of this network of local associations to something larger or external like an overarching cultural force (Latour 2005, 1).

In his book *Reassembling the Social* (2005), Latour outlines a new sociology of culture that can conduct such studies. Written like a travel guide, he maps the typical pitfalls of sociological studies and outlines the path one must take to avoid them. The pitfalls are mainly those temptations to depart from the local network of associations and to use a general, universal explanation to understand missing agencies—agencies that we often think must be global and social rather than coming from another local source (Latour 2005).

In order to overcome the second dilemma—the use of theories—it is necessary to understand that a group's *process of becoming* is not just a very local affair, but that it also involves a mediation between both cultural and natural spheres. This means that artifacts and actions are stimulated by natural as well as cultural phenomena, making them no longer purely subjective but based upon an objective reality too. If groups and their objects are based on natural as well as cultural information, then objects no longer have meaning merely in relation to one another, and sites and objects can be examined more empirically since there is a rational link with a common world. This allows interpretations to be built up without the imposition of arbitrary frameworks. However, access to this objective content and the ability to conduct such studies involves transcending certain traditional boundaries of study. One of these boundaries is the idea that humans are the only actors endowed with motive powers in society.

In his article "Where Are the Missing Masses?" (1992), Latour argues that in the same way that physicists have been looking for the missing mass in the universe to balance accounts of creation, sociologists have been searching for the "missing masses" that could balance their accounts of social construction. Whenever sociologists have attempted to study a social phenomenon, they have always sensed that vital information and agencies are missing from their local accounts. This has stimulated them to seek these missing agencies in invisible macro structures and cultural theories, but Latour argues that the missing agencies have been right in front of us all along, in the form of objects and artifacts. He states that "to balance our accounts of society, we simply have to turn our exclusive attention away from humans and look also at nonhumans" (Latour 1992, 227).

Thus, in order for studies to remain local and avoid seeking agencies in society, nature, individuals, or any external theory, it is essential to understand how objects encrypt natural and cultural information and are endowed with motive powers that then structure actions.

OBJECTS AS AGENTS

Taking a lead from Michel Foucault (1977)—but without reducing every-thing to mechanisms of social control—Latour outlines how human ac-tions and communications can be delegated to artifacts which then re-place humans and are able to physically constrain or enable others. Like a road bump that forces cars to slow down or a door closer that gently closes doors, objects can be entrusted with tasks and responsibilities in lieu of humans.

This investment of agency in objects is similar to the understanding in archaeology that material culture is active in its ability to constrain move-ment and maintain a setting for discourse (Thomas 1991; Barrett 1994), but Latour's understanding goes much further than this. Such an under-standing held by post-processualists uses the analogy of written "text" to explain object use (Hodder 1991). Objects in this analogy are compared to words that constrain discourse and communicate ideas within a gram-mar, or cultural "context" (ibid., 153). However, Latour sees objects not just as tools for ideas and actions, but proactive in their manipulation and empowerment of human activity.

In order to understand how this is possible, it is not enough to see objects as semantic tools. We need to understand *how* objects are formed, adopted, and used in order for us to see why they are so powerful. Viewing objects as inanimate tools moved only by human labor is similar to watching people drive cars and thinking that they are the motive pow-er behind them. People may be operating them, but an understanding of how cars are so powerful involves looking under the hood.

Objects are only the end point of a vast network of associations and relationships (both natural and cultural) that have culminated in a partic-ular form. The textual analogy for objects is misleading therefore because unlike words, objects can attain and maintain a much larger number of associations and thus are much more powerful. They are also not so universal in their meaning, often changing their meaning as they are adapted to other circumstances.

In examining the "process of becoming" for objects, it is clear that the traditional view of objects as emerging from a previous form, a functional necessity, or an external location does not begin to explain why they are used. Instead of viewing objects as solid things, Latour prefers to call objects "gatherings" or "collectives." One way to envision this new defi-nition of objects and to understand the process of their "becoming" is to see objects not as text, but instead as one would see a scientific formula.

OBJECTS AS FORMULAS

It was actually Latour's early investigations into how formulas arise in science that stimulated this new understanding of objects. His two-year anthropological study of a Nobel-prize-winning laboratory at the Salk Institute in California involved examining every stage in the characterization of a new entity—the TRH growth hormone (Latour and Woolgar 1979), a substance produced by the brain and believed to control body chemistry. Instead of coming to the traditional conclusion that the characterizing formula was a purely natural entity that had been discovered in the "book of nature," or to the social constructivist conclusion that it had emerged through some sort of social influence, Latour illustrated that it had come about through a local process of information accumulation (through tests), constant reduction, and combination. Such an explanation was confirmed as self-evident by the scientists involved (Salk 1979, 13; Latour and Woolgar 1986, 274).

During this process of characterization, the formula was a constantly evolving entity in the laboratory, constantly changing with every bit of new information that was accumulated. But once this process of characterization was arbitrarily stopped, and the formula was published in a scientific journal as a natural entity, the history of its development was forgotten, and the formula became a universal static entity. Rather than limiting this discovery to science, Latour argues that any object that is presented without the history of its characterization is prone to be categorized as "natural" or "cultural" and seen to be a solid, static entity.

This may also be the reason why objects and practices are so often characterized as solid, static entities in the social sciences as well. The social sciences rarely investigate purely local explanations for objects and practices, but commonly seek explanations in external theories and agencies, severely marginalizing the position of local history in explanation (Connell 1984). Despite its focus on the past, archaeology has also been poor at explaining change in local historical terms without resorting to external theories (Smith 2001). Therefore, it is not surprising that objects are viewed as static entities and mere tools in a functionalist or semantic tool set.

Nevertheless, this can be rectified by refocusing our attention on the process of accumulation, reduction, and combination of information behind objects, allowing the power of objects to be understood and for objects to be repositioned at the center of social construction and change. Nevertheless, such a process is a complex affair and, therefore, is best illustrated by reference to scientific practice.

The first step—accumulation of information about the world—involves experiencing the world, inscribing and mobilizing data back to a center of calculation, while retaining a degree of stability and context. This can be achieved in several ways: by experiencing objects and their relationship to certain elements in the environment, or by their relationship to trials in the laboratory. The second step—reduction of that information—involves the translation of that information from thousands of observations into symbols such as chemical elements, terms, or statistical variables and tallies, whose primary purpose is to reduce the volume of data. Reduction also enables that information to become more observable and combinable, with a minimum of contextual impoverishment. The third step—the combination of these symbols—again is no more of a cognitive activity than a further effort at reduction. Symbols are merely related to other encrypted observations via equations that juxtapose observations depending on their contextual association (Latour 1987).

An example that is given by Latour of this practice of accumulation, reduction, and combination is the calculation of turbulence by the nineteenth-century engineer Osborne Reynolds. This gives us a very good idea of the process behind the construction of an object—in this case a formula for turbulence. Reynolds collected hundreds of observations of turbulence from streams, rivers, and scale models (using various liquids). He then translated into symbols common observations such as, "The faster the flow, the more turbulence there is; the bigger the obstacle encountered by the flow the more turbulence there will be; the denser a fluid the more prone to turbulence it is; finally, the more viscous a fluid the less turbulence there will be" (ibid., 237). These were reduced to "T(urbulence) is proportional to S(peed), T is proportional to L(ength of the obstacle), T is proportional to D(ensity), T is inversely proportional to V(iscosity)" (ibid., 238). This reduced the number of observations considerably, translating them into symbols for easy manipulation. But a final combination of these symbols allowed the relationship between these observations to be most succinctly represented—T (is related to) *SLD / V*. While this final formula is merely the final translation in a series of reductions, it enables an individual to view many observations and relationships at once and to project what would happen in a particular instance given multiple factors (ibid.).

This also helps to explain the process of "becoming" for Roger Guillemin's TRH peptide, mentioned earlier. Like turbulence, TRH was a theoretical entity long before Guillemin formed his laboratory, but it was not an object until its relationships had been observed and these observations accumulated, reduced, and combined. Over many months, Guillemin and his laboratory put the object through hundreds of trials to determine its character. It was the observations of these trials and their reduction to a short but dense explanation in an academic article that created TRH as the distinct entity: Pyro-Glu-His-Pro-NH^2. The TRH growth hormone, like Reynolds' turbulence, was not a thing but a web of relationships that Guillemin had constructed from the observation of trials.

ANCIENT OBJECT FORMULAS

In a similar way, artifacts found in the archaeological record are the end result of a reduction of vast amounts of information and associations relating to the natural and social world. This does not mean that they stopped being adopted for other purposes once they were made (their further adoption and use would have continued the process of information reduction and combination). But it does mean that objects found in archaeological excavations should not be labeled as universal ancient or modern equivalents before the context of their deposition and use is established. Even purportedly utilitarian objects such as a bronze axe would have reduced information about the solidity of the item it was used for, the best materials for its construction, the best way for it to be constructed, hafted, and used, but it also would have reduced information about the history of previous forms and practices, associations and uses, and present needs and political circumstances. Many of these relationships were most likely recognized and enrolled when deciding upon its construction and later deposition, so it is essential that the contextual circumstances of objects are researched by the archaeologist before categorizing objects. Processes for achieving this are discussed in chapter 5. Researching the contextual circumstances of every object is especially important since objects may have been used outside of a network—in another place or time—meaning that the same relationships cannot be assumed for any two identical objects unless they have the same context.

CHARLES SANDERS PEIRCE

This conception of artifacts as integrated gatherings of local natural and cultural information is different from conceptions that attempt to bridge a supposed separation between universal nature and culture. As described in chapters 1 and 2, building bridges is a noble activity, but it maintains the modernist separation. The latest attempt to build bridges is through using another philosopher of science, Charles Sanders Peirce. Andy Jones uses Peirce's triumvirate classification of *signs* to conceive objects as: *indices* of past behavior (distinguished by studying object manufacture and wear), *iconic representations* of something actual, and *symbols* only understood through cultural convention, in order to suggest a way that nature and culture work together (Jones 2007, 18). This means, however, that analyses are recommended that study the object's composition, form, and use-wear along with their range of contexts to understand what function or meaning objects were given. In this way a combination of conventional scientific analyses of objects are used with conventional sociological analyses of objects, combining a belief in universal natural laws with a belief in universal cultural laws. In some cases this may be a fruitful approach, but because a general explanation for objects is sought rather than a local explanation (due to labeling objects "natural" or "cultural"), this technique will rarely give any faithful results. Objects change meaning with each local network, so apart from the problems with applying universal theories to them, the effort to understand some overall meaning (by combining objects from a general area in an analysis) is pointless unless arrived at from many local analyses.

Such a way of using Peirce's triadic system is not how Peirce used it. Peirce's actual understanding of science, expressed in *Man's Glassy Essence* (Peirce 1992 [1892]), is in fact very close to Latour's understanding. Yet without Peirce's understanding of the utter integration of nature and culture, those who have used Peirce, such as Jones (2007) and Alfred Gell (1998), tend to view nature as a patina of natural processes on cultural objects, not integrated in their form and content. Gell's understanding of the *human* networks behind objects is very useful by illustrating the oeuvres and agency of artworks that extend beyond the object, but the lack of natural elements in these networks hampers this understanding. A much better description of art would be a combination of vast amounts of knowledge about the world—about people, other paintings, the art market, paint, color, canvas, and the natural world (Boast 1997, 185; Preucel 2006). The artist combines this information about society and the physical world to create a piece of material culture that is not a representation of the physical world, but a representation of varied information about the world and its relationships.

In *Man's Glassy Essence*, Peirce argues that "it would be a mistake to conceive of the psychical and the physical aspects of matter as two aspects absolutely distinct. Viewing a thing from the outside, considering its relations of action and reaction with other things, it appears as matter. Viewing it from inside, looking at its immediate character as feeling, it appears as consciousness" (Peirce 1992 [1892], 349). Peirce actually believed that matter was constructed through the process of humans and non-humans working together (which means that matter is never a distinct natural entity), but because he does not clearly explain how this operated (except through his vague concept of sedimentation), it is easy for his semiotics to be misunderstood and misused (Kilpinen 2010). Over the past one hundred years, modernist and postmodernist concepts of society and nature have developed and solidified, and unless these concepts are deconstructed, it is easy for them to remain and get in the way of an integrated analysis such as Peirce advocates.

Although Latour rarely mentions Peirce, Latour's development of the concept of networks to explain the production of matter and his deconstruction of modernist and postmodernist concepts have greatly contributed to and clarified Peirce's understanding of matter. Latour has also applied his concept of networks to understand "cultural" objects and actions (not just "natural" objects), which extends Peirce's vision to the

sort of material that archaeologists deal with (something that Peirce unfortunately never got around to).

While Peirce's triadic system for reconstructing meaning (object—
sign—interpretant) is prone to misuse—with the category of interpretant
(or mind) often allowing humanist theories to slip into the equation—it
does provide a possible solution to the humanist criticism of Latour—that
Latour has dehumanized culture (Pickering 1995). In Peirce's triadic system, objects and signs are perceived through an interpretant who com-
municates their meaning to others, who perceive objects and signs and
communicate them on, and so forth (Bendixen 2006). This is different
from Latour's system of networks which insists that all connections must
be accounted for, and that detours through some invisible "mind" must
be avoided at all costs (Latour 1987, 247). Yet Peirce's "mind," like Latour's conception of the body (Latour 2005, 209), is not comprised of
universal mental laws, but actually consists of external local phenomena
arranged to form a unique mind through an individual's "self-control"—
control over what information to accept or reject (Colapietro 1989). Thus
in Peirce's view, a mind is made up of the information it has accumulated, reduced, and combined—much like Latour's notion of object encryption.

This conception has the effect of providing an alternative model of
rationality for explaining actions that stem from the mind. The common
model used by the social sciences, as discussed in chapters 1 and 2, is to
use economic, ecological, or social theories to explain actions. But Peirce's
model stipulates that the mind making judgments is only able to make
decisions with the local information and observations it has accumulated
(a sort of reasoning that he calls "abductive") (Peirce 1934). While it is
difficult to trace the local information that a mind has accumulated in
order to understand why it makes certain decisions (and this is probably
the reason why Latour is loath to include it), it is worth considering it for
two reasons. First, because the mind is clearly a part of action, and therefore it is important to factor it into our theory, and second, because it
improves Latour's explanation of how objects change meaning.

Regarding the first reason, while Latour's radical post-humanist
stance was important to shift sociology's anthropocentric attention away
from humans onto non-humans as well, his stance never quite held true
in practice. Yet his dramatic statements such as "you discriminate between humans and the inhuman. I do not hold this bias but see only
actors" (Latour alias Johnson 1988, 303), and his proposition of a "mora-
torium on cognitive explanations" (Latour 1987, 247) were not meant to
be permanently binding. Latour's analyses have almost always traced the
human association of objects with other objects, and his suggested mora-
torium was only for "ten years" (ibid.), suggesting that he did not intend
to ignore the mind forever, just long enough for universal cognitive or
social theories to lose their grip (Bendixen 2006). Now that over twenty-

five years have gone by, perhaps it is time for the mind to be part of the equation again, if only to correct our model.

Regarding the second reason, Latour generally views change as occurring through controversies (clashes over definitions of objects), and thus in all of his studies he follows controversies in order to trace the development and changes of networks. However, it is not clear how networks change through these interactions. By considering the mind as a nub during clashes, through which pieces of information from conflicting definitions are processed (producing changes to the existing network), and from which a counterdefinition is made (further processed by another mind and so forth), it helps to understand how controversies create change in networks and gives them a more human face (discussed further in chapter 5).

THE GREAT DIVIDE

While science may provide a model for how ancient objects and formulas are produced and changed (through Latour and Peirce), it is one thing for it to provide a model, and another to say that it is the same thing. Three hundred and fifty years of polemical arguments venerating science as modern man's greatest achievement—an achievement claimed to separate us from the barbarians of the past—are hard to reverse. Yet Latour's illustrations that "we have never been modern" and have continually mixed nature with culture, subjects with objects, science with religion, have helped to expose these divides as artificial. As a consequence, scientific practice can now be seen as immensely valuable for understanding how "cultural" objects were constituted. Using scientific practice to understand the process of object creation in the past, however, does not involve redefining the pre-modern in the image of the modern scientist. Levi-Strauss attempted something of the sort when he suggested that indigenous societies would come to the right understanding of the world if only they had the same instruments as modernist science (Levi-Strauss 1962, 268 in Latour 1993, 98). Such an attempt misapprehends the vast distance between pre-modern culture and the modernist conception of science. Instead, a comparison between pre-modern conceptions of culture/nature and a non-modernist conception of science holds more promise.

Nevertheless, Latour argues that this promise is not easy to accept because of the "Great Divide" between "Us" and "Them"—a divide that modernism effected between the West, who saw a difference between nature and culture, and pre-moderns, who could not recognize such a difference, and who therefore must be purely cultural. An example that Latour gives to illustrate how completely the West believes in a Great Divide are the categories in our own culture that anthropologists see as valid to study. For instance, until recently anthropologists rarely studied any group in our own society more mainstream than graffiti artists or other marginalized groups (Latour 1993, 101). It is only groups such as these that are considered purely "cultural" in our society, as opposed to "natural" groups and institutions who are rarely seen to have anything to do with culture and retain the *right* way of doing things, such as economists, scientists, or the judiciary. On the other hand, non-modern societies are generally considered completely cultural, and this belief has an equally corrosive effect on postmodern anthropologists and archaeologists studying other cultures. Instead of allowing them the same abilities, postmodernists strive to highlight the striking differences between other cultures and our own, to underscore their alienation from us (e.g., Thomas 2004).

However, Latour argues a crucial point: "if we take into account the networks that we allow to proliferate beneath the official part of our [Modernist] Constitution they look a lot like the networks in which 'They' say they live. Premoderns are said never to distinguish between signs and things, but neither do 'We'" in practice. Therefore, we have never actually been modern and "we can now drop entirely the 'Us' and 'Them' dichotomy, and even the distinction between moderns and premoderns" (Latour 1993, 103).

If pre-modern cultural practices are really as similar to the real practice of science—albeit with less ability to hybridize because of the modernist theoretical dichotomy between nature and culture—as Latour claims, then scientific practice (as a process of networking between the spheres of so-called nature and culture) can present a better model for archaeology than the sociological and anthropological models that now appear untenable. Not only does scientific practice provide a model to explain cultural change, but it also allows many other practices, not traditionally associated with science and culture, to be explained too, including economics (Callon 1998; Thévenot and Boltanski 2006) and law (Latour 2009a).

UNDERSTANDING OBJECT POWER

One of the most important lessons to learn from science is how, once objects have been formed and encrypted, they have enormous motive power. This is one of the most mysterious aspects of both science and culture, but it is not difficult to understand if the process of an object's creation has been followed. The ability of an automatic door closer to know just how long to remain open, how fast to close, and how much pressure to exert in keeping the door closed comes from information encrypted into the device about human and natural forces (Latour/Johnson 1988). Without our understanding of how this device was encrypted, its ability might be seen in the same supernatural light as the Victorians viewed early spectacles of mechanical engineering.

This power to act in the place of humans and the natural world derives largely from the arrangement of objects or facets of a machine in a particular combination that brings the information attached with one object in meaningful juxtaposition with others in order to communicate or predict the outcome of human or natural forces. Latour calls the places or laboratories in which these arrangements take place "centers of calculation."

To illustrate the power of objects in "centers of calculation," Latour turns to another example from science—a hydraulics lab in the port of Rotterdam that wished to design a new dam (Latour 1987, 230). Instead of going out and building a dam that would then have had to be modified or even knocked down to improve it, Professor Bijker of the Delft Hydraulics Laboratory first built a scale model. In a similar way to creating a scientific formula, he first accumulated information on every essential detail of the port, including the width of the river channel, the duration of the tides, the strength of their flow, and the proportion of salty and fresh water in the port. Then all these elements were scaled down into an accurate model of the port. The river was made to flow at the correct speed, a wave machine recreated the tides, and tiny video cameras and sensors were built into the model at regular intervals to monitor what happened with each experimental dam. In the space of a few meters, they managed to reduce the port to a scale model or "microcosm" in which all the forces "out there" could be observed in their lab.

Then because he had combined all relevant elements from both the human and natural world together in correct proportion, Bijker was able to add particular factors to the mix and predict what would happen to various relationships on the scaled model without the huge expense of doing it wrong in the real world (ibid., 231). By reducing real human and natural things in the port to miniature scaled objects, and by combining them in a microcosm of the port—representing the relationships between them—Rotterdam engineers saved themselves years of work and millions of florins (ibid., 231). Yet the power of these objects could not have been understood nor capitalized upon without the knowledge of what they represented in the real world or the relationships between things. With this knowledge, these objects became immensely powerful and could influence decisions that affected the lives of thousands of people. Latour (2009b) argues that it is just this sort of knowledge—a knowledge of the network of relationships behind objects—that gives objects power in pre-modern societies (also Haber 2009).

In archaeology and anthropology, cultural objects are so often denied a complex network of relationships between the natural and social world. This means that objects are essentially viewed (as the objects in the scale model would have been without their context) as ritualistic objects—tools that are seen as having social significance within the confines of their culture but that have no relevance to the real physical world (Bourdieu 1984). As a result, the power of such objects to control the world and influence action is vastly underestimated and objects are seen as peripheral to human activity.

By understanding archaeological artifacts as representing networks of real phenomena, and "ritual" contexts of deposition as networks of networked artifacts (akin to a "center of calculation" that pools information from the natural/social world to control that world), objects and "ritual" deposits become central, not peripheral, to human activity. In a similar way to the model of Rotterdam's harbor, the encryption of information from the human and natural world into various artifacts, and their placement in an assemblage to represent relationships between elements, would have created formulas or microcosms to understand the world. The further addition of elements to assemblages or the manipulation of encrypted objects already within assemblages would have enabled new information and relationships from the physical world to be incorporated into these formulas and would have helped to predict their effects. While the understanding of ritual sites and deposits as microcosms of the world is not new (Turner 1969, 39; Richards 1993, 149), the physical nature of encrypted information and the active and constant use of microcosms as "centers of calculation" means that these contexts would have been central influences on community actions. In the same way that science today is a central influence on everything we do—from what we eat, how we cook, dress, and maintain our health to how we build our houses, how we travel and avoid dangers—so it would have been in the past but integrated with, not separated from, cultural or religious institutions.

As centers of calculation, archaeological contexts of deposition would have been sites for the elaborate calculation of effects on the social and natural order caused by new factors introduced into society or the environment. Microcosms of the natural/social order would have greatly facilitated the highly complex pre-modern discussions of consequences caused by new factors (as described by Latour 1987, 204 and Levi Strauss 1962, 267) by enabling new factors to be physically added to the microcosmic mix and the consequences for various relationships with existing factors to be predicted.

In this context, ceremonies would have had a very special role (as illustrated below). Whether reaffirming traditional interrelationships or whether incorporating new relationships—resulting in what we see in the archaeological record—ceremonies would have crafted these microcosms (or cosmograms) through carefully choreographed narratives and the juxtaposition of objects around monuments or in contexts of deposition. Yet modernist (and postmodernist) notions of culture have meant that such an understanding of ceremony has been difficult to grasp.

SCIENTIFIC CEREMONIES

As discussed in the last chapter, anthropologists and archaeologists traditionally see ceremonies and their resulting configurations as purely social phenomena. This has meant that ceremonies are seen to have meaning within a cultural system but have little meaning in relation to the real world. Latour argues that this belief is compounded because anthropologists (and archaeologists) must always return to their own culture—either to write up a dissertation for academia or merely continue as a participant in their society—and therefore they cannot afford to accept the reality of contrasting scientific knowledge. Thus indigenous knowledge, as expressed in ceremonial rites, must always be considered social in opposition to natural truth (the status given only to Western scientific knowledge) (Latour 1987, 211). It is only when indigenous knowledge is seen to coincide with Western scientific knowledge that it is accepted as partly scientific—a state of affairs usually considered accidental rather than the result of a similar process of scientific analysis.

Yet indigenous science (or ethnoscience) has contributed significant innovations to Western modern science. The branch of ecological and biological science called Traditional Ecological Knowledge (or TEK) was formed to mine and evaluate traditional indigenous knowledge for material that might be useful to Western science (Keoke and Porterfield 2003; Weatherford 1988, 1991). Indigenous engineering, agriculture, nautical design, pharmacology, mathematics, architecture, ecology, and military science have all been mined for ideas over the past century, many of which have been employed and proven to be highly beneficial to Western modern science (Snively and Corsiglia 2000). The understanding of rubber manufacture, platinum metallurgy (Keoke and Porterfield 2003), grassland management (Turner 1991), and drugs such as quinine, aspirin, and five hundred other important drugs (Weatherford 1988, 1991) all originated from Native American indigenous science. Despite arriving at legitimate knowledge and making significant contributions to science, indigenous knowledge is often seen as being influenced by "a particular cultural perspective" and therefore as very different from Western science because it appears to be processed and communicated in different ways (Snively and Corsiglia 2000, 10). While indigenous sciences are clearly the result of objective observations, the information and relationships that are obtained are often encrypted into metaphors and mythic-sounding stories that are transmitted orally or ceremonially, giving the impression, to Western ears, that indigenous sciences are very cultural.

Even many of those studying indigenous science, with an actual interest in promoting its equity with Western science, see similarities between practices as merely superficial and related to the observation and accumulation of data rather than the processing of it. Masakata Ogawa (1995, 588) defines both modern and non-modern practices as consisting of a "rational perceiving of reality," while Snively and Corsiglia (2000, 10) defines them as a "rational observation of natural events, classification, and problem solving," but this is the extent of theoretical similarities drawn. Instead, those promoting indigenous sciences tend to argue that there are many different types of science of equal weight, with indigenous science and Western science as different but equal institutions (Snively and Corsiglia 2000; Aikenhead and Ogawa 2007). This is not dissimilar to the naïve postcolonial philosophy of multiculturalism (e.g., Giddens 2006, 485), which sees different cultures, ideologies, or religions as separate and incommensurable but equal in value (Gough and Gough 2003; Williams and Baines 1993, 16). The trouble with such claims of equality is that they ignore the glaring inequality between prevailing perceptions of different sciences or cultures. Since Western science is generally seen as all-powerful through what it has accomplished, the mere claim that indigenous knowledge is equal has no more than a token value and glosses over deep inequalities without resolving them. This leaves only the impression that other sciences or cultures are alien and incompatible.

Yet such differences between indigenous and Western sciences stem largely from comparing indigenous science with a modernist theory of Western scientific practice—a theory that sees no integration between nature and culture. This theory of science has resulted in claims that Western science is positivist, uniformitarian, Cartesian, etc.—terms that sound worlds away from definitions of indigenous science. Yet such representations of Western science are misrepresentations if they avoid mentioning the human element. Without a true understanding of Western scientific practice as a thorough integration of nature and culture—an understanding arrived at through breaking down Western scientific practice into its component parts and processes—the many ways that indigenous sciences intersect with Western science have been neglected. While vast differences do exist, these differences appear to be in the scope and scale of information processed rather than in the actual process.

Since Latour's reevaluation of the practice of science, it is much easier to see the connections between indigenous and Western science. Indeed, accounts of indigenous science, recorded by indigenous people themselves rather than by anthropologists, are very similar to Latour's understanding of Western science. The fact that indigenous scholars consider Western science to be very different from indigenous science and that they wish to describe their science as a separate science in its own right indicates that these accounts are honest and do not intentionally parallel Western scientific practice for political gain—although the effort to correct anthropological perceptions of their practices as "cultural" is evidently important to them (Aikenhead et al. 2006, 407). It is also apparent that none have heard of Latour's reevaluation of Western science. In order to illustrate the authenticity of these accounts I have drawn heavily upon quotations from indigenous scholars.

CORRELATIONS BETWEEN INDIGENOUS AND WESTERN SCIENCE

In recent years a few indigenous scholars across the world have climbed the ranks of academia to finally be able to articulate their cultural practices in Western terms (Cajete 2000, 2004; Little Bear 2000; Agrawal 1995; Kawagley et al. 1998; Battiste and Henderson 2000; Aikenhead and Ogawa 2007). But instead of adopting an anthropological model of culture, these scholars have severely criticized anthropological models for omitting the natural element of their cultures. Their understanding of cultural activities as indigenous science and their description of the process of indigenous science closely parallels Latour's account of Western scientific practice. The following description by native people of the scientific process of knowledge encryption and the parallel non-modern description of Western science is intended to illustrate this new understanding of archaeological objects and sites. Many non-native scholars who work closely with Native peoples (Christie 1991; Snively and Corsiglia 2000; Johnson 1992; Turnbull 2000a; Watson-Verran and Turnbull 2005) have also confirmed this alternative understanding of cultural practices.

Firstly, indigenous scholars see their science as localized and contingent (Snively and Corsiglia 2000, 10; Cajete 2004, 47; Aikenhead and Ogawa 2007, 560; Christie 1991). This is similar to science and technology studies (STS) which, after Latour, see Western science as a local production of knowledge. In fact, it was this understanding that led to the recent comparison of indigenous knowledge systems with science (Watson-Verran and Turnbull 2005, 346). Gregory Cajete, a Tewa American Indian and associate professor and director of Native American Studies at the University of New Mexico, has written extensively on Native American science. He writes, "Native Science bases its interpretation of natural phenomena on context" (Cajete 2004, 53).

Leroy Little Bear, professor emeritus at the University of Lethbridge, Canada, explains how this works. Changing combinations of factors in the environment result in different scientific understandings because everything is seen as related—"in a 'spider web' network of relationships" (Little Bear 2000, x). He writes that, "For the Native American, even regularities are subject to change. Native Americans never claim regularities as laws or as finalities. The only constant is change" (ibid., xi). This means that configurations of natural and cultural elements must be observed locally to understand the precise combination of factors influencing them. He states, "Events, patterns, cycles, and happenings occur at certain places. . . . Animal migrations, cycles of plant life, seasons and cosmic movements are detected from particular spatial locations; hence medicine wheels and other sacred observatory sites. Each tribal territory has its sacred sites and its particular environmental and ecological combinations resulting in particular relational networks."

An example of the usefulness of this approach is the example given by Corsiglia and Snively (1997). Among the Nisga'a people of British Columbia, specialists are trained to use "all of their senses and pay attention to important variables: what plants are in bloom, what birds are active, when specific animals are migrating and where, and so forth. In this way, traditional communities have a highly developed capacity for building up a collective data base. Any deviations from past patterns are important and noted" (Corsiglia and Snively 1997, 25). In 1982, native fishermen observed that mature Dungeness crabs were marching past a dock at the mouth of the Nass River rather than staying in deep water. Once reported to tribal council leaders, it was soon established that the ocean floor was contaminated by heavy metal pollutants from a new molybdenum mine that was disrupting the ecosystem. The understanding of the environment and the interrelation of factors that comprise it enabled them to perceive irregularities and trace them to their source (ibid.).

This example also illustrates that indigenous observers follow the actions and reactions of natural elements to other phenomena to create knowledge (Aikenhead and Ogawa 2007, 561; Battiste and Henderson 2000, 45). Such a way is not dissimilar to the way that Western scientists characterize objects through following the relationships between elements in laboratories (Latour and Woolgar 1979, 1987). Cajete writes, "Both Western science and Native science use research and data gathering. Over the millennia, Native people observed and experimented to understand how the world worked and to apply what was learned" (Cajete 2000, 44).

While the modernist theory of science sees Western science as operating within a supposed universal frame of reference (Durkheim 1972), a great number of studies by the sociology of scientific knowledge (SSK) and science and technology studies (STS) have found that Western science is essentially a local process too when it comes to creating knowledge (Hacking 1983; Latour 1987, 2004c; Star 1995; Collins and Pinch 1998; Shapin 1998; Turnbull 2000a; Rouse 2002). When comparing Western and indigenous science, Turnbull writes that both create "equivalencies and connections whereby otherwise heterogeneous and isolated forms of knowledge are enabled to move in space and time from the local site and moment of their production and application to other places and times" (Turnbull 2000a, 38).

This process, drawn from Latour (1987), is essentially how Western formulas are able to appear universal. Watson-Verran and Turnbull (2005) observe how this process—associated with Western science—is also used by indigenous people, although it does not make them think that knowledge is universal. In a number of case studies they illustrate how the Anasazi, the Inca, and Micronesian Pacific navigators encrypt information into objects and use them systematically to make connections and mobilize local knowledge. They illustrate, for example, that "The power of the Incan knowledge system [through *ceque* and *quipu*] lay in its capacity to provide connections for a diverse set of knowledges and to establish equivalences between disparate practices and contexts over a very large area" (ibid., 352). These systems differ from modern science in the kinds of strategies and object devices through which local knowledge is mobilized, but just because they lack elements such as writing, mathematics, and standardized measurements does not mean that they cannot mobilize knowledge in other ways.

Secondly, rather than being a haphazard accumulation of information by laymen, most indigenous communities have specialists who are devoted to generating knowledge and use techniques to maintain quality control (Snively and Corsiglia 2000, 10). Cajete writes that "Learning a Native Science, whether it is the use of herbs or star watching, is a long and arduous journey, in some ways equivalent of attaining a PhD in the university system of Western Culture. The neophyte passes through various levels of knowledge and knowledge transfer all the way to the doctorate" (Cajete 2000, 125). According to Aikenhead and Ogawa, "a knowledge keeper can only pass that knowledge (ways of knowing) along to others who have formed an appropriate relationship with the knowledge keeper" (Aikenhead and Ogawa 2007, 559). "All data are usually vetted collaboratively with wise knowledge keepers (often Elders) and all are tested out in the everyday world of personal experiences" (ibid., 562). "Elders also work together to create a consensus like Western practitioners" (ibid., 580).

In a similar way to Western science, the preparation for observation and accumulation is very important. Cajete writes, "Native science relies on preparation of the mind, body and spirit of each person as the primary vehicle of 'coming to know.' The mind and body can be used for careful, disciplined and repeatable experimentation and observation" (Cajete 2000, 69). The actual observation of phenomena is also very methodical. Cajete writes, "The coming-to-know process is nevertheless extremely systematic. For example certain processes must occur in a particular order, which in its way is similar to the precise ways that an experiment is executed within the Western scientific method. . . . Like Western science, indigenous science is sequential and builds on previous knowledge" (ibid., 80).

Thirdly, once systematic observations have been conducted, information about elements of the natural and human world and their particular relationships are reduced by being encrypted into objects in a similar way to the encryption of names and symbols in Western science (according to Latour 2005). Cajete writes, "Signs and formulas of thought appear in many forms, records in stone, clay, birch bark, hides, structures and hundreds of other forms. These representations record key thoughts, understandings and stories important to remembering aspects of Native Science" (Cajete 2000, 70).

The reduction of information into manageable signs, however, often takes an esoteric form. The incorporation of terminology that sounds religious often tempts Western scholars to see indigenous accounts as superstitious (Snively and Corsiglia 2000, 23). But the reduction of elements and relationships to single objects, patterns, animals, or characters in a story is no less esoteric than the reduction of information into the letters of Western scientific formulas or Latinate scientific names and abbreviations.

Native American anthropologist Robert Hall once explained one of the processes of Native American encryption. After the observation of particular natural phenomena, some Native Scientists use dreams to reduce the characteristics and relationships of various phenomena into particular forms. He explained that during the dream-state, the varied phenomena recently experienced—information about both human and non-human actions and relationships—are combined by the human mind into hybrid forms or sequences which provide the inspiration for the reduction of relationships into esoteric forms (Robert Hall pers. comm. 1999). This is not dissimilar to Charles Sanders Peirce's notion of "abduction" which Peirce argued was the mind's subconscious effort to make sense of a vast amount of internalized information. The scientific method has largely been attributed to Peirce, but he was only articulating what he saw occurring already in scientific practice. Peirce explained that abduction was the principle mechanism behind the integration and reduction of large amounts of internalized information and which produced the "eureka" moments so common in Western scientific experience (Peirce 1934).

Once objects are encrypted with information and relationships in indigenous science, they are then used with other objects within the context of ceremonies to link even larger amounts of information and relationships together to construct higher-order understandings. In this sense, they are the activity at centers of calculation that pool information and utilize it. In a similar way to the use of the model of Rotterdam's harbor, or even laboratory experimentations and demonstrations, ceremonies tie together many object formulas to predict, understand, or communicate phenomena. Cajete writes that "Native Science also has models . . . which are highly representational and elicit higher order thinking and understanding. An example of such a ritual process model is the Plains Sun Dance, which may include symbols such as the circle, numbers, geometric shapes, special objects, art forms, songs, dances, stories, proverbs, or metaphors" (Cajete 2004, 53). "Ritual and ceremony can be personal or communal 'technologies' for accessing knowledge, and symbols are used to remember key understandings of the natural world" (Cajete 2000, 65).

Creation stories, and other oral narratives, are central to tying together objects and their information during ceremonies, and act in a similar way to scientific articles. Cajete writes, "All the basic components of scientific thought and application are metaphorically represented in most Native stories of creation and origin" (Cajete 2000, 13). "Stories, particularly origin and culture hero stories are mechanisms by which these understandings are conveyed to the next generation. This process can be compared to the process in which a book is written and then disseminated" (ibid., 43). Robert Hall states that ceremonies and their material deposits and structures are often little more than material reenactments of such narratives (Hall 1997, 19; Hall pers. comm. 1999). Oral narratives, recited or reenacted during ceremonies, also help to elucidate the relationships between objects in ceremonial contexts. Scientific information is compressed into descriptive names and metaphors, proverbs, drama, or even jokes that can be decoded "upon appropriate reflection or contemplation" (Snively and Corsiglia 2000, 12; also Aikenhead and Ogawa 2007, 554). Cajete writes, "the greatest source of metaphor comes from nature, these stories are filled with analogies, characters and representations drawn from nature, metaphors that more often than not refer to the processes of nature from which they are drawn, or to human nature, which they attempt to reflect" (Cajete 2004, 51).

Even origin stories continually change through addition of new information. Cajete states that since "Origin Stories are predicated on, above all, their own experience, specific to a particular place on the Earth. . . . Each generation adds to it something of itself and of its experience" (Cajete 2000, 38). Other oral narratives can communicate information about changes to migration routes or changes in fish populations and contain specific information about "size, vitality, longevity of animal populations that provide biologists with long term observations that can be correlated with overfishing and pollution" (Snively and Corsiglia 2000, 13).

Scientific understandings of humans and non-humans, however, are expressed through their entire culture, not just inscriptions or ceremonies—illustrating the strong relationship in non-modern societies between nature and culture. Cajete explains: "A people's understanding of the cycles of nature, behavior of animals, growth of plants and interdependence of all things in nature determined their culture, that is, ethics, morals, religious expression, politics and economics" (Cajete 2004, 46). Architecture, especially, encodes these scientific understandings: "Traditional Native architecture presents yet another example of applied science. Each traditional structure evolved from the special relationship people had evolved with their environments" (ibid., 100). "The structure, story, symbol and meaning of traditional dwellings embody the view of and compassion for the natural world . . . woven through guiding stories that relate the events of the creation of the earth, plants, animals and the first people" (ibid., 206).

Scientific understandings, as communicated through oral narratives and ceremonies, are also very important for conducting everyday activities, including how to make a caribou snowshoe, an animal trap, or how to navigate home (Snively and Corsiglia 2000, 15). In the Yupiaq Eskimo culture "all important knowledge was preserved by oral traditions which were crucial to survival" (Kawagley et al. 1998, 137).

DIFFERENCES BETWEEN INDIGENOUS AND WESTERN SCIENCE

While indigenous processes of encryption are very similar to the West, the type of information encrypted and the form of indigenous encryptions can seem very different from Western science, and can include information about human behavior and spirituality, as well as physical laws. Cajete writes, "Native Science is a broad term that can include metaphysics and philosophy, art and architecture, practical technologies and agriculture as well as ritual and ceremony practiced by Indigenous peoples past and present" (Cajete 2004, 47).

The largest problem that Western scientists have with indigenous science is the incorporation of spiritual elements in explanations, which induce many to see indigenous accounts as superstitious (Snively and Corsiglia 2000, 23). Yet as Johnson (1992, 13) writes, "Spiritual explanations often conceal functional ecological concerns and conservation strategies." For example, in Canada's northern territory, the traditional Dene people see negative environmental events as caused by spiritual forces. Yet these spiritual forces are set in motion by human actions that misuse elements of the environment. The principles and rules that govern human actions toward the environment—that to us appear to be ritual observances—such as how much to hunt and where, are precisely developed to ensure that the environment is kept sustainable and balanced. Johnson states, "All of these practices are based on an empirical understanding of population dynamics and ecological linkages" (ibid., 60), but because natural processes are codified by religious terminology, Western scientists assume that these practices have no relation to nature.

Central to many indigenous cultures is a sense that everything is related (Cajete 2000, 73; Aikenhead and Ogawa 2007, 558; Snively and Corsiglia 2000, 11). As such it is essential to gain a holistic sense of an environment in order to understand the full range of factors and relationships that constitute its causes and effects. Because native people see no separation between human and non-human elements, human actions are included in calculations to understand the world. The inclusion of human and non-human elements in calculations by no means reduces the effectiveness of indigenous science, and may enhance it. The Hopi, for instance, have long understood that underground copper deposits in the Southwest are extremely important to bring essential rains to the desert by attracting lightning. By understanding the interrelationship between human and non-human factors in the environment, they campaigned against copper mining as having an enormous impact on weather patterns (Sahtouris and Lovelock 2000, 341). Through a similar understanding, the Kogi in Colombia have argued that deforestation is having a large impact on their climate by drying out the area around them and lessening the amount of snow that falls on the mountains—which dries out the rivers that their crops depend upon (ibid., 342)—an elaborate understanding that belies a complex series of scientific deductions.

Today, ecologists and biologists are starting to understand and respect the traditional indigenous wisdom developed by native specialists over centuries of scientific observance. With a more holistic, localized standpoint and without the constraints of disciplinary and nature/culture segmentation, indigenous science has provided numerous ideas for Western biology and more sustainable agricultural and ecological systems (Snively and Corsiglia 2000, 8, 10).

By working with indigenous people to understand their encrypted knowledge and by translating indigenous scientific practices into Western terms, it is possible to understand the information they encrypt, and for us to relate to the processes that they use. Eroding the false assumption that there is a diametric difference between indigenous or ancient cultural practices and Western scientific practice is essential in order for archaeologists and anthropologists to get beyond the Great Divide and the nature/culture separation and to start taking objects seriously. In the same way that Latour had to overturn every stone in science behind which universality had hidden, no stone should be left unturned in culture behind which social structure can hide. One particularly large stone is the practice of indigenous medicine. Nevertheless, even this practice has definite similarities with Western healing practices when understood from the indigenous perspective, and it provides a perfect illustration of the power of object encryption.

HEALING

In both Western and indigenous medicine, healing is believed to occur through reestablishing a balance in individuals. In the West, diseases (other than contagious diseases) are largely seen to be the result of chemical imbalances in the body and are healed through introducing chemicals that readjust that balance. Conversely, in indigenous societies, Native people see diseases as resulting from a spiritual imbalance. Donald Sanders, a scholar of Navajo healing practices, explains that disease is usually seen as resulting from an imbalance between humans and nature. This imbalance is created by violating taboos, disturbing plant and animal life, or even by holding malicious or selfish thoughts (Sanders 1979, 117–46 in Cajete 2000). These causes are not as removed from Western etiology (the science that studies causes of disease) as we think. Taboos relating to hygiene or careful handling of certain plant or animal life exist in our own culture, and current medicine is actively investigating the relationship between illness and negative or fearful thoughts (Benedetti et al. 2006; Mueller et al. 2012). Yet, as Cajete writes, indigenous healing "exemplifies an ecological dynamic revolving round establishing and maintaining relationships" (Cajete 2000, 122). Efforts aimed at balancing these relationships are traditionally conducted through spiritual means, and "ceremonies were choreographed to help both individual and community to come to terms with one's relationship to other life" (ibid., 117). These renewal ceremonies help to refresh the understanding of relationships in the human and natural world, which in turn are seen to reconnect people with them. Shamans generally have the job of conducting these ceremonies and readjusting balances because they have "the most complete understanding of the nature of relationships between humans and the natural entities around them" (ibid., 116).

One way that shamans reestablish relationships between humans and the natural world is to determine from patients which qualities are missing from their relationship with nature and then to acquire them from the natural world. Tim Ingold writes about how Inuit shamans examine patients and then use their ability to shape-shift (when in a trance) and visit particular animal species to acquire certain qualities that they feel are lacking in their patients (Ingold 1998, 186). A similar process occurs when herbs and medicines are used to cure sickness, but the power of these things has often been misunderstood by Western scientists as residing in their biologically active ingredients (which are then investigated for use in the West). James Sa'ke'j Henderson, a Chickasaw and leading Native philosopher, explains how these herbs, plants, feathers, and bones that shamans carry in their medicine bags actually help patients by bringing certain qualities and relationships associated with these items into people's consciousness (Sa'ke'j Henderson in Peat 2002, 140). For example, a bone from a certain animal "allowed a person to enter into a relationship with the Keeper of that animal" (ibid.) thus redressing the balance between them and nature. Cajete also writes that "Herbs provided a metaphorical and practical physical example for understanding human relationships to the order of nature" (Cajete 2000, 119). It is through the reacknowledgment of these relationships that healing is effected.

This power of association is close to how Latour, and many others who study the sociology of medicine, have explained the power of drugs. In the 1990s, Anne Harrington, professor of history of science at Harvard, assembled all available research on the "placebo effect," as well as current placebo researchers, to provide an understanding of the effect of association and belief on healing (Harrington 1999). Her findings also provided a valuable example of how pharmaceutical drugs work. The placebo effect was first discovered during the trial of mesmerism in the 1770s when Benjamin Franklin and a commission of doctors investigated the healing effects produced by a doctor, Franz Anton Mesmer, in Paris (although it was not called a "placebo effect" until 1920). Their conclusion was that it was the power of suggestion that led to these healings. In the nascent field of medical science, this finding actually caused an overt separation between legitimate medical practices and the exploitation of people's "imagination" to heal (Stengers 1995, 136). Placebos, or fake pills made of sugar, were still sometimes used by doctors in the late eighteenth and early nineteenth century, but they went out of fashion in the 1890s after one doctor was sued for giving false information.

Nevertheless, the placebo effect was reinvestigated during and after the Second World War when a doctor on the battlefield (Henry Beecher), who was short on morphine supplies, injected a patient with salt water as an anesthetic and it worked just as well (Harrington 1999, 2). Beecher's clinical article "The Powerful Placebo" (Beecher 1955), the result of considerable research and testing of the placebo effect, presented staggering evidence for the physiological potency of placebos. At first placebos only worked for 30 to 40 percent of patients. This prompted many investigations into who was and who was not susceptible to placebos. However, by the 1970s the field had concluded that no particular person was more or less likely to be susceptible to placebos, and subsequent investigations then focused upon interpersonal and situational factors (Harrington 1999, 3). Instead of the patient determining the outcome, it was believed that the doctor's manner and the form of the placebo used were important. Several studies proved that the confidence in administering the placebo, the "ritual" used, as well as the shape, taste, and branding of the pill were essential for their efficacy (Blackwell et al. 1972; Branthwaite and Cooper 1981). These studies produced even more effective placebo treatments and 40 to 50 percent of patients were healed with them.

During the 1980s, research shifted again—this time to the doctor's belief in the treatment. Researchers found that the doctor's body language often gave them away, and they demanded that the doctor administering the placebo also believe in the placebo too. It was found that patients in pain, who were given a placebo by doctors—who were persuaded to believe in them—suffered much less than those who were given an actual painkiller by doctors who were told it did not work (Gracely et al. 1985 in Goldacre 2008). At the same time, a number of medical anthropologists argued that the sociocultural framework was the most important factor for healing. They asserted that the use of symbols in Native healing rituals were just as effective as placebo pills. But instead of being something that was ingested, their power was in the sociocultural information encrypted into the symbols (Moerman 1983; Hahn and Kleinman 1983 in Harrington 1999, 7). They therefore argued that Western medicine was actually quite similar to Native medicine and rituals in that both constructed logical networks of reasons and associations—within the construct of their society—for why certain drugs would work, and this gave them power in the practitioner's and patient's minds (Hahn and Kleinman 1983). A similar conclusion is reached by Isabelle Stengers, who writes that the manipulation of the public's "imagination" in order to heal never really went away, but it did have to be aided by sociologic (Stengers 1995). Thus in both Western and indigenous cultures, it is the information encrypted into objects and practices that makes them powerful—not so much the objects themselves. This illustrates that instead of truth being "discovered," or "biased" by culture, truth is created through the networks of associations and relationships that are built up.

CRITIQUES

Close examinations of indigenous science reveal considerable similarities between the process of indigenous knowledge production and STS accounts of Western scientific processes, as well as differences between them in terms of their scale and scope. Such a comparison does not negate the value of either, but allows us to understand indigenous culture in a different light. However, a problem does arise when indigenous science is compared with modernist (and postmodernist) versions of science. Two tendencies are apparent when such comparisons are attempted: either Traditional Ecological Knowledge (TEK) is equated with timelessness and universality in order to be compared with a modernist account of Western knowledge as universal (Gough and Gough 2003), or TEK is seen as cultural and compared with a postmodern account of Western scientific knowledge that sees science as a culturally contingent phenomenon (Carter 2004). Sometimes both contradictory tendencies occur at the same time (e.g., Snively and Corsiglia 2000).

Several critics have rightly argued that portraying indigenous knowledge as timeless locks indigenous cultures into a position of stasis, while maintaining that both indigenous and Western knowledge are universal subsumes indigenous knowledge under Western science and legitimizes the hegemony of Western science without problematizing it (Gough and Gough 2003; Carter 2004). A similar problem arises with the multiculturalist tendency to pluralize knowledge systems, as discussed earlier. By ostensibly calling each system equal, but ignoring the degree of power behind each system (and the reasons for it), the unequal power relations between indigenous and Western science are kept intact (Carter 2004). Moreover, the argument that modern science is a phenomenon of Western culture requires special pleading and is hardly justifiable considering its results (Latour 2005, 101). Both of these types of comparison therefore result in ethnocentrism—the belief in the superiority of one system over others—whether they like it or not. As George Orwell illustrated so neatly in *Animal Farm*, to claim that we are all equal is not the same as demonstrating it.

Yet, by comparing indigenous science with STS accounts of Western scientific practice these problems are largely avoided because STS accounts also see Western scientific knowledge production as local and a combination of human and non-human elements. Instead of diminishing TEK by comparing it against a modernist notion of Western science, its comparison with a non-modernist notion of Western science better illustrates its parity and the timelessness of scientific method (rather than content). By problematizing the modernist claim that Western science is universal and an evolutionary advance for mankind, and by illustrating how it gains its power to explain the world through an increased scale and scope (facilitated by the alliance of a larger number of encrypted objects), rather than by an increased intelligence, a comparison with indigenous science can be made without the danger of ethnocentrism.

Once this difference is understood, science as a human activity should be seen as equally common to mankind as is "language, music, or dance albeit one that moderns and even some postmoderns may be slow to notice and acknowledge" (Snively and Corsiglia 2005, 909). For our purposes here though, the illustration that indigenous science parallels many processes of Western science enables anthropologists and archaeologists to benefit from insights into Western science that have emerged in the anthropology of science. These include insights into how objects are formed, used, and changed and the best methods to interpret them.

ABSTRACTION AND RITUALIZATION

Another valid critique of comparing culture to science is that in many instances throughout pre-modern societies, objects are used in a ritualistic way without a complete knowledge of their networks, especially in cases where the networks that led to the creation of objects were forgotten. These instances often occur during a period of stasis, when the current system is not producing enough anomalies to force it to change. Nevertheless, this phenomenon is also something that is quite common in science and therefore can be explained.

Latour refers to this process of abstraction as black-boxing, the creation of a thing that is no longer questioned and is separated from its history. Once entities are black-boxed, all that is important to people is that they work. Similar to the discrepancy made between formulas before publication and formulas after publication, objects whose history is neglected or forgotten quickly become reified, idolized, or used in other networks. They become solidified because they have been isolated from the fluid chains of associations and relationships that formed them. They can also attain a deific status because without the understanding that formulas merely represent a reduction of information and relationships, their power to explain the world and to predict experience becomes mysterious.

However, the practice of black-boxing an object or idea should not be limited to modernist science or technology. Latour traces the deification of cultural objects in a series of articles on iconoclashes (Latour 1998a, 2001b, 2002b, 2005). In such cases, objects have been severed from their histories and have become religious fetishes that are considered powerful due to the strength of their representation as nth-degree reductions of information—while what they actually represent has long been forgotten. Latour recounts several instances when such icons, paintings, or objects have been smashed by individuals because they were considered to have grown too powerful. Instead of referencing information elsewhere, they had become fetishes and ended up being worshiped themselves (Latour 2005, 39).

Without the knowledge of their correct associations, these objects can often be used for different objectives. The result of abstraction and deification of objects is that the contexts in which they are used can also become repetitive abstract practices or "rituals." Their meanings become lost and other elements may even be associated with them in ritual that do not have any relevance to their original meaning (Latour 1987, 242).

Because a discrepancy exists between the usage of artifacts with a knowledge of their history and network, and the usage of artifacts without such a knowledge (or usage in another network), a distinction also needs to be made in our own archaeological analyses. We need to distinguish between practices that are conscious acts designed to remember the process of an artifact's becoming, and other practices that are unconscious rituals (or appropriations of objects by other networks). The common assumption that all practices or objects of the same form carry equal weight in analyses of their meaning and function is highly problematic if there is such a discrepancy. While chapter 5 describes how to distinguish between conscious and unconscious usage, uses of objects must obviously be examined in the context of the network that uses them.

In accounts of indigenous science, one of the things that is often stressed is that once an artifact is "packed" with specific information and networks of relationships, it is essential that the "tribal group 'remembers to remember' the context, circumstances, and purpose of its creation" in order to maintain its meaning (Cajete 2000, 51). Cajete claims that Native American renewal ceremonies such as the Plains Sun Dance are just such efforts to remember the network of information behind objects. "Even traditional costumes reflect symbolic representations of their relationship to these [natural] entities and the people dance and sing their relationships to revitalize their understanding" (ibid., 68, 102). Battiste and Henderson argue that even if "Eurocentric researchers know the name of a herbal cure and how it is used, but without the ceremony and ritual songs, chants, prayers and relationships, it cannot achieve the same effect" (Battiste and Henderson 2000, 43) because it is the sociologic that gives it power. Thus renewal of associations and relationships behind practices is essential if the efficacy of practices is to be maintained. Without an understanding of the networks of associations behind practices, practices are in danger of becoming ritualized and lose their meaning.

MYSTICAL OBJECTS AND ANIMISM

One of the effects of forgetting the network of associations and relationships behind objects is that objects or object formulas often become mystical to people, modern and non-modern. Latour writes that if "'theories' are transformed into 'abstract' objects severed from the elements they tie together . . . [but] nevertheless have some bearing on what happens down below in empirical science—it has to be a miracle" (Latour 1987, 242). In Western science this mysticism is increased due to an interesting twist that occurs after theories are transformed into abstract objects. Scientists often allude to the mysterious application of an object equation to phenomena outside of the observations that led to its creation (such as the water turbulence equation relating to gas turbulence in other galaxies) (Latour 1987, 238). This sometimes leads to a deification of the equation as having a special quality of universal truth in itself. Since the object enables other phenomena to be predicted, it comes to be seen as exceptional, a mystical "universal" seen to be outside of the local networks that gave it life.

However, the mystery of such an application disappears once the process through which equations are extended to explain new phenomena is understood. The reduction of information to a simple object or equation involves the translation of many forms into a summary form, like the translation in the turbulence equation from many different types of obstacle to the letter L, which signifies the numerical length of the obstacle. By translating objects into a common form (i.e., letters and numbers) or a form that can easily be combined with other similar forms, they become commensurable with other reductions. Thus, the application of one equation to other phenomena is really only the additional reduction of information, through commensuration of elements from both, which results in an extension of the network. It is impossible to see the connections that have been made unless the detailed history of how those equations were created—the accumulation, reduction, and combination of data—is fully understood (or internalized). This is what makes them so mysterious to outsiders, or even to the scientists who connect them (through abduction), who have internalized their development (Latour 1987, 240; Star and Griesemer 1989, 393; Turnbull 2000a, 40; Peirce 1934).

This understanding is very valuable for comprehending the archaeological record. If object forms provide commensurability between different frames of reference while maintaining their capacity to explain, this explains the adoption of objects and their central presence in distant and culturally divergent regions (Latour 2005). Star and Griesemer explain how these "boundary objects" work by being "plastic enough to adapt to local needs and constraints of the several parties employing them, yet robust enough to maintain a common identity across sites" (Star and Griesemer 1989, 393). This is not dissimilar to how social theories are created and become plastic enough to absorb any information thrown at them (as described in the first chapter), or for that matter, how modern art manages to speak to people of many backgrounds once all reference points are removed.

Yet the most valuable insight from Western science (for us) is how natural and cultural objects become animate and powerful for many indigenous societies. The understanding that objects (like the TRH hormone) were created through the encryption of their associations and relationships with other elements, and that these encryptions (or formulas) become powerful by predicting the world, perfectly illustrate how objects become powerful for indigenous people.

Currently, animism is experiencing a renaissance in archaeology (Brown and Walker 2008; Alberti and Marshall 2009; Losey 2010; Porr and Bell 2012). While ethnographies of animism are valuable to describe the influence of animate beings on people and practices and to identify material expressions of animism, these observations are generally used to identify objects and deposits in the archaeological record and interpret them as involved in animism. While animism is definitely an important consideration in interpretation, this use of animism does not necessarily help interpretation. Like Viveiros de Castro's (1998) description of Perspectivism, it does not explain how animate objects or animate beings become animate and therefore cannot help interpret how they influence actions. Instead, animism merely becomes a theory to impose on similar-looking objects and practices, much like the term "ritual."

Rather than respecting indigenous perspectives, this categorization without understanding threatens to paint indigenous people as "savages" in the same way that early portrayals of animists used to do. Despite the well-meaning inclusion of animism in interpretation, we have to wonder what we would think if indigenous people wrote an anthropology of our culture and claimed that we slavishly worship an animate god called "science" whose priests wear white coats. . . .

Gregory Cajete writes that "along with words like 'primitive,' 'ancestor worship' and 'supernatural,' animism continues to perpetuate modern prejudice, a disdain, and a projection of inferiority toward the worldview of Indigenous peoples" (Cajete 2000, 27). Instead he explains animism as the view of everything "as having energy and its own unique intelligence and creative process, not only obviously animate entities such as plants, animals and microorganisms, but also rocks, mountains, rivers and places large and small. Everything in nature has something to teach humans. This is the indigenous view of 'animism'" (ibid., 21). The encryption of networks of information into objects and natural features through stories and rituals that tie together morals, natural processes, and relationships between objects and people is one way that these objects become coded and "teach humans." In Native American society artisans create objects that "have a power beyond their literal connotations. . . . Through the ceremony of art, indigenous artists 'pack' a symbol with specific meaning and intent. Petroglyphs represent a clear exemplification of such a packing process" and, as a result, they have an animate power (Cajete 2000, 50).

Thus, instead of labeling certain items as animate, or certain practices as influenced by animism, by considering the processes that lead to these entities and practices—that include the encryption into them of both natural and cultural information—we can begin to understand them and use them profitably in interpretation. Analysis can also remain on a local level this way without leaping to strange speculative conclusions.

WHAT THIS ALL MEANS FOR ARCHAEOLOGY

Once it is realized that objects are not mere inanimate tools from a semantic or functionalist tool set, but are highly powerful animate agents, objects can be reinstated at last at the center of social construction and change. Such an understanding of object power was not possible until recent correlations were made between cultural objects and objects from Western science, since artifacts have traditionally been viewed as merely cultural. It took an understanding of objects as natural/cultural and a realization of the process behind their encryption from anthropologies of science to fully comprehend their power. Without an understanding that local objects contain the agencies necessary for interpreting the past, agencies have been sought from external sources, such as macro structures and functionalist or structuralist theories, creating artificial histories and blinding us to the actual past.

What is needed now is a fresh look at objects with the understanding of how they are encrypted with information and used. If prehistoric burial practices or other ceremonies in the past can now be viewed as scientific expressions that helped to explain intricate relationships between elements in the natural and cultural world and predict them, then they should be interpreted with this in mind rather than as places for the dead or as places for other static social roles. In the same way that Native

Americans and many other indigenous cultures see ceremonies as reenactments of creation stories that link together various natural and human
activities to explain those activities (and the impact of new factors), burial
practices and other ceremonies at ritual monuments would have been
similar contexts for the reenactment of stories and natural/cultural relationships. Representations of these natural and human activities in artifact forms would have enabled elements of the world to be incorporated
and explained, resulting in the elaborate depositions, ceremonial and burial structures that archaeologists observe in the ground. Covering the
mounds with earth would have effectively sealed or "black-boxed" these
definitions in a similar way to the publication of scientific articles—reifying understandings and creating mnemonic devices for reference and
recall. Later manipulations of the sites may also have been attempts to
redefine these encryptions.

Such an understanding of artifacts and architecture allows us to place
so-called ritual sites and objects at the center of prehistoric social life, as
they are in indigenous life. This knowledge that objects are not merely
cultural, but encrypt information about nature and culture, helps us to
understand how objects in the past were powerful enough to structure
actions and even incite violence. This allows us to relinquish our macro
structures and external theories and to focus on the objects themselves for
information. Knowing that it is the objects themselves that were structuring actions should prompt more attention to be paid to how objects are
used in and around sites, and whether relationships exist between different local depositions. Most importantly, the knowledge that assemblages
and traits are often consciously constructed to represent crucial understandings of the world in explicit terms should encourage archaeologists
to try to decipher these representations—not from the perspective of
some theory, contemporary anthropological account, or ontology, but
from the perspective of the local prehistoric group that constructed them.

However, such analysis is rendered highly difficult from the first by
certain archaeological and anthropological assumptions, and the many
tools that are based on these assumptions. These assumptions and tools
have the effect of immediately categorizing objects and fixing them as
formal entities, and need to be reevaluated before we proceed to trace the
associations and development of forms.

FOUR

Group Formation, Dissent, and Change

One of the most insidious assumptions that arose out of the modernist separation of culture from nature, and the subsequent misunderstanding of objects, is the assumption that all cultures are unified, linear entities (Thomas 1996, 21). Such an assumption is most graphically illustrated by the many timelines drawn for cultures. However, once an invisible force called "culture" was adopted to account for the missing agencies of nature (actually encrypted into objects), it was only a small step to assume that culture was a unified force.

It is well known that the assumption of culture as unified has murky roots in the history of archaeology. The most thorough book on the topic by Sian Jones, *The Archaeology of Ethnicity* (1997), illustrates the development of this assumption and its pervasiveness in archaeological theory and methodology. As far back as the mid-nineteenth century, the idea of cultures as monolithic entities was used in debates to justify colonialist expansion and slavery. The Nazis also used it to homogenize their nation and legitimize the annexation of other countries by claiming ancient affinity with a larger interregional culture—formulated through drawing similarities between prehistoric assemblages. While both anthropology and archaeology have rejected the idea of culture as monolithic many times—on the basis of its ethical implications and the empirical problems with it—Jones argues that the assumption that cultures are bounded, unified entities continues to persist due to being encoded into many of our techniques (ibid.).

Thomas (1996) also illustrates how this normative notion of culture as monolithic has continued throughout the twentieth century—from Gordon Childe's Marxist philosophy, which saw every part of culture as understandable through the whole, to New Archaeology, which retained a holistic view of culture comprised of integrated subsystems. While arguing that Post-processualist approaches have superseded such a view, Thomas soon continues the tradition of criticizing monolithic culture while perpetuating such a conception by arguing for a British-wide habitus of social structures (ibid., 48), an ideology of power (ibid., 49), the practice of ancestor worship (ibid., 179), and other universal practices that unify the region.

While there have been many attempts to rid archaeology of this unilinear notion of culture, Jones (1997) argues that it has continued to return largely due to the continued use of nineteenth-century methods that were originally adapted to study cultures in the same way as natural organisms. The most powerful method, adapted from the natural sciences for archaeology, has been typology, which assumes that all its categories (like organisms) are unified. Typology has been the object of many attacks by archaeologists (Ford 1954; Hill and Evans 1972; Shanks and Tilley 1987a; Wylie 2002), but it is clear that merely removing this technique from analyses has not been enough to eradicate its influence.

Due to its ability to condense information, the typological method has permeated almost every aspect of the archaeological toolbox. Yet, without a critical reassessment of this method and the techniques resulting from it, it is likely that we will continue to perpetuate the view of culture as unified and the idea that objects and practices are fixed in time and space (Jones 1997, 129).

THE THEORY OF TYPOLOGY

While archaeology as a discipline has evolved considerably over the past two hundred years, the typological method has remained directly or indirectly at the forefront of archaeological investigation ever since its inception at the beginning of the nineteenth century. This method is essentially the identification of general artifact types, practices, or cultures based upon their similarity of form. The pervasiveness of this methodology is such that the very classification of artifact types such as an "axe" or "vessel" is based upon it (Shanks and Tilley 1987b). However, the typological method derives from two very old assumptions that few archaeologists would agree with today. The primary assumption is the nineteenth-century idea, mentioned above, that cultures are monolithic-bounded entities that evolve in a unified way, but related to this is the notion that types of artifacts and practices within a culture will have one proper function or meaning at one time (Jones 1997, 132–4). These assumptions have led us to expect similarities in correlations between many sites within regions and to use particular techniques that correspond with these assumptions (Adams and Adams 1991; Wylie 2002).

One of many archaeological techniques used to practice typology is the spreadsheet, or statistical database, derived from natural science. Since the above assumptions correspond so well with assumptions of the universal nature of natural elements in the sciences, the use of these databases was originally deemed acceptable. Artifacts or traits, like natural elements, are seen as having only one proper meaning or use and therefore are designated as variables to be correlated with others in order to find universal patterns of correlation. This is the theory at least, but there are difficulties with both the assumptions and practice of typological classification.

The persistence of the concept of culture as unified may, in fact, be explained by the fact that the practice of typology, based upon this assumption, actually perpetuates the myth of a unified culture. The very search for similarities to identify a common artifact or practice means that differences within those entities are usually ignored (Jones 1997, 130). The separation of artifacts and traits from their context for analysis by specialists and the entry of them as formal variables into a spreadsheet or statistical database makes it difficult to reconnect contexts for comparison. More than anything else, this impedes the observance of other artifact meanings or uses. The active search for similarities in correlations over large areas only exacerbates this neglect. Once similarities are found, these are arbitrarily nominated as the most important factors and are seen as evidence of a unified culture, prompting in turn the further use of typology (ibid., 131).

In the absence of such arbitrary selection, a significantly different picture emerges: an immense mess of variation within and between communities and regional areas. Such is the case anyway for many cultures, including the Early Bronze Age, where there is far too much complexity to allow a general overview.

EARLY BRONZE AGE STUDIES AND REVERSE TYPOLOGY

The history of Early Bronze Age studies is essentially a history of arbitrary selection. Stuart Piggott first defined the "Wessex Culture" by ignoring differences in structural or burial traits in favor of artifact "richness"—the similarity that bound "Wessex" barrows together for him (Piggott 1938). Although Gordon Childe advocated the study of all material, Childe also favored a few select artifact types that allowed him to define bounded cultural entities in the Early Bronze Age (Childe 1956, 121–3; Jones 1997, 18).

The use of selected objects to categorize bounded cultures or periods has been a common theme in Early Bronze Age archaeology. When Piggott's "Wessex Culture" became too unwieldy, ApSimon (1954) divided the culture into two chronological phases based mostly on daggers. The other most common artifact used to distinguish cultures or time periods in the Early Bronze Age has been pottery (Longworth 1961 and especially D. L. Clarke 1970), where ceramic typologies have been used largely to the exclusion of other information (Pollard 2002, 28). However, toward the end of the 1960s this use of typology began to be challenged. Differences in artifact styles were still seen as representing different cultural ideals (from Crawford 1921), but the attribution of cultural differences to alien cultures from France or Germany brought the search for cultural differences into disrepute.

After J. G. Clark's (1966) attack on Culture History and the search for separate cultures, the divisions within and between the Beaker and Wessex "cultures" began to be eroded. Nonetheless, a form of the typological method was still used—just in reverse. Instead of selecting a few artifacts and ignoring anomalies to define a cultural division, a number of anomalies were selected and the similarities ignored to deny that divisions existed. For example, when ApSimon's Wessex I and Wessex II division was questioned, it was through a study of the gold and bronze metalwork that the distinction was removed (Coles and Taylor 1971). Then through the presence of a handful of "Beaker-like" artifacts in "Wessex Culture" graves (stone battleaxes, V-perforated buttons, and barbed and tanged arrowheads), it was argued that the Wessex Culture had evolved from the Beaker Culture (Piggott 1973, 374; Case 2003). Later, due to the discovery of a significant overlap between the "cultures," this small group of similar artifacts and traits resulted in the Wessex Culture being viewed as merely a higher class of Beaker graves (Burgess 1980, 99).

The result was that while the concept of distinct monolithic cultures was vehemently dismissed, by using a form of typological method or "reverse typology," the concept was actually perpetuated. The effect was to create even larger monolithic cultures with fewer distinctions—cultures that extended across the whole of Britain. This prepared the way for prehistory to be explained "in terms of general theory rather than special circumstances" (Bradley 1984, 13). Despite archaeologists' best intentions to avoid explanation in terms of general cultural distinctions, this new era of archaeology continued to emphasize the cohesiveness of large monolithic cultures. By emphasizing a few similar traits over many differences in support of functionalist or structuralist theories, archaeologists have effectively returned to earlier practices.

Such an impasse perpetuated by typological classification is still evident in Early Bronze Age studies today. Ann Woodward, in her book on barrows, uses a form of typological method to review similarities between barrows in Britain (Woodward 2000). When defeated by a few anomalies, Woodward resorts to the only general pattern—barrow location on high places. These locations are explained as determined by a need to view other barrow cemeteries and monuments (Woodward 2000, 130). Although a possible reason for barrow location, intervisibility neglects the rich diversity between barrows and thereby conflates several periods as well as regions into one monolithic culture (Garwood 2007, 44).

TYPOLOGY AND ARCHAEOLOGICAL THEORY TODAY

It may be that this typological method has persisted because it corresponds so well to current theories about prehistoric culture. While most archaeologists working on the Neolithic or Bronze Age would disagree with the idea that these cultures each represented a single body of beliefs (Thomas 1991, 36, 1996; Barrett 1994, 50), there is a general consensus that social codes and rules of behavior were maintained over large areas through formalism and restriction of movement in monuments (Barrett 1994, 15; Gosden 1994, 24).

This notion again stems from Bourdieu's concept of the "habitus," whereby codes and rules of behavior are instilled from birth in individuals who further perpetuate them in structures and practices (Bourdieu 1977). These codes are seen by British prehistorians to be different from conscious meanings invested in artifacts and traits, which are believed to be more variable (depending upon the individual's sum of experiences) and result in "surface" symbolism. Codes of behavior are more unconscious and provide continuity between times and places since they are restricted by convention and monumentality. This means that some correlations can be expected between sites within bounded regional areas, but the great variation within them can be explained as so many fallible conscious interpretations.

While some general correlations are found between sites and regions during the Neolithic, significant variations between and within individual regions also occur (Thorpe and Richards 1984). Once in the Bronze Age, this concept of culture runs into even greater problems since burial practices and structures become radically diverse. It would be logical if there existed one consistent pattern throughout all barrows, but any line of similarity runs only through a small percentage of the barrows at one time. Even for those lines of formal similarity, it is hard to imagine that codes of behavior were identical over such large distances and periods.

SUBCULTURES

Fortunately, such variability is more understandable if cultures are considered less monolithic than in the above conception and if a conception of object change is brought to bear on them. Perhaps the closest that archaeologists have come to explaining both similarities and differences within cultures is through the concept of subcultures.

The recognition of subcultures in the archaeological record is not a new phenomenon—minority groups in the ancient past have been given voices since the 1970s (Leone et al. 1995), but rarely have subcultures been seen as separate from mainstream culture. Subcultures are usually seen as part of an overarching culture, not in opposition to it, and their material culture as part of a constellation of emblems, not as statements of disagreement. Again, the problem lies in our assumption that culture, and its associated material culture, is unified—an assumption perpetuated by typology.

Yet in the 1990s more radical theories of subcultures were proposed (Wiessner 1990; Hodder 1991; Matthews 1995; Jones 1996, 1997) that drew on decades of work by cultural anthropologists (Hodder 1982), gender archaeologists (Gero et al. 1991; Gilchrest 1994), and historical archaeologists (Leone et al. 1995). While this resulted in a small debate and a recognition of subcultures, few of these theories were groundbreaking, essentially being renderings of partisan theories of culture, reformulated for subcultures.

One of the first to produce a general theory of subcultures for archaeology was Keith Matthews (1995), who equated them with contemporary social categories such as age, sex, class, sexuality, etc., drawing on work conducted on subcultures by sociologists (Hebdige 1979; Argyle 1992; Brake 1985). Matthews highlighted an important observation from these studies, and one that has huge ramifications for archaeology: that subcultures use traditional objects for subversive purposes (using subaltern resistance theory). Drawing on the example of punk subculture, he illustrated how traditional objects like business suits and British flags were torn up and worn to signal dissent and promote an anarchic ideology. This iconoclastic use of traditional symbols makes rigid typological classifications of artifact forms difficult to justify. Unfortunately, by equating subcultures with social categories of sex, class, sexuality, etc., he reduced subcultures to arbitrary twentieth-century structures that determined their actions, while maintaining the concept of a unified culture by integrating subcultures together in society. Furthermore, when applied to the past or the present, such categories often do not relate to the actual demographic of particular subcultures. Gender archaeology has already had to redefine gender categories to include both men and women (Meskell 1999, 89; Voss 2000, 186) after realizing that so-called gender subcultures do not relate exclusively to particular sexes. In a similar way, the punk subculture cannot be related exclusively to the working class, itself having been manufactured by upper-middle-class artists (Savage 2001, 11).

Sian Jones (1996, 1997) deals with the above problems by expanding the definition of subcultures and referring to cultural and subcultural entities as "ethnicities," drawing on work done in anthropology (Bentley 1987; Eriksen 1992). These she compares to Bourdieu's "habitus"—a set of unconscious rules (or doxa) that govern how individuals perceive and act in the world (Bourdieu 1977). Therefore, instead of defining culture as one united "habitus," she argues that subcultural "habituses" also exist, whose identities arise from political or other contextual situations (Jones 1997, 91). While this model of subcultures, defined as *primordialist* theory, gives a deeper explanation of material culture and promotes diversity within cultures, it again reduces subcultures to invisible structures that rigidly control their adherents. As such, it is difficult to clearly explain the origins and development of material culture, or to understand how groups coalesce and form hybrid groups (Stone 2003, 39).

Instead, Tammy Stone (2003) argues that we must allow ethnicities more fluidity (after Barth 1969), claiming that individuals consciously emphasize or de-emphasize their ethnicity for economic, political, or social benefits depending upon the historical and social context they are in (Stone 2003, 35). While this model, defined as *instrumentalist* theory, allows individuals more agency, individuals are instead merely controlled by standard functionalist urges. By reducing subcultures to a political or economic currency, this model similarly omits to trace the origins and development of material culture, forcing the use of external theories such as migration. It also cannot explain why individuals persist in holding to their ethnicity in the face of hostility and violence.

Recently, in *The Archaeology of Ethnogenesis* (2008), Barbara Voss attempts to solve these problems by combining the above approaches. Drawing from her work on gender theory, and the mutability of such categories, Voss further de-essentializes ethnicity (as well as race, nationhood, and class) by illustrating the contingency of identity. She argues that identity is always unique and constantly evolving through changing historical circumstances. Pulling together the three strands of subculture theory above, she explains that identity is constructed to subvert dominant identities (using subaltern resistance theory) by drawing lines of similarity between heterogeneous individuals (using primordialist theory), while simultaneously drawing contrasts with others (using instrumentalist theory). Objects are claimed to be central to this process, helping to subvert, create, and stabilize identities by establishing relations of similarity and difference.

Unfortunately, Voss still avoids explaining the origins and development of object forms, seeing them as merely a cultural capital of symbols used to resist and attain domination (from Bourdieu 1984 and Foucault 1980)—a fairly reductionist explanation itself (Gero 2000; Brück 2006). While the combination of postcolonial, primordialist, and instrumentalist theories may appear to be a good solution, these theories are still all based on the assumption that nature is separate from culture. Their combination therefore cannot solve all the problems that this separation creates. The observation of activities such as subaltern resistance and the use of objects to establish similarities and differences are useful, but without an understanding that these activities refer to the real world and not just the social one, the origin and development of forms and the reasons for people's emotional attachment to them (hidden in the process of their becoming) will continue to be overlooked and external social explanations will continue to be sought for them.

Instead of seeing differences between subcultural entities as unconscious, expedient, or defined by contrasts (with objects used to express these differences), by acknowledging the relationship between the real world and objects, differences between subcultural entities become cosmological. Objects as formulaic understandings of the world become the reasons for differences, not the tools of differences, and arguments are fought over the descriptive power of their objects, not over supposed social or territorial tensions (although these may result from them).

This understanding of groups and their differences not only allows the insights of previous theories to be incorporated, but also addresses their inadequacies. If new groups arise from different understandings of the natural/cultural world (encrypted into new objects and practices) rather than from vague social or functionalist influences, this explains the fervor with which groups maintain their differences, despite hostility. It also explains why contrasts are drawn and why hybridization sometimes occurs. As Stone argues, politics is still central to the interaction between groups—with the co-option of each other's forms for polemical purposes, and even the manipulation of central object forms and practices to stabilize controversies (Stone 2003). But because the objects are formulas and not tools, they cannot be equated—as Stone attempted—with expedient political or economic currency. It is not the similarities or contrasts in object forms and practices that individuals draw upon when they use them to illustrate their affinities or differences with others, it is the differences in relationships between information encrypted into objects that they are referring to. In this scenario, the history of object creation is of central, not peripheral, importance in the understanding of both the origin of groups and their definition.

This understanding of objects also better illustrates why groups dissent so violently against them. In the earlier example that Matthews (1995) gave of punks in the 1970s, the roots of their antagonism were more related to anti-mainstream sentiments born of a real-world lack of employment and opportunities, and reactions to the inadequate portrayal of their situation by music and cultural representations, than to a vague class struggle or a direct reaction to some ideology (Savage 2001, 163). Thus the destruction of traditional suits, flags, and portraits of the Queen, as well as their destruction of references to other bands, defined punks in relation to other representations and entities, but it was in relation to the encrypted *content* of those other representations.

SYMBOLIC CONFLICT BETWEEN AND WITHIN TRIBES

In his paper "Symbolic Conflict and the Spatiality of Traditions in Small-Scale Societies," Matthew Chamberlin (2006) provides several ethnographic examples of coexisting groups in active opposition. In the case of the Trobriand and Dobu tribes from Papua New Guinea, they both build their identities through the active devaluation of each other's artifacts and practices. This devaluation refers to the encrypted content of each other's artifacts and practices, content that is the result of a network of real-world information and relationships between the natural and cultural world. The Dobu indulge in such devaluation by ritually consuming fertility symbols important to the Trobrianders while flaunting their "knowledge of paternity" through other symbols. Similarly, Trobrianders reject the Dobu's "knowledge of paternity" while decorating their war shields with their symbols of fertility (from Glass 1988, 57 in Chamberlin 2006, 43).

Even in areas where objective differences are absent, such as in the Middle Zambezi Valley, different versions of cultural origins are used to assert differences and commonality—in this case between Goba, Nyai, Chikunda, and Tonga groups (Chamberlin 2006, 42). This results in symbolic conflict where the groups "appropriate external traditions or fend off such attempts, continually transforming tradition and adjusting their position in a hierarchy of meaning" (ibid. from Lancaster 1974, 711–5). More warlike symbolic conflict can also occur, such as between the Baktaman and neighboring tribes where temples and sacra (required for rituals) are destroyed or taken (Barth 1975, 64 in Chamberlin 2006, 43).

Examples of desecrated temples and shrines are especially indicative of controversies over encryptions. Many are recorded in early historical accounts of Native American tribes (e.g., the Hernando de Soto expedition) (Milner 1999, 124), and numerous examples are also evident in the North American archaeological record. While the desecration of temples or shrines has largely been overlooked in the archaeological literature, David Dye and Adam King have identified numerous incidents of desecrated temples and mortuary sites from the Mississippian Culture of the Southeast and Midwest (Dye and King 2007).

Unfortunately, Dye and King interpret this desecration from the perspective of objects as symbols of wealth and power—the easiest theory to impose because it "never fails to explain" as Latour argues (Latour 2005, 251). Thus they interpret these desecrations as attacks on the power-base of neighboring elite rulers to undermine them. However, from the premodern perspective of objects and ritual structures as encryptions of information about the social and natural world and therefore representing differing interpretations of the world and the identities of groups, it is natural that attacking groups would want to focus their energy on suppressing those differing representations.

As Leroy Little Bear states, "Events, patterns, cycles, and happenings occur at certain places. . . . Each tribal territory has its sacred sites and its particular environmental and ecological combinations resulting in particular relational networks" (Little Bear 2000, xi). This means that there is rarely a contradiction in the variance between one area's knowledge and another's because knowledge is local. However, the observation of certain regularities at many different localities creates higher order regularities that have in turn resulted in wider reaching encryptions of these patterns in symbols, rituals, and ceremonies. As Little Bear writes, "From the constant flux Native Americans have detected certain regular patterns, be they seasons, migration of animals or cosmic movements" (ibid., xi). These are some of the commonalities that tie groups or tribes together. Hence, while there may be shared cultural elements between groups, representing shared understandings of the world, differences in cultural elements stemming from different local perceptions of the real and social world can create potential controversies within or between groups.

James Snead writes that the social and natural order were highly entwined with sacred places such as temples or mortuary grounds that then played "a central role in reifying that order, particularly in the face of dissident perspectives" (Snead 2008, 138; also Ashmore 2002, 1178; Tuan 1979). Snead writes that Western Apaches told of "being 'shot' by stories related to places in the landscape and thus compelled to conform to the culturally-constructed ideals they embodied" (Basso 1996, 56 in Snead 2008, 138). Thus, he argues, these places were often a focus for conflict, both from outside groups and from dissenters within.

Snead cites numerous historic accounts from the Southwest of internal dissent resulting in a sundering of communities and the desecration of temples (ibid.). Such a process even has a name, termed the "Orayvi Split," after the Hopi Third Mesa village of Orayvi in which discord over the Orayvi ceremonial system (Whiteley 1988) and possibly other issues (Titiev 1988; Levy 1992) led to the departure of half the population and the founding of new villages elsewhere. Destruction of the temples is one common facet of an Orayvi split (Snead 2008, 149).

Ian Frazier writes of Native American social dynamics that, traditionally, "social problems were resolved geographically. . . . [S]plitting up into smaller groups was an efficient way to use the wild resources of the land" (Frazier 2000, 11). Yet intragroup conflict has received little or no attention in archaeology, with groups continuously seen as static, monolithic entities. Perhaps the reason for this is that until recently anthropologists and archaeologists did not even accept the existence of intergroup conflict either.

Conflict has commonly been explained away to avoid portraying Native Americans as bloodthirsty (Arkush 2008). In the 1960s, conflict was portrayed by archaeologists as an intelligent solution to combat resource scarcity and population pressure, and then in the 1980s as a means to appease the gods or maintain social equilibrium (ibid., 561). Evidence for extreme violence such as trophy head taking has even been seen as healthy cultural behavior and "simply a difference in mortuary practice" as recently as 2007 (Demerest 2007, 609), ignoring the violent nature of decapitation. As a result, certain prehistoric eras have been claimed to be completely peaceful, such as the North American Hopewell or the British Neolithic. The notion that the Hopewell people might be a peaceful folk, or Pax Hopewelliana as they are known, was actually a notion that was derived from Gordon Childe's view of Neolithic people as peaceful traders, applied to the Hopewell by Thorne Deuel (1952 in Seeman 2007). Pax Hopewelliana is still in use today (e.g., Hall 1997, 156 and Milner 1999 in Seeman 2007), although advocates have recently conceded that a certain level of conflict did exist (Milner 2007).

The idea of insurrection within communities or regions has actually been around for a long time in archaeology, even though this has not been equated with conflict. The use of traditional objects by individuals to disrupt the consensus was a major theme in Ian Hodder's seminal work on active material culture (Hodder 1982, 69). It is surprising that it has not been more comprehensively acknowledged in archaeology (Jones 1997, 114), but "active" material culture symbolism has largely been seen as symbolism expressed by individuals within a unified monolithic culture, not in opposition to it (Thomas 1999, 163). The focus on more general codes and rules of behavior, instead of on symbolism (which was considered too variable), has meant that material culture has been seen to "act as props for the strategies of social life," while monolithic society was quietly reproduced (Barrett 1994, 169). The word "active," however, in Hodder's original meaning of the word designated the use of cultural objects by certain Baringo tribespeople to subvert the consensus.

The understanding that groups are defined by their dissent is central to Latour's work. Latour sees society as composed of various groups vying to present the ideal view of the world rather than constituting a unified culture with class distinctions vying with each other for power. This is also the defining theme in Isabelle Stengers' concept of "Cosmopolitics"—her word to describe a society's workings toward creating an ideal representation of the cosmos (Stengers 1996). This term helps to illustrate the ideological nature of groups as well as their activity to organize and implement their opposing understanding. It is a much more fluid and active perception of entities than the more static, unified terms of "culture," "subculture," or "ethnicity." It also requires a close observation of their actions to determine the particular, local causes of their difference.

Perceiving groups as political entities also has the interesting effect of reorienting our concept of culture and material culture. According to such a perception, cultures are no longer monocultural, and groups within them are no longer subliminal, monolithic entities, but are continually changing through conscious reaction to others and their notion of the truth. Objects are no longer the symbols of groups but actually their political manifestos. Such a conception embraces Hodder's understanding of active material culture more productively than the idea that objects maintain or reproduce social organization.

We can best understand the political nature of groups and the role that objects play by following the process through which groups and their objects come into being. The most analytical study that has been done of this process is probably Latour's anthropological study of scientist Roger Guillemin and his laboratory in *Laboratory Life* (Latour and Woolgar 1979).

Understanding that "we have never been modern" means that the processes through which groups and their objects emerge in science can be useful in understanding parallel processes through which groups and objects emerged in the past. It is of no little importance that this understanding has come through studying object emergence under laboratory conditions. After two centuries of studying non-industrial societies that were powerless to control anthropological interpretations of them, it was only through the collaborative study of Western knowledge production that the actual process of object creation was discovered, illustrating the adage that in order to understand another culture, you really need to understand your own first.

CHALLENGING KNOWLEDGE CLAIMS

In his book *Science in Action* (1987), Latour describes the results of his 1979 anthropological study by explaining the process through which a dissenter (Roger Guillemin) must pass in order to challenge a representation of the world—in this case the representation is the GHRH peptide established by the scientist Andrew Schally. Guillemin was an eminent French scientist who was introduced to Latour in France and invited him to come to San Diego to study his laboratory while he attempted to challenge Schally's conclusions. Over the space of two years, Latour laboriously followed the controversy that unfolded in Guillemin's laboratory. In generalizing this controversy, Latour illustrates the steps a dissenter must take.

The first hurdle that the dissenter faces is the article in an academic journal that describes the representation that he disagrees with. The article is a very difficult hurdle in itself when it is backed up by the reputation of the scientist, the reputation of his laboratory, and the institutions that funded him. It is even more difficult to challenge the article if it is well established and used by many others in the field. If the dissenter wishes to question the article, he must face all of the allies and sources that the scientist has used to back up his claim. If he still wishes to dissent, he must then face all of the instruments and their readouts that illustrate the scientist's claim. This is already a formidable array of evidence, but even more formidable is the next step: disputing the replication of the experiment and the demonstration of its results in a laboratory. If this stage does not convince the dissenter, then the only way to challenge the representation is to set up an even greater laboratory and replicate it himself.

In Guillemin's case, he had to set up an even more powerful laboratory than Schally, with even greater funding and the same, if not better, instruments. To come this far and to organize the allies and funding for a new laboratory obviously requires enormous determination. But the task becomes impossible if there is more than one claim to dispute. This is because each of the claims approved by the field upon which Schally constructed his claim would have needed to be disputed, requiring equal amounts of effort and cost expended on each. It is impractical, if not impossible, to do any more than build a different representation from the building blocks already in place and used by the opposing claim.

This illustrates the solidity of knowledge systems and why systems are so rarely changed in their entirety—it is far too much effort to overthrow more than one or two claims. This means that more than a few changes represent a sizable shift in knowledge even while some elements remain. Such a conception of variation challenges the belief in archaeology that if a few artifacts or structures remain unchanged, despite other significant changes, they represent unruffled continuity between periods.

Even to build up such a limited dissenting representation, Guillemin had to shake up the entire structure of the field in order to allow him to proceed with a new logic. This involved redefining the entire TRH subdiscipline (Latour and Woolgar 1979, 119). Once this was done, he was able to recommend the substitution of differing elements, and while replicating Schally's experiment with a different bioassay, he found that the peptide did something entirely different. Instead of increasing the production of growth hormones, he found that the peptide decreased them. Guillemin was able to argue from this that Schally had mistaken his results, and he was also able to claim that he had discovered a new object—one that could do something different. As a result of this research, he earned the Nobel Prize for science.

The process of dissent and object creation, described by Latour, illustrates the level of politics and the cost involved in challenging the status quo and producing a different representation. This process is not, by any means, just a matter of claiming that a new representation is true and of being validated by "nature." Neither is the process influenced by "culture" or a universal social theory. It involves painstakingly reorganizing previously validated knowledge and using the same or more elaborate tools to come up with a different conclusion. It requires seemingly endless amounts of networking—enrolling allies such as multiple material elements but also professional colleagues, previously validated knowledge, and funding in a seamless whole, and making them all work faithfully.

This process is not unlike the medieval feudal system in which the lead scientist, like a feudal lord, must prove himself and gather funding to support a large retinue of loyal followers and resources to work his/her way politically into a position of influence. This network of human and non-human allies must be maintained all the way since any weak link may erode that authority. Neither do the politics get easier once one is in a position of influence. The rules of this political game "are simple enough: weaken your enemies, paralyze those you cannot weaken . . . help your allies if they are attacked, ensure safe communications with those who supply you with indisputable instruments, oblige your enemies to fight one another; if you are not sure of winning, be humble and understated. These are simple rules indeed: the rules of the oldest politics" (Latour 1987, 37).

In the same way, the pathways open to indigenous people who wish to change understandings of their Native science are few and tortuous. The steps to a position of influence are expensive and highly political. Even to know the scientific knowledge encrypted in rituals or objects involves an apprenticeship and often money or goods paid to the shaman or keeper of indigenous knowledge. Cajete states, "There are both formal and informal pathways to certain levels of Native Science. For instance, in the Midewiwin Society of the Ojibwa there are four stages of initiation, each involving extensive training, learning of songs, ceremonies, stories, interpretations of special scrolls, and petroglyphs" (Cajete 2004, 53).

For the maintenance of this knowledge, Cajete writes, "Sanction and commitment acted as foundational safeguards for both individual and tribe and formed a kind of 'check and balance' for important knowledge" (Cajete 2004, 55). "Sanction of knowledge through appropriate ritual and tribal society acknowledgement, and commitment to gain and share knowledge are important, since knowledge of the natural world and how best to relate to it is not just a matter of individual understanding but is gained and shared for the benefit and perpetuation of the community" (ibid.).

The structures of scientific knowledge that emerge from Latour and Cajete's descriptions are vastly more rigid and indestructible than commonly held beliefs about Western or indigenous science allow. The idea that just anyone with a new idea can overthrow a scientific "falsity," however distinguished they might be, or however truthful the new idea appears, is deeply naïve (Latour 1987, 95). The only way to change a knowledge claim, however small, is to form a large group of allies, human and non-human, and restructure the field with the same building blocks in a different configuration. Such a perspective helps to understand why pre-modern material culture and practices changed so slowly.

The scientific practice that runs parallel to this political process is, of course, the topic usually focused upon by historians and philosophers of science, but it is no more important than the politics and actions that originate and support it. Thus one cannot rely purely on nature for explanations of scientific practice. Conversely, ceremonial practices and material culture cannot be interpreted as purely religious, social, or political phenomena, but must also be understood as having a relationship with the real physical world.

However, while Latour and his colleagues in science and technology studies have demonstrated how to follow objects in science, there have been few Latourian studies of cultural or religious groups that can serve as practice models to help anthropologists or archaeologists break out of their modernist approaches. To redress this imbalance, the following section offers one such study of a recent group formed to ferment dramatic religious change—a change that illustrates the influence of local natural and cultural factors and the political actions that were central to its instigation. This was the introduction of cremation, promoted in the nineteenth century as an alternative to the Christian practice of inhumation burial.

A NON-MODERNIST HISTORY OF
NINETEENTH-CENTURY CREMATION

While religious changes have often been given a purely social explanation, the biggest change in conventional religious practice in the last century—the rise of modern cremation and its adoption by churches—was largely due to the very material threat to health that the large-scale inhumation of bodies in cities posed after the Industrial Revolution. Modernist sociologists may still claim that such a change was the product of a social process, such as secularization, but on closer examination it is evident that neither explanation is sufficient.

While functional necessity may be one reason for the origin of cremation, it cannot fully explain how cremation became popular. Multiple factors, both natural and social, were at work, factors that were too deeply enmeshed to be separated out. Changes in theology brought about by experiences of real-world phenomena, as well as political actions designed to promote cremation, were central to this process of change. Like the character of natural objects in a scientific study, the eventual character of British cremation once it was adopted was very different from the character of cremation originally proposed by Italians or the meaning that was later given to it by sociologists. Instead, it comprised a network of actions and ideas that enabled it to be the powerful option for people that it is today. Yet these multiple factors are easily missed, and the full process is forgotten if change is attributed to a single external theory from either nature or society. It is also a pretty good story.

The first major appearance of cremation in nineteenth-century Europe was the result of a very deliberate scheme to secularize society. In the mid-nineteenth century, Italy experienced the effects of a broad movement led by freemasonry to undermine control of society by the Catholic Church (Novarino 2005). Freemasons identified cremation as a powerful symbolic and practical way to break the Church's monopoly on death, a monopoly widely seen as the lynchpin of their control. The grand master of Italy himself, Giuseppe Mazzoni, is quoted urging "all the lodges and all the Masonic bodies to energetically engage in this major issue, as nobody could avoid its extraordinary importance" (ibid., 209). Freemasonry in Italy at this time was generally composed of freethinking individuals such as liberals and doctors, many of whom held high positions in society and government. Their huge influence in parliament enabled parliamentary debate on cremation to start as early as 1869, and over the next sixteen years, hundreds of cremations were conducted across Italy with tacit support from parliament. The arguments for cremation were ostensibly functional and hygienist, but there is much debate among historians as to whether the functional value of cremation was actually a disguise for the political actions of these doctors, many of whom were freemasons (Mates 2005, 339).

It is interesting that during this time the Catholic Church was not actively opposed to cremation. This may have been due to the special care taken by masons to cloak their intentions. But all of this changed very suddenly in 1886. When the grand master of Italian freemasons died, instead of being cremated—which had been his desire—he was buried according to the wishes of his family. The Italian cremation societies, suspecting Catholic intervention, stirred up a violent protest in the press and demanded his cremation, openly exposing their secularizing intentions. In reaction to this protest the Catholic Church launched the most violent attack on freemasonry to date, excommunicating all those who belonged to cremation societies (Novarino 2005, 209). This decree drove freemasonry further from the Church and turned Catholicism away from cremation for almost eighty years. It was only in 1963, after cremation societies strove to make it clear that cremation was not a subterfuge to undermine the Church, that the Church finally lifted its ban (Mates 2005, 342). Thus, in the same way as the origins of cremation were not primarily functional, the Church's reaction and change of heart were not primarily theological, but involved a network of natural, ideological, and political factors.

The origins of British cremation—ostensibly the same practice—were quite different although they stem from an Italian exhibit on cremation at the Vienna World's Fair in 1873. Sir Henry Thompson, Queen Victoria's surgeon, was at the fair and was so impressed by the exhibit that he published an essay promoting cremation as a more hygienic burial practice than inhumation (Kazmier 2005, 398). At this time there was a severe lack of space for the dead in many of the burgeoning cities in Britain. While the population of cities had drastically increased due to the Industrial Revolution, the Anglican Church had stubbornly refused to expand their cemeteries. Grotesque stories abounded of gravediggers digging up the recent dead to bury others, as well as other stories that the dead were polluting the ground water and the air surrounding cemeteries (Jupp 2005a, 114).

Thompson's solution, however, was not embraced as a sanitary solution by all in the medical profession, and many articles were written by doctors, including the medical inspector of burials for England and Wales, opposing the innovation as unnecessary. And, to be sure, it is likely that many of the grotesque stories about burial were urban myths, catering to the Victorians' penchant for the gothic. The main critic of cremation, the eminent doctor Francis Seymour Haden, actually argued that burial was a much less polluting way to dispose of the dead than cremation and that it did not result in air pollution as the British complained that Hindu cremations in India did.

The idea that cremation had a functional advantage, therefore, was far from universally evident from the start, and it is clear that it was something that had to be fought for. Soon after his article, Thompson formed a society for the promotion of cremation. The Cremation Society, as it was known, first focused upon persuading and recruiting eminent individuals in support of the cause, including the celebrated novelist Anthony Trollope and numerous celebrities from the world of high culture. Encouraged by this support, the society precipitously built a furnace in 1878 and unwisely experimented by first cremating a horse. Unfortunately this caused huge public outrage, which impelled the Home Office to officially ban cremation.

The next step therefore was to address popular opinion. One of the society's attempts to promote cremation occurred in August 1882, when England was first beaten by Australia in cricket. The editor of *Sporting Times*, the son of a founding member of the Cremation Society, published an obituary for English Cricket saying that "The body will be cremated and the ashes taken to Australia." The ashes of a bail or cricket ball were duly sent to Australia in a cremation urn, initiating a legend and the famous cricket series, *The Ashes* (Jupp 2005b, 135–42; White 2005c, 397). Other attempts by founding members of the Cremation Society, such as Hugh Haweis, included publishing thinly disguised fictional descriptions of grotesque burial ceremonies in order to turn the public off burial.

By far the most successful event to publicize cremation, however, occurred in 1884. An eccentric doctor from South Wales shocked his village by openly cremating his son in a barrel of petrol just as villagers were leaving church after a Sunday service. William Price was a gifted man who had been the youngest member of the Royal College of Surgeons, but he was also flamboyantly subversive and an Arch Druid, advocating, among other things, free love and naturalism. His interest in cremation, fostered through an interest in contemporary antiquarian accounts of Bronze Age cremation and its purported links with Druidic practices, interestingly illustrates the influence of prehistory in nineteenth-century British cremation.

By the age of eighty-three, when Price performed the cremation in full Druidic costume, he had fathered three children with three different women, two of whom he had named Jesus Christ. It was the death of one of these children that led to the notorious cremation event, which he believed would precipitate a return to Bronze Age burial practices. However, in the middle of his chanting, as the flames were growing higher, the police descended and halted the cremation, arresting Price (White 2005a, 350).

The judge for the case against Price was a clever choice, probably influenced by the Cremation Society itself. James Stephen was a non-religious intellectual whose brother was the father of Virginia Woolf. Having served in India, where cremation was common, his liberal opinion was that while different people may do things differently, that did not make those things illegal (White 2005b, 388). To the delight of the Cremation Society, Stephen's judgment was that it was not illegal to cremate a body as long as it did not cause a public nuisance (White 2005a, 351).

This spectacular judgment laid the foundations for the Cremation Society to proceed with cremations legally. Thus it was neither functional necessity nor social politics by themselves that helped cremation's legal acceptance, but both. It was also helped along by particular subversive and political actions.

Price's startling public cremation and court case not only brought about legal acceptance, but also stimulated enormous curiosity. Even though Price lived in an obscure Welsh village far from the centers of influence and power, his actions sent shockwaves throughout the nation and around the world. Newspaper articles covering Price's sensational cremation and the subsequent court case spurred public debate about cremation, which in turn aided in its popular acceptance. A significant result of this controversy was that, for the first time in nearly two thousand years, people were suddenly forced to think about why they buried their dead. As Latour states, "it is only when there is a dispute, as long as it lasts, and depending on the strength exerted by dissenters that words such as 'culture,' 'paradigm,' or 'society' may receive a precise meaning" (Latour 1987, 201).

At first, commentators argued that burial was practiced because it was imperative for the body to be preserved for resurrection on the Last Day, when the Bible stated that the dead would rise. But then people argued that attitudes to the soul and afterlife implicit in this practice had changed since the third century AD. Since the 1840s a secular movement had existed that pushed for the immortality of the soul or the "belief in a human soul which leaves the body after death and continues into another dimension" (Davies 2005, 31; also Jupp 2005c, 353; Badham 2005, 376; Dartigues 2005). Through the Spiritualist movement and the frequent publications of after-death experiences, people had long entertained the idea that the soul was separate from the body. Others argued that if God's will were thwarted because there were only ashes and not decomposed bones to be revived, then God's will was not very omnipotent (Love 2005, 358–9). Thus popular theological discussion led many people to agree with cremation in the first years of cremation, although this did not translate into official theological change.

It took a good deal longer for the Anglican Church to develop any sort of consistent or coherent policy on the matter of cremation. Nevertheless, change in the Church was also driven by events. The experience of violence during the First World War brought to an end many people's belief in resurrection, and the Church was soon forced to take notice. The horrific obliteration of hundreds of thousands of people by mines and explosive shells meant that there was little left of people to bury or arise on the Last Day. This was a huge problem for the bereaved, who started doubting the doctrine of resurrection. Many in the Church also followed suit rather than challenging the bereaved in their parishes.

Remarkably, such challenges to church doctrine led to heresy trials against senior Anglican and Methodist pastors in the 1920s. But the trials actually had a positive result in that they stimulated healthy Church debate. In debates at church congresses over the next fifteen years, it became evident that many in the clergy no longer believed in the doctrine of resurrection nor thought that it was a necessary part of Christianity either (Jupp 2005a, 115). In 1938 the Church of England Doctrine Commission finally published a report stating that Christians should reject a "literalistic belief in a future resuscitation of the actual physical frame laid in the tomb" (1938, 207 in Badham 2005, 377). Soon afterward the Cremation Society stepped in and proposed a motion that cremation was not a problem for Christian Identity, with the Bishop of Oxford supporting them. In 1944 the Convocation of Canterbury finally declared (ironically after cremation had thoroughly transformed the Church's concept of the soul and its relationship to the world) that "Cremation had no theological significance." Four weeks later the Archbishop of Canterbury died and was himself cremated, giving a huge impetus to the cremation movement (Jupp 2005a, 115).

Thus, the story of modern-day cremation illustrates the multifaceted nature of change in religious practice. Cremation originated for different reasons in different places—either as an effort to secularize society, to clean up the natural world, or even to reinstate a primitive Bronze Age practice. It became legally accepted through sociopolitical actions and was popularly accepted through basic theological change. Theological change, in turn, occurred largely through experience of the world—either through hearing of after-death experiences or through experiences in World War I—and all changes were precipitated by events. The point that emerges from this illustration is that change cannot be explained by reducing multiple enmeshed agencies to singular separate factors, either human, social, historical, natural, or political. The only way to understand them properly is to follow them all. Similarly, as archaeologists, we must accept that experience of the natural world and its changes or challenges can prompt theological changes and sociological phenomena. Above all, this history illustrates that the best place to start such investigations of change is to look for significant events and political actions, and start examinations there. These are often the points of convergence for networks of factors and often bring about change. More importantly for us, they also stimulate rare instances of explicit conscious meditations on abstract, "black-boxed" practices (Beck et al. 2007, 834).

Unlike many archaeological interpretations of change in religious practices, the history of nineteenth-century cremation illustrates that change does not occur easily. Simplistic ecological, prestige-goods, or risk-management models fail to address the complex local networks of factors that bring about change. To identify all the factors involved, such networks need to be followed without prejudicially defining in advance the spheres of possible influence.

FIVE

A Method for Analyzing Cultural Action

In the first part of this book we learned from historiographies of science and social science that the artificial separation of nature from culture has created deep flaws in our understanding and description of how objects and practices originate, and how change occurs. In order to get to a non-modernist understanding of these processes without being influenced by the nature/culture dichotomy, it was necessary to first observe how non-modernist societies view change. Central to their conception of change is the idea that objects form active agencies, agencies that are usually attributed by modernists to invisible social or natural forces. Latour's explanation of how objects are endowed with agency, through their associations and the process of information encryption that creates them, and how they become powerful agents in science and society, has greatly improved the awareness of object agency in the social sciences. More importantly, it has begun to undermine a belief in the existence of "society" as an invisible force.

Nevertheless, it is also important to understand how modernist notions of "nature" and "society" have structured many of the research tools that we use, and how these tools must also be altered so that they do not perpetuate modernist notions. Only this way can we allow local experiences, history, diversity, and dissent (previously marginalized by seeking invisible social or natural forces) to take center stage in the explanation of change.

The second part of this book is an attempt to outline some of the problems with research tools and to apply a methodology that remains open to local interpretations. This methodology was acquired by studying the practice and methods of anthropologists of science, and is adapted for the study of archaeological data. Like any methodology

111

adapted from another discipline, problems arise that are unique to archaeology together with problems that apply to other disciplines too. The individual solutions worked out at each point may therefore help non-archaeologists as well. Most of these problems involved finding an alternative to statistical methods for the reduction and presentation of qualitative data. As discussed in chapter 4, statistical methods are problematic for following actors over time as they are based upon the assumption that culture and its objects are unilinear while forms actually change meaning constantly with different usage. Yet archaeology is in a unique position to help develop solutions to these problems with its experience straddling the physical and social sciences and producing quantitative methods that can present qualitative data.

CONTROVERSIES

Perhaps the most important contribution of the anthropology of science to the social sciences is their solution to the age-old problem: how to interpret without theories. As it was made clear in the story of nineteenth-century cremation — nothing can be reduced to a determinative social or natural theory. Instead, each stage of change was the product of hard work by individuals who created the links between events, history, theology, and the natural and social world. Nevertheless, anyone trying to understand the process of this activity, and what was associated and connected to bring about this change, would have had a pretty hard time without access to the history of this process. Such is the position of archaeologists trying to understand change in the past. When attempting to interpret material from the ground up, we find ourselves confronted by a mass of seemingly unconnected archaeological data. Without an understanding of the missing agencies that tie this data together, archaeologists are invariably forced to invent or seek invisible social or natural forces to explain them.

This is the dilemma that archaeologists have always confronted when wishing to develop a method to understand the past (Hodder 1986, 138; Binford 1982, 160; Childe 1949, 24; Taylor 1948, 143). While many have wished to obtain a faithful explanation of material in the ground by following the data precisely, Hodder, Binford, Childe, and many others have all confronted the difficulty of choosing which dimensions of variation were relevant and which were not. With thousands of pieces of disparate data, it is virtually impossible to reconstruct the functions or ideas behind objects and sites (Binford 1982, 160). Like thousands of jigsaw pieces from many different puzzles (without any cover pictures to reference!) the archaeological record appears to be a total enigma. The only solution to this dilemma has been to use theories — artificial cover pictures — to help select pieces that can be used productively to gain some sort of picture, even if that picture is artificial. Migration and diffusion theories, middle-range theories, ethnographic analogies, and sociological theories have all been used to create pictures that are more or less "exemplifications of ethnographically documented practices and beliefs" (Brown 1997, 470).

Today, archaeologists are faced with the same problem with very little improvement. Theories of the body and the brain are the most recent in attempts to find a universal theory that will provide arbitrary dimensions of variation (Boivin 2008), but unfortunately they still provide arbitrary explanations as well. Nevertheless, the problem of finding the relevant dimensions for groups has been a common problem for other social sciences, and we can learn from solutions found by some of them to avoid the use of theories. While most in the social sciences have adopted theories to determine the relevant dimensions, anthropologists of science have long been forced to reevaluate their methods because of their spectacular inability to impose social theories on hard scientific data.

Their solution has proved a game changer for the history of science and for parts of sociology, and could provide archaeology with a valuable approach to understand objects and sites in archaeology from the ground up, without the use of theories. Instead of searching for the right theory to attain the relevant dimensions of variation, historians of science realized that the real problem was finding the right data to study (Barnes 1982; Golinski 1998, 20). It was realized at an early stage that not all data is equal. As Latour argues, most objects and actions are black-boxed—or no longer linked to all of the associations that gave them meaning. If objects are used abstractly without expressing the relationships between associations that gave them meaning, then it is clearly impossible for social scientists to identify the relevant dimensions of variation from them, and any data from these objects merely ends up muddying the analysis (Latour 1987, 3, 242). This lack of useful data from the majority of human actions, more than anything else, has given social scientists the impression that it is impossible to attain explanations except through theories. Without explicit data to counter our own speculations, we become like pre-experimental natural philosophers, imposing our own assumptions on material.

Yet, historians of science discovered that there were certain occasions when the encrypted information and associations of an object were made explicit (Collins 1985; Rudwick 1985; Secord 1986). The first was the occasion when an object was first encrypted. Unfortunately for archaeologists, it is not easy to find the occasion of an object's inception, let alone to study the process of thought behind it. Nevertheless, a less rare occasion was also discovered that provided historians with a clear window into the process of thought behind objects. These were occasions when controversies, like the above controversy over nineteenth-century cremation, blow up between groups over the ability of objects or practices to represent the world (Golinski 1998, 21).

Latour writes that such controversies over objects generally occur when objects that represent information about nature/culture fail to explain that information accurately or do not explain it as well as they used to (Latour 2005, 81). This can occur when new information emerges that invalidates the representation or when different representations emerge that explain the information better. Different representations of the same phenomenon rarely exist together in peaceful harmony because of the impossibility of holding two conflicting understandings of the same (significant) phenomenon at the same time. Psychologists call the distress this position causes "cognitive dissonance" or "cognitive disequilibrium"—a state of mind which forces individuals to accept or challenge new representations (Festinger et al. 1956; Piaget 1985). Due to the potential cost of throwing out the old and accepting new representations that have not been tested, new representations generally cause some level of controversy. During these controversies, proponents of representations desperately try to illustrate to others why their representations are the correct ones, thus providing explicit networks of references that detail the relevant associations of objects, as well as the connections made between associations (Latour 1987, 26; 2005, 52).

Controversies therefore provide the equivalent of a series of scientific *tests* of objects, the essential practice that determines the character of objects in scientific practice and is the very essence of science (Latour 2005). Studying controversies is thus the research equivalent of using a time machine, enabling us to go back to any period and test the parameters of objects and practices from that period.

Such an understanding follows Thomas Kuhn's declaration that when a difference is critical enough to threaten a worldview, opponents build explicit cases for their conflicting representations (Kuhn 1962, 148). Because opponents dig deep and elucidate the reasons behind objects and practices to the best of their ability, the work for the historian or prehistorian is largely done for them. Latour writes that "when we approach a controversy more closely, half of the job of interpreting the reasons behind the beliefs is already done!" (Latour 1987, 26). The character of these illustrations is almost always material and therefore highly traceable (ibid.). By following the process of controversies between protagonists, following every action and reaction, the *relevant* dimensions of variation can be traced from the representations themselves and their associations, rather than having to find artificial dimensions through a social theory.

Following controversies is the central methodology in most of science, technology and society studies (STS), and in all of Latour's books. In his book *Science in Action* (1987, 26), he argues that following the development of controversies about objects (formulas, rituals, structures, or anything encrypted) is the best way to observe the information and relationships encrypted into objects—after the process of their becoming has been neglected and they have become "black-boxed" (abstract and reified). When such controversies result in the development of new objects and practices, it is also the best way to observe the process of becoming for these new forms.

Latour explains that controversies can occur as the result of a number of reasons. If the representation has been used to understand, control, or predict the world and it no longer works effectively (like a machine, a formula, or a cosmogram) due to too many anomalies that cannot be explained away, some individuals or groups can become dissatisfied with it and may come up with alternatives—new representations of the world used to predict and control it. These new representations can sometimes be completely new forms, but they are usually adaptations of old forms.

Kuhn argued that the majority of people for whom the old representations worked fairly well are generally loath to reject their tried and tested forms for untested alternatives just because of a few anomalies (Kuhn 1962, 24). They tend to expend enormous amounts of effort in order to explain the anomalies away, or just ignore them (ibid., 52). Unless the problems with representations are very bad, any attempt to replace them will be viewed as *iconoclastic* and not at all welcome. This is contrary to modernist theories of change, which usually see new attempts to understand the world as progressive and embraced (ibid., 93).

Truly iconoclastic actions are actually different from disputes that are stimulated by anomalies, but nevertheless appear to stimulate reactions similar to controversies (Latour 1998a). Iconoclasm against representations is generally motivated if the representation has been separated from the information and relationships that gave it meaning and it has become fetishlike—or accorded mysterious truth-giving powers without the knowledge of how it came by them. Many instances exist of individuals attacking an image or statue to merely destroy its seeming power. Latour follows several iconoclastic acts against religious and artistic icons in a series of articles to examine why this occurs (Latour 1998a, 2001b, 2002b). Without a knowledge of the associations and history behind artworks, artworks often become fetishes and are worshiped themselves (in a way). Instead of directing thought away from the artwork and toward the ideas and things they represent, religious and artistic creations can come to be seen as mediators for "God" or "truth" and become very powerful as a result. Individuals, angry with what objects or structures represent, or angry with the power that images hold, can sometimes direct that anger toward images that have become fetishes (Latour 2002b, 32).

Whether violence toward objects is stimulated by the desire to replace those objects or merely destroy them, in both cases it results in controversies that bring people together in defense of objects or against them, forcing people to explain the meaning behind them.

CONTROVERSIES AND CHANGE

Historians of science have also found that controversies are the catalysts for the development of new representations or amalgamations of conflicting representations. In the same way that scientific developments occur largely through controversy and competition—with differences of opinion that force traditional representations to be reevaluated and elaborated or changed—Latour argues that cultural developments are similarly influenced by differences of opinion (Latour 2005).

One of the criticisms of ANT has been the difficulty of actor-network theory to explain change (Spinuzzi 2008, 22; Harman 2009, 130; Latour et al. 2011, 27). This is odd since ANT was designed as a way to follow change, but the criticism is understandable if Latour's philosophy is taken into account to the exclusion of his methodology (the problem with Graham Harman's account). If matter is the reduction of relations, and analyses purely aim to follow these relations to map out the cartography of information that it comprises, then ANT analyses would result in a map of an actor's network that grows in size over time, but doesn't change. In order for change to take place, it is necessary for something to be introduced to the network that is not simply additional information (ibid.).

While many ANT accounts do unfortunately end up with such a static map of associations, the reason is usually that they deviate from Latour's methodology. By focusing on controversies, studies are guaranteed that conflicting ideas will impact networks and that some change will occur. In this way, Latour takes a fairly Darwinian view of change, although without Herbert Spencer's notion of the "survival of the fittest" (which was actually added to Darwin's *Origin of Species* in its second edition) (Latour 2001a). Latour illustrates with Shirley Strum (Strum et al. 1987) how objects from dissident networks, like genetic mutations, act as the mechanism of evolution in traditions. However, this is not technological evolution in the usual neo-evolutionary sense. Latour's mutant objects or representations are those that accumulate, combine, or encrypt more or different information about nature or society. These are the most threatening to the majority view and create controversies. Nevertheless, it takes much more than this for evolution to occur.

In every tradition there are multiple differing opinions and resulting mutant representations (or mutineers), but these rarely affect the opinions of others, even if they are better at expressing the world. Proponents of different representations succeed or do not succeed in changing the majority view depending upon the political actions they take to promote their representations. These actions or political maneuvers, like Darwin's non-functional yet sexually attractive traits, are as important for change as the practical value of representations, by enabling them to be contenders (Latour 1987, 98). Thus Latour argues that in addition to mapping the associations that individuals enroll to justify their representations and the elements of opposing representations, it is equally important to follow the political actions of individuals during controversies to understand how representations get accepted.

THE FREQUENCY OF CONTROVERSIES

For the past thirty years, many in the history and philosophy of science have studied historical controversies and confirmed that they expose fundamental values and unspoken rules. However, they also realized that such disputes occurred far more frequently in the past than Kuhn's picture of controversies as infrequent disputes over paradigms suggests (Golinski 1998, 21). Latour has argued that science actually moves forward as the result of constant ongoing controversies over representations (Latour 1987, 4). However, there is a great difference between controversies over "science in the making" and controversies over "ready-made science" (which is rarely touched). To question "ready-made science" requires opening a tightly sealed black box of entrenched knowledge, and it demands enormous willpower and resources. This is why those with differences in opinion usually try to align themselves with current knowledge in order to contribute to "science in the making." Kuhn's perspective on controversies—as infrequent disputes over paradigms— was probably the result of seeing only the seismic scientific changes blazed into history, when differences of opinion came from individuals (usually outside the scientific academy) who attacked "ready-made science" head on. As Latour argues, "there is a direct relation between . . . the angle at which the claims clash with other claims and . . . the number of allies one has to fetch" (Latour 1987, 210).

For the vast majority of controversies, therefore, proponents of differing opinions will approach their opponents at an oblique angle and go out of their way to prove that they are part of the academy, presenting their ideas as similar to "ready-made science." They will tend to use the same objects as traditional representations, albeit in different ways. As illustrated in chapter 4, traditional objects are also used in different ways by dissenters who attack "ready-made science" head-on and wish to define themselves as different. This means that whether controversies are overt or muted, the use of traditional objects by dissenters often renders their own existence invisible, at least to the historian who is looking for differences in object forms to identify change.

Furthermore, the majority of modern controversies are also missed by historians because they were purposely forgotten and actively erased. Because the victorious characterizations that emerge from controversies are declared "natural" facts, the messy scientific controversies behind them, together with the process of scientific practice, are usually neglected as inconvenient contingent history and conveniently forgotten. The same Whiggish attitude is applied to modern controversies over cultural and religious changes once they are resolved. As illustrated by the history of cremation in Great Britain, once cremation had finally become accepted by the Anglican Church, having radically transformed the doctrine of resurrection and the concept of the soul, it was declared that "Cremation had no theological significance" (Jupp 2005a, 115). Due to the complications that controversies present to modernists, they are often conveniently neglected, and together with attempts by dissenters to make differences appear as traditional as possible, it is quite hard for the historian (as illustrated by Kuhn's ignorance of the majority of scientific controversies) to identify them. Thus it is only recently that controversies have been restored to their rightful place in historical theory and methodology as the premium data source and driver of change.

Yet, despite their awareness of this problem with identifying controversies, historians of science have not come up with an analytical way to identify them. This means that many historical controversies that are ripe for analysis have gone neglected by historians of science. It also means that for archaeologists, there is no method that we can adopt to identify controversies in the archaeological record and distinguish them from non-controversial episodes and deposits (or "normal science," in Kuhn's terminology). For this reason, I have devised an archaeological method to identify controversies (described later). This takes into account differences in artifact use as well as differences in artifact form in order to perceive controversies that are hidden by the use of traditional objects.

In addition, while historians of science are good at detailed descriptive narratives of controversies and may identify the significant dimensions of variation by following the actors they study (as they interact, enroll allies, and negotiate), they have not come up with an analytical way to identify these dimensions without following actors. This means that significant dimensions of variation are sometimes missed or discovered too late, and without a method to identify them, Latour has been criticized for arbitrarily selecting these dimensions (Dolwick 2009, 39; Sismondo 2004, 72). For archaeologists this is especially problematic, since it is only by knowing the significant dimensions of variation that we can identify controversies in the first place.

Adapting our classification methods to locate and study controversies, however, is only one step in a large overhaul of basic research methods required to follow controversies. This does not mean that modernist research methods need to be thrown out. Latour argues that since "we have never been modern" in the first place, most of our practices can remain intact, while only those that have been tainted by modernist and postmodernist theory need to be reevaluated or adapted. It is important though that these basic research methods be adapted first in order to pave the way for controversy studies.

A METHOD TO AVOID THEORIES

In his book *Reassembling the Social* (2005), Latour refines his method of following controversies in science and applies it to cultural groups and their objects and practices. In this way, Latour provides the social sciences with a method to understand old and new worldviews, their objects, and practices. Latour first disagrees with the sociological practice of attributing social actions to invisible social forces and theories that individuals are unaware of (but that the omniscient sociologist alone can see—a view largely perpetuated by Bourdieu). "This is conspiracy theory not social theory," Latour argues (ibid., 53). Instead, he demands that not only non-humans be granted actor status—with powers of influence that come from the networks of information encrypted into them (Latour 2005, 10)—but also that human actors be credited with knowing why they do things (ibid., 12).

However irrational these human informants may sound, Latour argues that they will always have a logic, even though that logic may be unfamiliar to us. Our job is to discover their logic in order to understand their actions. "By letting actors deploy controversies and tracing connections between them and the aggregates assembled you can let actors define the order rather than impose it beforehand" (ibid., 23). This means being "prepared to cast off agency, structure, psyche, time, and space along with every other philosophical and anthropological category, no matter how deeply rooted in common sense they may appear to be" (ibid., 25). Thus, for Latour, the definition of a good account is an account in which the explanations offered by the actors are allowed to be stronger than the explanations of the analysts (ibid., 30).

BASIC PROBLEMS WITH RESEARCH METHODS

The biggest hindrance to such an analysis is the method (in the social sciences) of utilizing the largest amount of information possible about similar objects, activities, or structures (Law 2004, 2). Such a method stems from two assumptions. Firstly, if general forces are seen as responsible for individual actions or sites, it is assumed that information from singular sites is not enough to form a general interpretation. For practical purposes this assumption appears true, since most sites rarely produce enough information to produce an interpretation nor could they be seen as relevant enough to speak for many sites. But a difficulty arises in choosing which sites to pool information from without fouling the analysis. Using random samples or total datasets ignores the individuality of sites and contexts, and thus rarely produces enough general patterns to form a productive interpretation. This is why focusing on controversies has great value. Controversies are not just another unproductive, abstract, or irrelevant site. Controversies tend to be situations in which a great deal of relevant information is presented and coherently linked together by proponents.

Secondly, if large areas are seen as monocultural, then it is assumed that a large amount of information about objects, taken from a wide catchment area such as a region, will give a better interpretation. As discussed in chapter 4, the assumption of cultural unity for an area sees similar objects or structures in a region used for the same reason over time and space and not for local temporal reasons. This assumption supports the view that each object, context, or site is equal to others of their type and encourages the use of as much data about particular forms as possible from a wide area. There may well be similarities in object use over a large area, but these similarities cannot be assumed to exist purely on the basis of form. They can only be categorized together on the basis of context.

The value of focusing purely on controversies is that analyses are automatically focused on context—on particular times and places (Latour 2005, 52). As Gabriel Tarde wrote, "In general, there is more logic in a sentence than in a talk, in a talk than in a sequence or group of talks; there is more logic in a special ritual than in a whole credo" (Tarde 1999, 115 in Latour 2002a). If studies do not focus on particular times and places, then studies will be trying to understand the reasons for object use with contrasting data. To include all similar forms from an area would muddy the analysis and produce confusing and contradictory results rather than help to discover a correct correlation for one community at one time (Law 2004, 3). It is not the largest amount of data that enables the best conclusions, it is the most relevant data. More data can end up decreasing contextual quality (Latour 2005, 176).

For example, excavation reports often conclude with a chapter in which they situate the site within the context of a whole region in order to interpret it. By detailing the various uses of similar artifacts and structures at other sites, the idea is to triangulate the contexts in order to reach some sort of conclusion about the artifacts in general. However, this method rarely arrives at any successful correlations because of the variety of uses that artifacts or structures have over a large area. What emerges is usually just a *potpourri* of different uses. While occasional similarities are explained as confirming the existence of a much deeper, unconscious habitus that extended far and wide, such a diversity of uses (without the context behind each one) helps to feed the belief that objects and traits, especially within ceremonial sites, were superficial expressions and used irrationally. Such findings in sociology (as a result of this research method) are largely the basis for theories such as Anthony Giddens' Structuration theory, which sees variation as merely the result of unintended consequences of action (Giddens 1984).

Yet, these "superficial" configurations are often replicated more than once within a single community, which indicates that logic is much more consistent within a community than communities are given credit for. For instance, clusters of contemporary burial mounds in Bronze Age Wessex often share similar configurations of artifacts and traits that are not found elsewhere (see appendix A). This suggests a rationale behind these configurations, which makes sense if the mound is the unique representation of a community's cosmology. Such important differences are lost, however, if mounds are grouped together from a whole region and similarities are sought across a wide range of sites.

BROADER CONGLOMERATES OR "CULTURAL GROUPS"

While sites may be encryptions of an individual's or a community's rational understanding of the world, which changes over time and space (and therefore needs to be carefully studied by itself), it is also true that broader constellations of ideas exist too. Similar contextual associations between objects, traits, and structures do exist in multiple communities at once over a wide area, which suggests that while variation exists between them, there is some consensus of ideas over large areas. While these broader constellations can be roughly mapped out, the secret to analyzing both scales without diminishing local conclusions, however, is to remain local—not to think that important information can be found by resorting to a general level. Once a series of several specific local analyses have been conducted, broader generalizations can be built up about these constellations from commonalities between these local interpretations, which can help to understand broader dynamics.

Nevertheless, these broader analyses should not interfere with further specific analyses. Information missing in one representation cannot be assumed to exist just because it exists in another similar representation (Latour 2005). Through building up interpretations from individual sites separately, many more differences at those sites can be explained than if one site's interpretation were imposed upon another's. Searching for similar patterns in other sites only blinds the researcher to other more important local differences. Local sites are local representations and not the exemplars of a whole culture, but at least analyses of several local sites (if other controversies can be found) can shed light upon one or more versions of a cosmology.

Without actively seeking controversies, it is easy to fall into the trap of searching for one overarching cosmology. By identifying the significant differences between representations in order to identify controversies, and by focusing on how those differences interact with predominant representations, researchers are also able to gauge the influence that dissenters have had on change. However, in order to identify differences and follow their interactions with others, archaeological techniques need to be adapted to facilitate such an analysis.

STEP 1: LOCATING CONTROVERSIES

The first step in analyzing controversies is to actually identify controversies. As discussed in chapter 4, the reason controversies are rarely recognized in the archaeological record is that they are never expected. With the belief that culture is unified and separate from nature, any changes in burial practices, object assemblages, or structures (however radical) are assumed to relate to different periods, cultures, classes, or functions, never to dissident ideas about the natural/cultural order. The use by dissidents of traditional objects or structures (albeit in different ways) to make powerful statements about their difference (like in the example of British punks), has unfortunately made it easier for archaeologists to explain away these radical differences as superficial or gradual changes made by a traditional monolithic culture (due to the similarities in forms used). As argued earlier, the central culprit in perpetuating this misapprehension is typology, which was formed from the assumption of culture as unilinear and has permeated most archaeological techniques.

For example, whenever an archaeologist classifies an artifact or structure within a region as a certain type, the typological method is being used. By focusing on the forms of objects or structures to classify them, the analysis automatically assumes that similar forms have similar meanings and different forms have different meanings. This neglects the fact that similar forms of artifact or structure are used by proponents of alternative representations to make different statements. Such uses of typology perpetuate the assumption that culture is unilinear—that traditions exist as monocultural entities over time and space.

Instead, what is really needed is the classification of similarities and differences in the *use* of artifacts and structures in order to identify the variety of ideas and cultural groups within an area. Identifying the different groups or constellations of ideas within an area is actually essential in order to locate controversies because controversies are located by finding where two different groups, or contrasting ideas, interact. Without identifying the variety of different groups, it is impossible to locate the interfaces between them. Identifying the similarities and differences in artifact and structure use—or particular configurations of contextual associations—requires classifying objects and structures by form *and* context rather than purely by form.

In archaeological practice, the typological method has again made this effort very difficult. Because of the interest in classifying artifacts by form and not by context, objects are separated from their context almost as soon as sites are excavated and sent to different analysts for examination, making it extremely difficult to reconstruct individual contexts for comparison. Ceramics, metals, bones, and organic material are all examined separately by form. Component parts of the context are then entered into a typological database as general formal variables that enable cross tabulation with other generalized formal variables. Such a separation of objects from contexts assumes that each piece of a site is part of a larger whole that comprises all contemporary contexts of an area and often a whole region. This stems from the same assumption of cultural unity that sees all deposits as part of an unconscious expression of that unified culture.

In order to locate controversies, therefore, the typological method and its accompanying research methods both need to be reevaluated to enable differences in the use of objects and structures to be identified. Until recently it was fairly difficult to classify sites by context. Apart from the difficulty in knowing the relevant dimensions of variation, the combinations of contextual factors for those dimensions can themselves number in the thousands. Yet again, this problem has been encountered by other disciplines and their solution can be of great use to archaeologists.

Culture Attribution

In English literature it has long been known that different writers have signature writing styles. In the same way that particular cosmological expressions are expressed through particular contextual configurations of objects and traits, individual authors express themselves through their unique use of language, and in particular, their configurations of words. One of the great intellectual challenges of literary scholarship, ever since critical scholarship of the Homeric canon in Ancient Greece, and especially since the great eighteenth-century forgeries, has been to accurately attribute poetry, plays, and prose to the correct author. Since the advent of information technology in the 1970s, over nine hundred papers have been written about computational methods to identify the signature writing styles of authors and to find their imprint on anonymous works (Rudman 2010).

The premise behind attribution methods or "stylometrics" in English literature is that individual authors can be identified by their use of a set of words and phrases common to them, not just by a few unique words (Vickers 2011, 117). This avoids the problem that scholars encountered with authors who copied unique words from each other (ibid.). This is similar to the above solution to the problem of the identification of cultural groups in that groups are also better identified by their unique set of associations (context) rather than by particular objects that might have been co-opted. On the basis of this premise, many scholars in English literature have devised computer programs and statistical methods to identify the frequency of authors' words in works of unknown authorship and to compare them with the frequency of other authors' words in the same works.

The linguist Ian Lancaster, for instance, has proven that from 1597 to 1604, Shakespeare repeated 892 different phrases over 25,700 times in his works (Lancaster 1996 in Vickers 2011, 138). By analyzing the frequency of these phrases in other works, Brian Vickers was able to prove in 2009 that Shakespeare was the co-author of several anonymous plays (ibid., 141).

While archaeological sites are very different from texts, representations of worldviews in burials, structures, or deposits are assemblages of associations that encrypt meaning through the contextual relationship of one to another. In a similar way to text, therefore, a representation is characterized by its contextual configuration and can only be attributed to particular worldviews through its contextual similarity.

However, while recent programs designed to identify similar texts are very good, there are enormous problems with using author attribution programs to identify similar archaeological contexts. Stylometric programs that identify sets of common words and phrases for an author and determine the frequency of that set in other works rely on a known set of works by that author to determine their style. For archaeology, that would mean arbitrarily selecting a group of contexts to form the archetype for a group. The problem with this is the possibility of selecting an erroneous context that misleads the analysis. It may also exclude a context type that is instrumental in defining a difference. The common contextual assemblage for a group is what the analysis is trying to achieve in the first place, and without running the analysis, it is difficult to arbitrarily determine it.

Also, because proponents of alternative cosmologies are constantly shifting their arguments and allegiances to forms—adopting traditional elements and using them differently in their polemic—it is very hard to pin any group down to particular objects or structures. However, the ways in which they "use" different objects and structures differs far less. This "use" can be translated into "context," or the assemblage of various artifacts and traits held by a group.

Modes Technique

For these reasons, a unique method was devised to identify the relevant dimensions of variation and common contextual assemblages of groups, using techniques from stylometrics, but adapted for archaeological data. The relevant dimensions of variation were first selected by determining which context types differed the least. This was based upon Latour's understanding that groups may constantly shift their arguments and allegiances, but always maintain core non-negotiable configurations that define their difference from others (Latour 1987, 201). It is largely over these differences that controversies are fought. In order to identify which context types differ the least and find these non-negotiable configurations, it is imperative to list all the elements that are present in representations and identify which context types are the most constant.

It was found that certain databases allow for more freedom of categorization than others. Museums use a type of database that preserves detailed artifact and structural context data while enabling that data to be indexed and compared. Modes 1.99 is the database recommended by the British Museums and Libraries Association (see www.modes.org.uk), and it is the one used here, but there are many to choose from. In setting up a database it is essential that each representation be broken down into three or four tiers of contextual information and many types of context. Each representation is first described sequentially and given a site context record. Then, each structural part of representations or action within that representation is described in detail and given its own subsite context record. Next, each artifact context is described and given its own artifact context record. Another tier in which individual artifacts and their immediate contexts are recorded may also be created. Subsets of records from each type of context, from the smallest up to the largest, can then be created and compared on a grid that allows their details to be viewed. By analyzing the common associations of each type of context, each context type can be analyzed for its stability over a whole area.

The great value of such an analysis is that mundane traits such as clay or limestone inclusions, structural traits, and organic deposits can be analyzed at an equal level with objects, rather than arbitrarily selecting one or two object types as the arbiters of affinity. At this stage it is important to consider every aspect as legitimate and not to see some as more significant than others based upon our own judgment (Latour 2005, 121). It is especially important not to translate a group's actions or objects into social forces of our own making and thus impose our own interpretations on our informants before we have finished listening to them. If we reject our subjects' relevant dimensions and associations as insignificant (based on our own assumptions) and attribute actions to invisible social forces or theories (that make sense to us) then we miss the real reasons for their actions (ibid., 48).

Once the most stable contextual types are identified, the variations within those types should be listed and grouped to identify different groups (ibid., 32). Identifying different groups is important in order to locate the interface between groups—the location of most controversies. Because objects are constantly being adopted and repurposed in controversies, this analytical way of determining the relevant dimensions of variation (or non-negotiable configurations) is essential in order to ascribe representations to groups. Determining the array of associated traits or contextual relationships of a group, rather than particular traits or objects, enables groups to be identified even as they move fluidly from object to object in a drive to legitimize their existence (ibid., 58). Such transitions would create confusion for formal typologies but are easier using a contextual typology that utilizes multiple contextual elements to classify groups. In order to illustrate the process of group characterization, all data from analyses along the way should be placed in charts or appendices for reference.

Once groups are identified, together with their significant elements and approaches, controversies can be located by mapping the geographic locations of representations and focusing upon those sites in which both groups are represented and interact. These sites are also often the location of amalgamations of traits from both groups as each group attempts to borrow elements from the other to aid their polemic.

STEP 2: FOLLOWING CONTROVERSIES

The second step is then to follow these controversies precisely—to describe the elements and associations that groups deploy to justify themselves, the way that objects are used, adopted, and repurposed and the sequence of these actions (ibid., 121). If controversies are prolonged and exist beyond counterstatements, then an opportunity exists here to understand groups (Latour 1987, 26). Efforts should be made to record every reference to each other, every action against each other, and every effect of actions on each other (Latour 2005, 121). These messy interactions often trace the core issues of groups, flesh them out, and illustrate the political movements involved in grounding them. Elements are borrowed from groups being opposed or from other mainstream traditions to show their affinity with the status quo and to legitimize themselves— illustrating their roots in traditional culture or other historical movements (ibid., 33). These help researchers to identify the historical associations (real or fictitious) of groups and any heterogeneous elements that illustrate even more distinctly the process of their becoming. The negotiation of elements by each side as both sides attempt to resolve controversies is also extremely important to understand the process of becoming for any new groups that emerge from controversies.

This is also where Peirce's triadic system for reconstructing meaning (mentioned in chapter 3) can contribute. Instead of treating each representation as a disembodied entity that structures itself and somehow manages to change throughout the controversy, by placing Peirce's "interpretant" between each translation of object to sign, it is possible to humanize the controversies and understand how each opposing representation causes feedback to the network and structures further representations. By separating out each action in the controversy and structuring the account in a linear fashion, it is possible to reconstruct the information available to each interpretant at each point and thus understand why choices were made and how their representations evolved.

STEP 3: SITUATING CONTROVERSIES

The third step is to follow the history and broader associations of significant elements referred to during controversies. Although controversies perform a valuable cartographic service — mapping the networks of associations that comprise representations and their groups — the meanings of all associations are not always found during controversies. Latour writes "it is perfectly true to say that any given interaction seems to overflow with elements which are already in the situation coming from some other time, some other place, and generated by some other agency. This powerful intuition is as old as the social sciences" (ibid., 166). While social scientists have commonly assumed that these agencies come from a macro society or social and natural laws and thus have concluded that they need to resort to a macro analysis to understand them, Latour insists that studies must remain local.

Most of Latour's book *Reassembling the Social* is concerned with making sure that the agencies deployed by actors to explain their actions are not reduced to deterministic modern agencies by the urge to resort to "hegemonic versions" of the truth such as social theories or theories of nature (ibid., 118). This is no less the case once analyses move beyond controversies and interactions to the wider world. Instead of opting for a compromise between the macro and micro scales of analysis, Latour demands that we "remain as myopic as an ant. . . . One must travel on foot and stick to the decision not to accept any ride from any faster vehicle" (ibid., 171). This means laying connections from one local interaction or controversy to other local places and agencies. Understanding where objects have been used before and in what context helps considerably to shed light on their meaning within that controversy (ibid., 172). However, it must be realized that only controversies can produce the clearest array of signifiers in defense of objects or practices, and therefore objects elsewhere may not be as clearly represented and may even be understood differently. This is the reason why the first step of seeking contextual similarities between objects in controversies (and their cousins elsewhere) before the investigation is so valuable. Such broader studies are necessary to get an idea of their common associations and other associations that might explain their meaning.

WRITING DESCRIPTIONS

Addressing the structure of such an account, Latour argues that instead of providing a hypothesis and fleshing it out with data that agrees with that hypothesis (as is the case for so many sociological studies), research along these lines must be faithful to the actors studied. This means that "it is not the sociologist's job to decide in the actor's stead what groups are making up the world and which agencies are making them act. Her job is to build the artificial experiment—a report, a story, a narrative, an account—where this diversity might be deployed to the full" (ibid., 184). Sticking to description helps to avoid explanations, and, if it is a good description, it should not need an explanation (ibid., 137).

As in a good story or narrative, nothing should be included that does not have a direct relationship to the plot, that does not create a reaction or have some sort of agency (ibid., 128). Latour's definition of a good narrative, in the same way that a scientific report or a novel is defined as good, is one that deploys the largest number of mediating actors, human and non-human, in a network of relationships (ibid., 129). "Agencies are always presented in an account as doing something, that is, making some difference to a state of affairs, transforming some As into Bs through trials with Cs. Without accounts, without trials, without differences, without transformation in some state of affairs, there is no meaningful argument to be made about a given agency, no detectable frame of reference" (ibid., 52). Latour's definition of a bad narrative is one that designates only a handful of actors as the causes of all others—actors that are not part of the plot or seen to have a direct influence on events. "If an actor makes no difference, it's not an actor" (ibid. 130). Any effort to claim invisible forces such as Nature, Society, Power, or Capitalism as actors and to avoid overly descriptive narrative (claiming it as unscientific) is contrary to how science is really practiced. "An invisible agency that makes no difference, produces no transformation, leaves no trace, and enters no account is not an agency. Period. Either it does something or it does not. If you mention an agency, you have to provide the account of its action, and to do so you need to make more or less explicit which trials have produced which observable traces" (ibid., 53). Good scientific accounts are the products of immense descriptive efforts of accumulation, reduction, and combination of information, every word being a network of local data and relationships with a bearing on the subject matter. Hypotheses in science are not anticipated forces applied to account for missing agencies, they are important final tools to combine all these strands of reduced data—usually in an abductive way, not inductive or deductive (Peirce 1934). In a similar way, final explanations should merely be efforts to tie together all strands of information at the end.

METHODOLOGICAL RELATIVISM

The problem with all methods, good or otherwise, is that whenever they produce a good result, that result is so often universalized and applied to all similar cases. We must understand that while the history of an object, structure, or practice may be shared, its use in other contexts may be quite different, especially in controversies. Therefore, in order to understand objects in their contexts it is preferable to avoid giving them a function based on their similarity with other forms. This belief is destructive to interpretation since it causes a premature closure of analyses before they can get to the essence of objects and structures. We must understand that each case has different relationships and associations and only if these sets of relationships are shared can objects and structures be categorized together.

While relativism has received a bad name from cultural or philosophical relativism that denies the existence of truth, methodological relativism is the vital suspension of object definitions before the conclusion of a study. In this case objects must be viewed as encrypted networks of information rather than as solid things. Latour argues that the foremost practitioners of methodological relativism are actually scientists who refuse to be definitive about natural entities before entities are characterized by tests and published (Latour 2005, 146). As an approach to understanding why particular objects are used, it is a much better approach than viewing objects as fixed entities, although there is still a place for this static view (Law 2004, 2). Latour writes that

> in most ordinary cases, for instance situations that change slowly, the pre-relativist framework is perfectly fine and any fixed frame of reference can register action without too much deformation. . . . But as soon as things accelerate, innovations proliferate, and entities are multiplied, one then has an absolutist framework generating data that becomes hopelessly messed up. This is when a relativist solution has to be devised in order to remain able to move between different frames of reference and to regain some sort of commensurability between traces. (Latour 2005, 12).

This is why it is so important to define the type of situations under study—whether they are the result of abstract, ritualized actions or conscious actions within the context of a controversy. Yet, even when it appears that actions were abstract and an object is used outside of its normal context, these objects may not be as abstract as thought—just used in different networks of action to the one they were created within. Therefore choosing a relativist approach to study objects is the only safe way to follow these objects as they change shape and context, and the only way to identify abstract objects, or any changes of network.

By keeping whole sets of relationships and associations in mind rather than one or two arbitrary facets, it is also easier to follow groups as they drop facets, adopt other associations, appropriate traditional forms and change them, avoiding the dead ends that purely formal analyses often reach. By giving universal terms to objects in the past—and especially by giving them equivalent terms from today—objects are homogenized, and we are prevented from understanding what those objects were used for in their specific contexts.

Although it is nearly impossible to fathom from archaeological excavations or analyses of burial mounds what ideological meanings were or what changes meant, the process of change is one avenue that we *can* follow. In a similar way to scientific experiments that subject new elements to multiple tests in order to determine their boundaries and characteristics, we can also follow how new ideas impact traditions, and observe their reactions. In this way we can also trace the boundaries and characteristics of new ideas and practices, forming conclusions not from imposed hypotheses or premature definitions, but from particular reactions at the local level.

The next two chapters attempt to identify and follow several controversies in the archaeological record with tools adapted for non-modern cultures. Chapter 6 examines the jumble of burial practices and mound forms from the area of Wessex in Great Britain. These mounds comprise much of the information that we have about British Late Neolithic and Early Bronze Age society, but have been vastly underutilized due to flawed modernist assumptions about burial and ritual. Chapter 7 examines a similar jumble of burial practices from the Lower Illinois Hopewell—a culture confined to a narrow valley, which flourished for little over two hundred and fifty years. Both chapters illustrate the great value of identifying and studying controversies in the past—illustrating how such a focus on these events can bring an entire culture to life.

SIX

Fragmenting the Bronze Age

In 2010 I organized the annual British Prehistoric Society conference to bring together the leading researchers of the Early Bronze Age (EBA) in order to discuss the emergence of the Wessex Culture. This was a period of flourishing metal, ceramic, and bone artistry that coincided with dramatic changes in burial practices, burial mounds, ceremonial monuments, and agricultural practices. The period began fairly suddenly with very different burial mound types built directly beside earlier Beaker Culture mounds. These burial mounds also contained cremation burials instead of inhumation burials and a range of very different artifacts. Even more spectacular was the fact that the "Wessex Culture" emerged at the same time as the last and extant phase of Stonehenge before it rapidly went out of use. Yet, this conference was the first conference for almost forty years to focus on the "Wessex Culture." There has been a similar dearth of academic articles on the "Wessex Culture" over this time, despite a voracious public appetite for research on Stonehenge.

Why such a lack of interest in the "Wessex Culture"? One reason may be that shortly after J. G. Clark's (1966) attack on Culture History and the search for invasive cultures, the divisions between the Beaker and Wessex "cultures" began to be eroded. The conclusion that was reached, by a process of reverse typological reasoning, was that if certain elements of the Beaker Culture assemblage persisted into Wessex Culture burials, such as stone axes and arrowheads, then the Wessex Culture must be merely an evolution or a separate hierarchy of the Beaker Culture and not really a change at all (Piggott 1973). It has already been illustrated in chapter 4 how reasoning from arbitrary differences is as bad as reasoning from arbitrary similarities since this ignores the larger picture and context of artifacts. However, once a separation between the Beaker and Wessex Culture had been eroded by this type of reasoning, the very different practices of both were conflated and homogenized into a general *mélange* of Late Neolithic/Early Bronze Age practices, effectively eliminating the "Wessex Culture" as an entity in its own right.

The conference in 2010 sought to reexamine this interface through the study of a variety of other aspects than just burial mound types. The title of the conference was "Wessex Culture 'Revolution' or Late Beaker 'Evolution'? Defining Changes in the Early 2nd Millennium BC." Speakers were asked to research the data from their area of expertise and to determine whether or not they could find radical changes that occurred around the time of the "Wessex Culture" mounds. The first day consisted of talks that focused primarily on the area of Wessex—an area of Southwest England including the counties of Berkshire and Hampshire in the east, and Dorset and Wiltshire in the west. The second day consisted of talks that focused upon Wessex Culture artifacts and influences from further afield, including parts of Northwest Europe.

The aspects analyzed by specialists within the area of Wessex were mound types (Paul Garwood), artifacts (John Hunter and Ann Woodward), burial practices (Jo Appleby, Andrew Martin, and John Gale), agriculture (Mike Allen), and ceremonial monuments (Jan Harding). On the first day of the conference, the data from each of these aspects were presented and shown to demonstrate spectacular changes at this time, which even surprised several of the specialists (Allen and Harding), who had assumed a more gradual change or even no change. Mike Allen discovered enormous changes in soil erosion across Wessex that occurred soon after Wessex Culture burial mounds were built, indicating a large-scale division of the landscape and intensification of agriculture at this time. Harding also discovered a sharp drop in the use of Beaker henge monuments and even the abandonment of many henges at this time.

For the second day of the conference, experts spoke about objects and associated traits in the "style" of the "Wessex Culture" from other parts of Britain and Northwest Europe. These areas included Somerset (Jodie Lewis and David Mullin), Scotland and Ireland (Alison Sheridan), Avebury (Ros Cleal), Brittany (Anthony Harding), and Germany (Sabine Gerloff). However, apart from in Somerset, little evidence could be found in these other areas for large-scale changes.

The discussion at the end of the conference then tried to understand why changes could be found at the local level, but not further afield, despite the presence of similar artifacts.

From the perspective of culture as a local understanding of the world, this difference is quite understandable. As has been illustrated in chapter 3, the context in which objects are presented is everything—object meanings cannot exist outside of the network of associations that give them meaning or else they will come to mean something entirely different. In order to maintain this network of associations, the network must be extended perfectly—a costly and exhaustive effort by twentieth-century AD standards, let alone twentieth century BC. The only way that facts and meanings appear to be universal in modern science is through an enormously costly effort at extending the conditions for facts to mean the same thing (Latour 2005, 229), and similarly, nothing less could have extended the meaning of prehistoric artifacts either. The formal similarities between artifacts across Great Britain and Ireland are no more indicative of a common culture than a lack of formal similarity. Only a confluence of various contextual factors can prove that a similarity in local understanding existed between different groups.

Therefore, the internal Wessex expression of material culture and contextual factors, and the external use of Wessex-style artifacts can be understood as enormously different. This is not to say that they are any less interesting. In fact, most of the "Wessex" artifacts appear not to have originated in Wessex at all, but to have come from outside of Wessex and therefore had original meanings that were likely changed when adopted in Wessex. The reconstruction of local meanings and uses, from their contextual associations, is a separate and equally interesting enterprise for each area. The only reason that objects are termed "Wessex" artifacts is because the Wessex area has received the lion's share of attention by British archaeologists in the last two hundred years, and because it contains some of the most abundant deposits—an abundance that is probably due to the economic success of Wessex rather than any sort of hierarchical position of Wessex within Britain. Yet, the contextual patterns of other regions and their associated artifacts and monuments are even more interesting for being neglected since they promise brand-new understandings of this period to be discovered (A. M. Jones 2011). It is only sensible, therefore, that the term for this new style of artifacts, where they appear outside of Wessex, should be changed to something more generally applicable than "Wessex Culture artifacts," such as "prestige period artifacts" instead (Needham and Martin 2010).

However, the fact remains that within Wessex there were a number of changes that coincided with the arrival of new artifact and burial mound types, which suggest that a revolutionary change of some kind did occur in understandings of the Early Bronze Age world of Wessex. While the observation that changes occurred at this time in artifact assemblages, burial practices, burial and ceremonial monuments, and agricultural practices is profound, it does not tell us very much about who brought about these changes and how they occurred. Such an observation is only the beginning in a study of the process and character of change.

The first step is to identify groups. With any major change, there will always be groups that approve and implement that change and groups that disapprove and resist that change, even within individual communities. In chapters 1 and 2 it was illustrated how in pre-modern societies, change is seen as extremely dangerous for the natural order. This is a major reason for the relative stasis of many pre-modern societies (Levi-

Strauss 1962; Descola 1993). Therefore, the existence of a major change is even more likely to have produced controversy and resistance.

While a theoretical distinction between a Beaker and a Wessex Culture is clear, this distinction has been muddied by not knowing the exact dimensions over which they differed. In the same way that natural elements like the TRH growth hormone or the Higgs Boson may be theoretical entities at first, but do not actually exist until their exact character is defined through tests, so too must the Beaker and Wessex Culture practices be defined and characterized. In the following case study, four studies were conducted on Early Bronze Age burial mounds from the area of Wessex: a study to distinguish different groups, a study to clear up taxonomic problems, a study to locate where the different groups interacted, and a final study to follow their interactions in order to understand the groups better.

The first study aimed at establishing the broader groups in Early Bronze Age Wessex by categorizing their different burial practices. Instead of using the traditional typological method to study variation, an alternative typological method (described in chapter 5) was used that took into account detailed contextual variation, as well as object forms, so that similarities and differences in practice, as well as in form, could be identified. This was important since opposing groups often use similar material culture to define themselves in opposition to others by using it in contrasting ways. A typological method that classified objects and structural traits merely according to their form would fail to notice any dissident differences in usage. Therefore it was perceived that this distinction in practice could be a way to identify differences between groups. By sorting the mounds by *context*—the manifestations of use—it was believed a much more reliable taxonomy could be produced that could define the character of each group and follow them through any transformations that occurred during interactions. Identifying the rough outline of broader groups was necessary to identify specific controversies, but has little bearing on the actual beliefs of individual communities, determined individually in the fourth study.

The second study examined the anomalous practices that did not fit any of the general types. On the basis of these few anomalies, archaeologists have rejected the existence of separate groups, but by investigating the contexts of these anomalies, from the general to the very specific level, an interpretation of these anomalies was arrived at. The third study then investigated all instances of interaction between groups at the interface between practices, for signs of controversy. The fourth study then examined in detail three contexts of controversy to understand what each group held as most important and how they expressed it.

As part of the ongoing Wessex Barrow Project at Bournemouth University, excavation reports of all barrows excavated in Wiltshire, and many from Dorset, were compiled and records created for them. The database is available at Wiltshire Museum and contains records for over eight hundred excavated mounds.

RELEVANT DIMENSIONS OF VARIATION

Before any analysis could be conducted, a better system than arbitrary selection had to be found to select the relevant elements for categorization of the mounds (Hodder 1991, 139). These elements needed to be relevant to each burial practice, but also be the dimensions over which each differed. In order to prevent these dimensions from being arbitrarily selected, the relevant dimensions were chosen by identifying the particular context types that varied the least in usage. This was based on the assumption that the most significant elements of worldviews would be less changeable than elements that were less significant (Latour 1987, 208; 2005, 31).

In order to find the context types that varied the least, it was necessary to calculate the frequency of correlations between every trait and every other trait, regardless of their apparent significance. Ten years ago such a comparison would have been fairly difficult, but the information technology now available allows us to process enormous amounts of information in contextual ways. Using Modes 1.99 was perfect for this because it preserves detailed artifact and structural context data and enables that data to be indexed.

First, every aspect of each burial mound was described and entered into a full-text site record. Then context records were created for each construction episode within individual mounds, and all aspects of these were separated out into micro-context variables within each context record. Separate records were also created for artifacts that enabled their different associations to be recorded too. This enabled each micro-context type to be indexed and variations to be quantified. The context types with the least variations were chosen as significant dimensions of variation. By comparing the indexes of indexed traits (one at a time), a list of the context types that varied the least was compiled. A selection of dimensions that differed the least were:

1. The type of burial within primary graves (inhumation or cremation).
2. The type of burial within secondary graves (inhumation or cremation).
3. The mound structure (bowl, bell, disc, or saucer barrow).
4. The pottery types (beaker, incense, collared urn, and food vessel).

The lack of other artifact types in this list supports one of the conclusions that Anne Woodward (2002) reached from her analysis of Early Bronze Age artifacts. This was the conclusion that many artifacts appear to be heirlooms, relics, or ornaments and therefore problematic for defining identity or change (Woodward 2000, 109; 2002). The further possibility that artifacts may be trade goods or plunder, which then could be used to make a statement about an opposing group (see chapter 4), confirms that object forms are too fluid to be considered as variables for defining groups. By using their *opponent's* artifacts in different configurations, powerful statements of difference can be made. According to the above classification, traits such as mound structure and burial practice appear to have much less variability and therefore are better indicators of identity (Latour 1987, 201).

CHRONOLOGY

Paul Garwood and others have often pleaded that the most important factor to consider when studying barrows is chronology; otherwise you end up conflating barrows from different time periods (Garwood 2007, 44). Chronology is particularly important in trying to understand the precise sequence of change in individual cemeteries. However, radiocarbon dates for barrows are scarce and have very broad spans of accuracy—150 to 200 years. Even if we could get down to fifty- or twenty-five-year accuracy, it might give us a rough idea of the barrows involved in a change, but not enough accuracy for determining a very swift sequence of events. In fact, radiocarbon dating may have adversely influenced our perspective of change as something that occurs very gradually, rather than swiftly, by presenting us with an enormous window for change. Fortunately we do have more precise, although relative, methods for determining the sequence of events.

Taking a cue from Sabine Gerloff (1975), Koji Mizoguchi demonstrated that in linear barrow cemeteries, linear alignments of barrows often extended sequentially from early to later barrows (Mizoguchi 1995). The first barrows in these alignments were often Beaker barrows, placed on the highest point of a ridge. This mirrors a similar conclusion by Douglas Charles for the mounds of the Lower Illinois Valley (discussed in the following chapter) (Charles 1985). A second means of determining chronological equivalency within (or even between) barrow cemeteries would be to identify those mounds that contain similar contexts (a process similar to the one used here to identify groups, but on a finer scale). Similarities of contextual associations for several objects and traits should be accurate determiners of chronological equivalence since associations are so hard to maintain over time (Latour 2005, 35). Nevertheless, the most accurate means of determining chronological sequences is through the examination of controversies. Structural manipulations and redefinitions of mounds, within the context of a controversy, help to develop a detailed sequence of interactions within a mound. If the controversy continues over several mounds, then physical and contextual proximity often allow a rough sequence to be traced.

In the following studies, "Cenotaph" mounds without burials were excluded from analysis, as were bowl barrows with cremations that had no Early Bronze Age affiliations (since these could have been from the Middle Bronze Age), and barrows that had no burial because they had been looted. While there have been several classifications of barrow types—eight by Colt-Hoare (1810) and fourteen by Grinsell (1957)—I have followed Ashbee (1960, 24) and classified bell and disc barrows together as "Wessex" barrows—also including the saucer barrows due to their similarity in structure and deposits (Ozanne 1972, 53). The difference between bowl barrows and these "fancy" barrows is essentially that bowl barrows are simple-shaped mounds while Wessex barrows are platforms with (or without) mounds on top of them (Darvill pers. comm. 2012). Differences also include a pronounced size, elaboration, and structure—criteria often difficult to express on paper—but leading Leslie Grinsell (the great surveyor of mounds) to rarely question his classifications of them.

THE FIRST STUDY: GROUP ATTRIBUTION

The first study attempted to identify the predominant burial practices from the group of mounds studied. This was achieved by identifying the common combinations of the above context types. Modes 1.99 was also invaluable for this. Modes uses a form of Natural Language Processing software similar to a Google browser that allows subsets of similar context combinations to be formed using an advanced search feature.

Through correlating the significant dimensions of variation, three groups of mounds stood out (see appendix B). The first group (of 156 barrows) relates to inhumation burials under bowl barrows (with fifteen anomalies). The second group (of 122 barrows) relates to cremation burials in bell, disc, or saucer barrows (with twenty-two anomalies). There were also fourteen anomalous secondary inhumation burials in these cremation bell/disc/saucer barrows. While the second group originated much later than the first, a significant chronological overlap exists with the first group. A third group (of 118 barrows) relates to cremation burials in bowl barrows that occur later in cemetery sequences and can be assumed to be a later development.

So far, these correlations are commensurate with Grinsell's and Ashbee's divisions of the Early Bronze Age and earlier interpretations (Piggott 1938; Childe 1956). Their understanding of this period was that a dynamically different burial practice emerged during the late Beaker period. Early Beaker period burial practices consisted of inhumation graves in bowl barrows while the Later Beaker period saw cremations placed under bell, disc, or saucer barrows. The practice of cremation also coincided with the abandonment of many ceremonial monuments (Harding 2010) and the introduction of new agricultural practices (that divided up the countryside) (Lawson 2007; Allen 2010).

Yet the exact relationship between the "Wessex Culture" and the "Beaker Culture" is still poorly understood. This is because archaeologists have had great difficulty in distinguishing the characterizing differences between the "Wessex Culture" and the "Beaker Culture." Although radically different in many ways, the particular ways they differ sometimes change from cemetery to cemetery. This means that any general analysis that has tried to pin down their characteristics has always run into a number of exceptions.

Largely on the basis of these anomalies, most researchers since the 1960s have rejected the classification of barrows into groups in favor of studying general elements that all barrows have in common, such as topographical location (Woodward and Woodward 1996). However, instead of dismissing the predominant groupings on the basis of these anomalies, as recent users of typology are apt to do, it is worth investigating whether any local explanations for anomalies exist. Thus the second study examined the context behind each anomaly in order to find any general correlations between them.

THE SECOND STUDY: THE CONTEXT OF WESSEX ANOMALIES

According to the above classification of 122 Wessex barrows, Wessex barrows should have had cremation burials only (see appendix B). Yet the first study highlighted two sets of anomalies—specifically fifteen Wessex barrows that had primary inhumations and fourteen Wessex barrows with secondary inhumations. Largely on the basis of these anomalies, many prehistorians have understandably claimed that cremation and inhumation were practiced interchangeably by one cultural group (Bradley 1984, 84; Woodward 2000, 23) and that the Wessex Culture was merely a "maturation of the Beaker rite during the Early Bronze Age in Britain" (Needham et al. 2010, 363).

The second study started with an examination of the *general* context of these anomalies. Over half of the anomalies (sixteen out of the twenty-nine) were first found to occur in the same cemeteries as other anomalies. This led to a comparison of the cemeteries that had anomalies with cemeteries that did not have anomalies. Of the twenty-nine anomalies, twenty-two were found to occur in cemeteries that had both Wessex and Beaker barrows (75 percent). This was fairly unusual since Wessex and Beaker barrows occur together in only 30 percent of the cemeteries studied (seventeen of the fifty-five cemeteries with over four mounds).

The next step was to examine the *immediate* context of the anomalies. Where anomalies occurred in the same cemetery as other anomalies, they often occurred near each other as well (43 percent). But the most striking correlation was observed when the positions of Wessex anomalies were compared to the positions of rare Beaker barrows in their cemeteries (see appendix C). Sixteen out of the twenty-nine Wessex anomalies studied (55 percent) occurred adjacent to, and usually immediately adjacent to, Beaker bowl barrows. A further two more were located one barrow away, and five more were located next to undetermined bowl barrows, which would make it 79 percent if these were included too.

This is a significant correlation when the low number of Beaker barrows in Wessex cemeteries and fairly random patterns of excavation over the past two hundred years are taken into account. On the basis of these correlations it is clear that many of these anomalies had something to do with being at the temporal and spatial interface between the two practices. While Wessex barrows and Beaker barrows normally contain radically different burial practices, where they occur together in the same cemeteries there was a distinct fusion of traits.

A similar correlation was noticed by Koji Mizoguchi in the 1990s after examining the interface between Beaker and Wessex barrows at the Shrewton cemetery (Mizoguchi 1995). However, Mizoguchi took the resulting anomalies to indicate a gradual change from one burial practice to another. He remarks that "the gradual nature of this process of change came about through the accumulated effect of the unintended consequences of action" (Mizoguchi 1995, 248), a view of change derived from Bourdieu and Anthony Giddens. The basis of this argument, however, is that the change from inhumation to cremation burial practice represented only a negligible change taken by a monolithic culture. He states that "In situ cremation practices only generated an increase in the size of the 'audience' able to witness the episode which signified the transformation of the body, even if the same audience could not participate in the deposition of the human remains. Change was therefore subtle and possibly unintentional" (ibid.).

While cremation featured in the burial practice of a few Neolithic long barrows, and at Stonehenge almost four hundred years earlier, the Early Bronze Age practice of cremation was a very different burial practice from Beaker practices and unlikely to be unintentional. It was also part of a broader change involving a brand-new preparation and burial rite, internment procedure, containment structure, artifact assemblage, and barrow form. The very idea that Beaker burial practice, which had continued largely unchanged for over four hundred years, could suddenly change radically in a few years so that more people could participate in it, belies the great problem with a unilinear concept of culture—it ignores differences.

Reconfiguring Mounds

If this change was not a subtle growth from one practice to another due to showmanship, then the question arises: what did produce the anomalies? An examination of the barrow structure of the anomalies provides some explanation.

A few of the fifteen Wessex barrows with primary inhumations appear to be the result of an attempt to physically transform existing Beaker bowl barrows into Wessex-style barrows. Winterbourne Stoke G43, Wilsford G70, Winterslow G3, and Amesbury G71 were originally Beaker bowl barrows that were later transformed into Wessex bell or disc barrows. This left inhumation burials under mounds that had a final Wessex appearance and resulted in several of the above anomalies if not more. Structural transformation is hard to surmise from the outward appearance of mounds or from most excavation reports since excavators have only started to look for structural manipulation fairly recently. However, almost all of the episodes of manipulation of barrows recorded in recent years occur at this interface between practices.

Of the other fourteen anomalous Wessex barrows—cremation barrows that have Beaker-style inhumations inserted into the top of them—all also occur at the interface between burial practices. This indicates that multiple efforts were made by Beaker groups at the beginning of the Wessex Culture to resist the changes introduced by early Wessex groups, by countering their representations with their own Beaker narratives.

Several cases also exist of early Wessex bell barrows being physically transformed into Beaker bowl barrows. These include Aldbourne G3, Aldbourne G4, Laverstock, and Ford G3 and Wilsford G36f, which left cremation burials under bowl barrows (two of which also have secondary Beaker inhumations actually inserted into the top of them). This may explain many of the anomalies of the third group—primary cremations under twenty-two bowl barrows placed at the interface between practices (immediately next to Beaker barrows).

Thus, there is reason to believe that many of the anomalies were actually the result of an interaction between two groups and not the result of a gradual evolution of practices or a reason for the dismissal of the Wessex Culture as a distinct entity. Of the hundreds of barrows with primary cremations excavated in Wiltshire, only two have solid evidence of primary burials containing an inhumation and cremation (Collingbourne Ducis G11 and Amesbury G61). These two instances may represent a rapprochement between the two cultures in a few communities, but for the majority of cases the burial practice changed radically and quickly.

THE THIRD STUDY: THE CONTEXTS OF INTERACTION

Having established the significant dimensions of variation for each group and a reason for many of the anomalies, the next study then focused upon all instances of interface between Wessex and Beaker mounds in order to identify any controversies and define the character of interactions.

Out of 172 Beaker barrows (or barrows with primary inhumations) a third (53) were located directly beside Wessex cremation bell, disc, or saucer barrows, many starting linear alignments of Wessex barrows (see appendix D). However, a large number of other Beaker barrows (sixty-one) were entirely isolated from cremations, indicating that cremation was not introduced into every community. A fraction of Beaker barrows were next to cremations in simple bowl barrows (the twenty-two anomalies explained above). Thus the adoption of cremation was a patchwork affair, and the extent of changes differed from place to place. It also indicates that cremation and the new Wessex barrow forms were resisted in places. A map of the Stonehenge landscape illustrates this (see figure 6.1). The landscape can be divided into a western and an eastern part with Stonehenge in the middle. In the western part there are over eighty bell, disc, or saucer barrows (the black dots) while in the eastern part there are only three. The fact that many other important henge monuments including Woodhenge, Bluehenge, and Durrington Walls are also located in this eastern part of the landscape indicates that this may have represented a Beaker stronghold.

The next comparison was of the size and structure of barrows at the interface between practices (see appendix E). Of the seventy-five (twenty-two plus fifty-three) Beaker barrows at this interface, forty are of identical size or within ten feet of the diameter of the cremation barrows beside them, despite barrows varying in size from 12 to 150 feet wide. In fact many appear to be so similar to the new barrows that they are often considered paired, creating an interesting dichotomy between inhumation and cremation practice. This concerted attempt of the new Wessex barrows to appear similar to the Beaker barrows next to them indicates an attempt at diplomacy, or as Latour puts it, a reduction of the angle at which different ideas meet in order to prevent conflict (Latour 1987, 208; Golinski 1998).

A study was then conducted to see whether barrows, other than the anomalies, contained evidence for structural transformation at the interface between groups. This was based upon the hypothesis that if there were any other controversies between groups, they may involve manipulations of each other's mounds.

Apart from efforts to transform Beaker bowl barrows into Wessex bell barrows, Beaker barrows were also redefined through the insertion of Wessex cremation burials into the top of them (see appendix F). Over 70

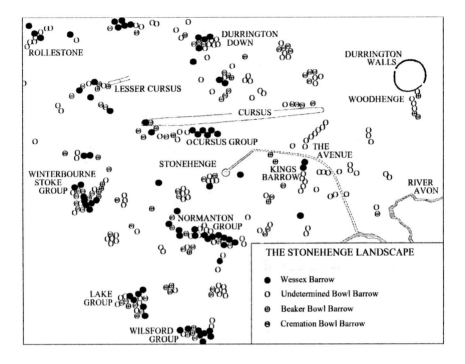

Figure 6.1.   Barrows in the Stonehenge Landscape

percent of secondary EBA cremations were inserted into the top of Beaker
inhumation barrows, in contrast to only 14 percent in Wessex cremation
barrows. A total of fifty-four Beaker barrows, or a third of all Beaker
barrows in Wiltshire, have secondary cremations, thirty-nine of which
are at the interface between Wessex and Beaker practices.

It has been argued that the insertion of secondary cremations into the
top of barrows resulted from families wishing to associate with earlier
barrows and their genealogy (Mizoguchi 1995). Indeed, the practice of
inserting burials into older mounds was also a Beaker practice, with
Beaker burials placed in older Beaker graves. Jonathan Last has illustrated that many barrows were opened up in this way to place additional
inhumation burials with the primary burials (Last 1998, 2007). However,
these instances may also represent attempts to redefine barrow narratives.

Refreshing the networks of information and relationships encrypted
into objects and structures through ceremony is largely what ceremonies
are about (Cajete 2000, 68, 102). Paul Garwood has also illustrated how
secondary construction phases at Beaker barrows took place within a
narrow space of time (c. 2100–1800 BC) (Garwood 2007, 36), overlapping
considerably with the introduction of Wessex Culture mounds (c. 1950

BC). Several examples even exist of Beaker inhumation burials inserted into Beaker mounds after secondary cremations had been inserted into the top of them (Amesbury G22, Wimbourne St. Giles G2, Winterbourne G56, Durrington G35 and G36). This indicates that the insertion of further inhumation burials into Beaker mounds may have been an attempt to renew or assert Beaker understandings of the world at a time when those notions were under threat.

In terms of the intrusive Wessex cremations, a quarter of these intrude directly into the central graves of Beaker barrows, often damaging the primary inhumations—a practice that seems more destructive than commemorative. Another fourteen secondary cremations were inserted into empty bowl barrows—several with large graves that may have held primary inhumations that were removed, possibly during the episodes of secondary cremation burial (see Ogbourne St. Andrew G11 and Highlea Farm 4, Dorset, Gale et al. 2008). In fact, Sir Richard Colt-Hoare, the excavator of over four hundred barrows, often remarked that when he found cists that had been opened before, they had no remains whatsoever "not even the fragment of a bone having been left behind" (Colt-Hoare 1822, 91). It would have been strange for an earlier antiquarian or looter not to have left any bone behind at all, which leaves open the possibility that some of the mounds may have been looted in antiquity to redefine the mounds.

Violence

Whether or not these instances of redefinition and counterdefinition were accompanied by violence is difficult to say without osteological studies of trauma. Since the vast majority of burials buried at the time of these interactions were cremations, and no way has been found to determine whether cremation burials suffered violence before their cremation, it may be even more difficult to find evidence for violence. However, an osteological examination of the Beaker inhumation burials that occur at the exact time of this interaction would give us some indication of whether violence occurred or not. The only Beaker burials that we know for sure that occurred at this exact time are those fourteen Beaker burials intrusive into Wessex graves.

While osteological studies have not yet been conducted, a surprising number of these fourteen anomalies have evidence for what might be seen as violence. This includes the presence of an arrowhead with one of the secondary inhumations (Ogbourne St. Andrew G7) that possibly was a cause of death, and two inhumations that were buried facedown (Codford St. Peter G1 and Wilsford G36f). The presence of violence in these few key instances of interaction indicates that this period was not a time of peaceful transition. The fact that these inhumations were inserted into the top of Wessex barrows at the interface between practices indicates that they may have been part of a suppression by a Beaker group that used members of the Wessex group for their counterdefinitions of mounds (see appendix G).

Most indicative of violence, of course, are the highly functional weapons with individuals of both practices at this interface between practices—indicative of the first arms race in British history. The enormous grooved daggers, often found with burials at this interface, not only have rigid supports running down their length, but also contain elaborate grooves along their length. These grooves are often found on bayonets and military knives today and allow blood to run out of the wound in order to break the suction caused by their penetration. This enables the dagger to be withdrawn with less difficulty. The existence of such a functional trait on these daggers precludes the possibility that they were purely for show.

The manipulations of burial mounds at the interface between practices, and these instances of violence, suggest that the rapid change from Beaker burial practices and mound forms to Wessex burial practices and mound forms was not always the work of one group evolving into another, but sometimes of two groups in conflict. Where the two practices came together, conscious attempts appear to have been made to reface each other's barrows, resulting in two contrasting burial practices in one barrow and an anomalous record. Such manipulations were not always associated with violence though. There are many historical and anthropological examples of iconoclasm and redefinition of ritual structures or symbols without blood being shed. Early Christian and Puritan iconoclasts defaced statues and removed icons from walls, resulting in the transformation of churches without violence to people. It was only when there were others in the vicinity that disagreed with the changes that violence sometimes occurred.

As we saw in the above ethnographic accounts, when worldviews interact there are often attempts to use each other's symbols or traditions to define their differences (Matthews 1995; Latour 2005; Glass 1988) or to illustrate their affinity (to avoid conflict) (Lancaster 1974). Such an appropriation of traits can also result in a temporary hybridization of structures, practices, or assemblages (Barth 1971, 184). This could also explain the appropriation of some Beaker artifacts in Wessex graves and Wessex artifacts in Beaker graves. In the same way as the Romans appropriated British Iron Age gods and assimilated them with Roman gods (e.g., Sulis Minerva), groups and their symbols can change affiliation through political intervention. This captures Hodder's understanding of active material culture in a much better way than the idea that objects purely maintain or reproduce social organization.

THE FOURTH STUDY: THREE BARROW CEMETERIES

We can best understand the political aspect of groups and the roles that objects played in practices by following a few of the interactions between practices that resulted in controversy. The fourth study follows the interactions between Beaker and Wessex groups in three cemeteries in Wessex. These are the best excavated or analyzed of Wessex cemeteries that have both practices, and they appear to have been involved in some degree of controversy. By following the sequences of interaction at the interface between practices, several interesting maneuvers and associations were discovered that shed considerable light upon both cultures. The significance of these maneuvers and associations would never have been realized without their context, and they illustrate the importance of following controversies to gain insights into past cultures.

Net Down, Shrewton

The first case study was of an interaction between a Beaker group and a Wessex group at the Net Down cemetery in Shrewton. A similar study was conducted by Mizoguchi (1995) to illustrate his conclusion, and the following study draws partially on his work. However, because he tried to identify the similarities between the mounds—using formal typology to make genealogical links—the differences between mounds were not fully addressed. This left a couple questions insufficiently answered. The first was: why did the Beaker burial practice change so radically in all aspects in such a short time; and the second was: why did two supposedly earlier Beaker inhumation graves intrude into the top of the supposedly later Wessex bell barrows?

Net Down is one the best excavations of a complete barrow cemetery in Wessex (Green and Rollo-Smith 1984, 255). Eleven of the fourteen mounds in two linear alignments were excavated in 1960, comprising three Beaker bowl barrows, five Wessex bell barrows, a disc barrow, and two later bowl-shaped barrows. Mizoguchi illustrated that the sequence of mounds in linear alignments from one end to the other was largely chronological (Mizoguchi 1995).

The position of the two anomalies at this site is significant in that they occur exactly at the interface between the Beaker and Wessex traditions. By carefully following the sequence of interactions between the Beaker and Wessex mounds and focusing on both the similarities and the differences, a different picture from Mizoguchi's is apparent. Several instances of transformation, physical destruction, and subsumption of one cultural type of mound by another illustrates that what occurred was not necessarily progressive evolution at all.

The first activity on the ridge started with Beaker barrows 5a and 5e to the west of the site and 5k to the east (see figure 6.2a). At the beginning of the Wessex period each barrow then attracted considerable attention. Barrows 5a and 5e to the east contained inhumations with Beaker vessels buried in central pits under bowl-shaped mounds. Barrow 5a also contained a stake setting. Quite soon after barrow 5a was built (considering its silt deposits), the ditches of both 5a and 5e were recut at their outer edges (the ditches around 5e having been filled with chalk rubble first). This appears to have created a slight Wessex-style berm around the Beaker mounds (see figure 6.2b)—a platform between the mound and the ditch. The secondary ditch around 5a also contained an infant covered by a small cairn of flints, a common deposit in the ditches of later Wessex barrows at the site.

This appears to be an effort by a Wessex group to transform both Beaker bowl barrows into Wessex-style bell barrows (like Wilsford G70 and Winterslow G3). At the same time (according to the excavator), a Wessex cremation was also inserted into the top of Beaker barrow 5e right into the central grave, disturbing the primary burial (Green and Rollo-Smith 1984, 269).

The next step was the placement of two Wessex bell barrows 5c and 5d immediately beside Beaker barrow 5a, both copying its structure and size (see figure 6.2b). Both contained a stake structure and a ditch with an identical diameter to 5a. Wessex bell barrow 5c contained an adult male cremation with a Wessex slotted cup, and Wessex bell barrow 5d contained an adult male cremation with a satellite female cremation in a collared urn. The similarities between 5a, 5c, and 5d were so prominent that the excavator was led to claim that all three mounds were contemporary (Green and Rollo-Smith 1984, 267). These similarities cannot be mere coincidence, but like the apparent transformation of the Beaker barrows into Wessex barrows, it seems that a statement was being made.

Another interaction between Beaker and Wessex barrows occurred at Beaker bowl barrow 5k. Barrow 5k was placed on the highest point of the ridge and contained an adult male inhumation, a beaker, and a copper dagger in an oblong central pit. Three further pits were dug with two young females buried in two of them and an adult male and a beaker inserted into a pit above the central burial.

Two Wessex barrows were then built on two sides of this Beaker barrow (see figure 6.2c). Again, both barrows copied the Beaker barrow next to them in size and structure. Wessex bell barrow 5j contained a male cremation in an oblong central pit with three satellite pits around it (similar to the Beaker barrow)—but which were empty. Wessex bell barrow 5l also had a central cremation with three satellite pits, two of which were empty. In one of the pits, however, was placed a female cremation with a rare composite Wessex-style necklace of beads including shale, faience, amber, and a periwinkle shell (see figure 6.2d).

The next stage of activity actually created two of the anomalies noted earlier. This occurred after Wessex barrow 5j had been constructed and

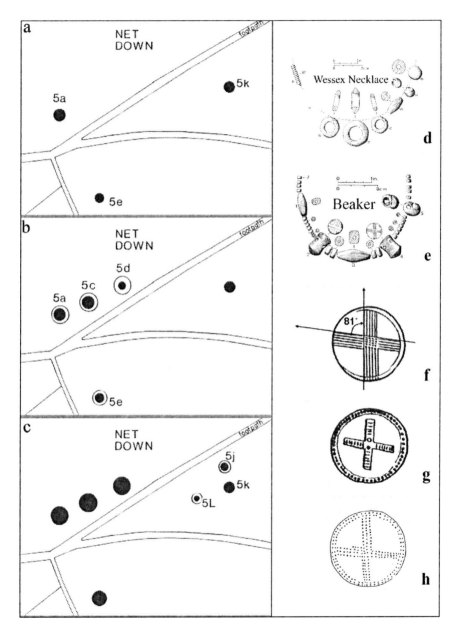

Figure 6.2. (a–c) Net Down Cemetery Sequence (from Green and Rollo-Smith 1984, 257); (d) Wessex Necklace from 5L (ibid., 309); (e) Necklace from 5J (ibid., 310); (f) Beaker Oblique Cruciform Symbol from Shrewton 5j (ibid., 310); (g) Beaker Oblique Cruciform Symbol from Mere G6 (Annable et al. 1964, 92); h) Beaker Oblique Cruciform Symbol from Wilsford G40 (ibid., 115) (Courtesy of The Prehistoric Society)

reveals that this interaction was not a one-sided exchange. Crouched in-humations of Beaker type were inserted directly into the chalk caps of both Wessex barrows 5j and 5L. These are the only cases of secondary inhumation in Wessex mounds at the cemetery and indicate a Beaker response to the introduction of Wessex ideas at the site.

At the same time as this intrusion, something significant was deposit-ed with one of the intrusive inhumations: the female inhumation in 5j was found with a necklace of beads including shale, amber, and a peri-winkle shell—very similar to the Wessex necklace with the female crema-tion mentioned earlier. This is one of the finest necklaces to be found in Wiltshire (see figure 6.2e). Even more significantly, this necklace had two dumbbell-shaped beads, beads that only occur with burials intrusive into Wessex barrows—that is to say in Durrington G14 and Snail Down G3 and G8. Onto the base of both of these beads were inscribed oblique cruciform symbols, a well-known Beaker symbol that occurs on gold sun discs and other items in some Beaker barrows. The obliqueness of these cruciform symbols is odd until you realize that the angle of the transept, eighty-one degrees, is the same for many of them (Darvill 1997) (see figures 6.2f–h). This angle is also replicated in other Beaker symbols such as the Bush Barrow Lozenge from Wilsford G5, a barrow also at the interface between practices.

We may never know for sure the significance of this angle, but its presence in contexts of contention indicates that it held some importance. Many archaeologists have associated it with the angular distance be-tween the midsummer and midwinter sunrise—eighty-one degrees at the latitude of Stonehenge (ibid.; Thom et al. 1988). Indeed an angle of eighty-two degrees is found on the sky disc of Nebra, the angular dis-tance between the solstices at the latitude of Saxony-Anhalt, where the sky disc was found (Meller 2004, 27).

Although Mizoguchi interpreted similarities in deposits as an indica-tion of diachronic continuity, the discrepancy between the Wessex bar-rows in the two interactions indicates that there was something more than a community continuing to practice its Beaker principles in the Wes-sex period. Instead, the similarities between the Wessex barrows and the earlier Beaker barrows appear to be influenced by the configurations in the barrows that they were built beside.

The appropriation of structural traits and the possibility that two of the Beaker barrows were refaced to resemble Wessex barrows indicates that an attempt was made to redefine earlier ideas, not to continue them. Such redefinitions, whether made by dissenters within the Beaker com-munity or from without, indicate that a separate worldview had emerged—a different one from Beaker mounds. The contemporaneity of this difference and its ideological divisiveness is illustrated by the subse-quent intrusion of Beaker inhumations into the top of the first Wessex barrows—an intrusion that may have been an attempt to counter the Wessex redefinition.

What is interesting about this exchange is the use of similar objects to express differences in ideas. On the one hand the Wessex barrows use the Beaker barrows' size and structural configurations, and on the other, the Beaker counterdefinitions explicitly refer to deposits in the Wessex barrows. Like the use of Wessex barrows for Beaker inhumations in the anomalies identified in the first study, this also appears to be a political move in the context of a cultural interaction. Without a contextual analysis of this interaction, such a manipulation of structures and artifacts would continue to confuse typological analyses.

Another interesting facet of this exchange is the fact that the necklace placed with the intrusive Beaker grave was one of the most striking artifacts in the Wessex region and contained explicit Beaker symbols. This can also be understood within the context of interactions. Bruno Latour explains that when groups are confronted with a threatening difference in opinion, both sides end up vying with one another in elaborate ways to illustrate explicitly why their representation is better (Latour 1987, 205). Such a drive to match the definitions of opponents may explain why these and other interactions have produced some of the richest as well as the most anomalous deposits in Wiltshire and Dorset. This includes the most famous barrow deposits at Normanton, Winterbourne Stoke, and Oakley Down cemeteries.

Radley Barrow Hills, Oxfordshire

The only other well-excavated cemetery with both Beaker and Wessex deposits is Radley Barrow Hills. This is a cemetery with similar linear alignments to the Shrewton cemetery and an almost identical process of change. Like Shrewton, Beaker barrows (12, 201, 3, and 4a) were built first in the most prominent positions on the ridge (see figure 6.3a). These barrows all contained primary Beaker inhumations. Barrow 12 contained a Beaker bronze awl, barrow 3 contained a Beaker knife-dagger, and barrow 4a contained a beaker, three barbed and tanged arrowheads, and two gold basket earrings. The last Beaker barrow to be built, barrow 201, contained a beaker, a bronze awl, five barbed and tanged arrowheads, and an individual who had been shot in the back with an arrow (Barclay 1999).

At the time of the first Wessex barrows at the site, Beaker barrow 12 (like Net Down Beaker barrows 5a and 5e) was enlarged with a secondary ditch around it, creating a Wessex-style berm around the Beaker mound (see figure 6.3b). According to the excavator, this was created at the same time as a secondary cremation was inserted into the top of barrow 12 (Barclay 1999, 102).

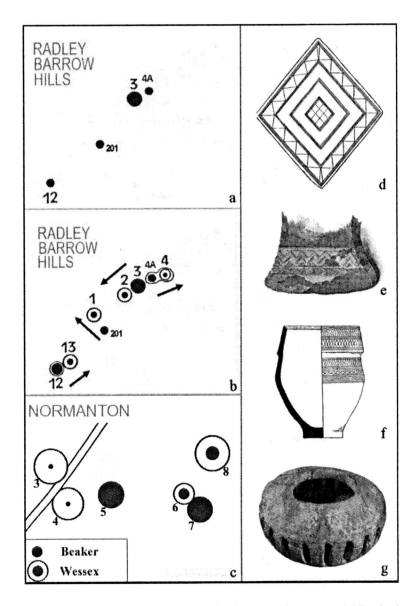

Figure 6.3.   (a–b) Radley Barrow Hills Initial Cemetery Sequence; (c) Beginnings
of the Normanton Cemetery; (d) Gold Lozenge with Zig-zag Motif from Wilsford
G5 (from Annable et al. 1964, 99); (e) Dagger Pommel with Zig-zag Motif from
Wilsford G5 (from Colt-Hoare 1810, 205); (f) Collared Urn with Beaker Decoration
from Wilsford G7 (from Annable et al. 1964, 98); (g) Photo of Stonehenge cup
from Wilsford G8 (Courtesy of Wiltshire Museum)

Then, each of the Beaker barrows (barrows 12, 201, 3, and 4a) were overshadowed by barrows 13, 1, 2, and 4 built immediately beside them, copying many of their traits (see figure 6.3b). Barrows 1, 2, and 4 were Wessex bell barrows while barrow 13 was likely a Wessex barrow too, judging from the shape of its ditch and central cists, although it was completely destroyed by the plow.

Barrow 1 was placed next to 201 and contained a cremation with a bronze knife-dagger, bone tweezers, and a bone ring-headed pin. Immediately beside barrow 3, a bell barrow (barrow 2) was built containing a cremation in a subrectangular pit with a very similar assemblage to 4a, including two gold bead covers and a bronze awl. The ditch around barrow 2 was also the same diameter as the ditch around barrow 3.

Another Wessex bell barrow (barrow 4) was then erected immediately beside barrow 4a, which contained a cremation with a dagger. At the same time, the space in between barrow 4 and 4a was infilled and a ditch was dug around both of them—subsuming Beaker barrow 4a and turning it into a bell barrow.

Here again, therefore, the Wessex barrows appropriated traits and deposits of the earlier Beaker barrows and presented them in a new context, effectively redefining them. The traits and deposits in barrow 2 are very similar to 4a—two Wessex Culture gold bead covers are deposited instead of two Beaker gold earrings, and one barbed and tanged arrowhead instead of three, in a similar subrectangular pit. A child cremation was even placed by the ditch, instead of a child inhumation. The use of a Beaker knife-dagger in Wessex barrow 4—similar to Beaker barrow 3—appears to be another appropriation.

Such a similarity of deposits cannot be a coincidence and their slightly different formation may be significant. It certainly indicates that both occurred within a short time frame, although there is no evidence for any counterdefinitions by a Beaker community. Nevertheless, this redefinition took an even more physical role than at the Shrewton cemetery, with barrow 4 subsuming barrow 4a within its ditch and mound. The evidence for violence in barrow 201—a Beaker individual shot in the back with an arrow, dated to the same time as the introduction of Wessex barrows at the cemetery—also indicates a tumultuous transition.

Three things are clear from these barrows at the cusp of change. First, the replication of traits from adjacent Beaker barrows suggests that the builders knew the long history of the barrows and what was in them. This indicates that it was members of the community that were dissenting from traditional Beaker practices, not some marauding tribe imposing a new tradition. Second, attempts to transform earlier Beaker bowl barrows into Wessex-style bell barrows suggests some form of revisionism. Third, the new representations match their counterparts in size and richness—with barrow 2 containing two beautiful gold bead covers instead of two gold earrings.

The Normanton Cemetery

The realization that rich deposits and elaborate structures occur at times of competition or during threats to social stability is not a new one. Michael Parker Pearson noticed that conspicuous consumption frequently occurs at times of stress (Parker Pearson 1982; also Bradley 1984, 75; Kossack 1974; Childe 1945). However, such rich deposits have commonly been seen as political displays of strength that could rally a monolithic population and overcome social instability, rather than as cosmopolitical contests between rival groups over what is true. Consequently, reasons for stress have been sought in wider, general explanations, rather than in material expressions within the radius of a few meters, and so the immediate contexts of such displays of wealth have often gone unnoticed.

To illustrate this, one of the richest displays in Wessex—the Bush Barrow assemblage—occurs exactly at the interface between Beaker and Wessex practices at the Normanton Cemetery (see barrow 5 in figure 6.3c). This was likely one of the first barrows in the cemetery, placed at the highest point and toward the beginning of the alignment of barrows. Bush Barrow (or Wilsford G5, as it is technically called) is a particularly odd barrow in that it perfectly matches the requirements for the Beaker tradition—an inhumation in a bowl barrow, with a possible Beaker dagger with rivet-studded hilt (Needham et al. 2009)—but it also contains many Beaker items with characteristically Wessex Culture materials. These include a large gold lozenge-shaped breastplate with zig-zag markings, another miniature replica of the gold lozenge, a rectangular gold plate with belt hook, a flat bronze axe, two large flat bronze daggers hafted with gold pins in zig-zag patterns, one smaller bronze dagger, and a hafted macehead with zig-zag bone fastenings (see figures 6.3d–e).

Bush Barrow is also next to a similar mound, Wilsford G7, a bowl/bell barrow with an inhumation accompanied by a large number of Wessex-style artifacts. These include a decorated collared urn, a "grape" cup, two spherical gold beads, striped and plain amber pendants, shale beads, some fossils, and a miniature jet replica of a double-headed axe.

While these two mounds are often cited as the premier examples of the Wessex Culture, with the Bush Barrow even giving its name to the first phase of the Wessex Culture, there are a number of problems with this cultural designation. First, the Bush Barrow lozenge symbols and zig-zag decorations have numerous associations with the Beaker culture. Apart from the aforementioned association with Beaker gold "sun disks" and the angular distance between the solstices represented by them, the lozenge and thick zig-zag decoration occurs on almost all surviving late Beaker pottery from this area and on a few related food vessels, but rarely on Wessex urns. Furthermore, a recent study by Humphrey Case (2003) has shown that the Bush Barrow daggers are more associated with Beaker knife-daggers than Wessex daggers.

Wilsford G7 also has many Beaker-related artifacts including a Beaker shard that was found included with the collared urn and a pendant in the form of a battle-axe, a form with Beaker associations (Case 2003). The collared urn is the most interesting association here, though. The decoration in linear zones over the body and shoulders with lozenge symbols is quite unique for collared urns, but is commonly associated with Beaker vessels (ibid.) (see figure 6.3f). These affiliations indicate that Wilsford G7 was also a Beaker barrow.

It has been suggested that the burials in both Wilsford G5 and Wilsford G7 were actually intrusive into older Beaker mounds (Needham et al. 2009; Case 2003, 167). Recent surveys of the barrows also suggest that both mounds comprised more than one phase of mound construction (Barrett and Bowden 2010, 10, 11). Whether or not these burials were intrusive, they were clearly strong reaffirmations of Beaker values with the latest Wessex metallurgical and ceramic technology.

They are also among the seven finest assemblages from this period. However, their ostentation and association with Wessex iconography may have something to do with their particular location in the Normanton cemetery rather than their association with some elite individual. While excavation of the cemetery was conducted over two hundred years ago and is very patchy, some indications exist of interactions between these predominantly Beaker graves and the ascendant Wessex Culture that was making incursions into the area. At both sides of Bush Barrow were placed Wessex barrows—two of the finest cremation disc barrows in Wessex on one side, and Wilsford G6 and G8 on the other (see figure 6.3c). Wilsford G6 is classified as a bowl barrow with an outer ring, but is almost indistinguishable from a Wessex barrow (ibid., 11; Grinsell 1957, 136). This barrow was looted before it could be excavated properly, so no records exist, but because of its form and its position—intruding upon the ditch of Wilsford G7—this barrow indicates that an interesting exchange existed in the vicinity of these barrows.

Wilsford G8, the barrow beside G6, was the third of the seven finest barrows in Wessex. Yet this was a Wessex bell barrow with a primary cremation and numerous Wessex artifacts, including amber pendants, a miniature halberd pendant set in gold and amber, gold-covered bronze horns, a gold-covered bone plaque, a gold-covered shale cone, and two gold-covered amber disks (that look a lot like Wessex mounds with golden berms around them). It is likely that this exotic and rich assemblage, placed in such a critical location overlooking Stonehenge, may have actually stimulated the Beaker group to be so competitive and explicit in their deposits in Wilsford G5 and G7. As Latour states, controversies stimulate opponents to match each other's representations and exceed them, "mapping for themselves, for their opponents, and for the observers, what they value most, what they are most dearly attached to. 'Where thy treasure is, there will thy heart be also'" (Latour 1987, 205).

With the Wilsford G8 deposit was also a beautifully wrought slotted cup that was originally named the "Stonehenge cup" because of its likeness to the stone configuration around Stonehenge. The only difference from Stonehenge is that it features a slanting roof from the outer ring of trilithons up to a higher inner ring of supports, decorated with lines not unlike thatching (see figure 6.3g). If this is a replica of Stonehenge, then that inner ring would not be unlike the inner horseshoe of higher trilithons within Stonehenge.

Depositions similar to the above barrows exist in four other impressive barrows of Wessex: Preshute G1, Hengistbury Head 3, Clandon Barrow (Winterbourne St. Martin G31), and Upton Lovell G2e. Preshute G1 was an inhumation burial in a bowl barrow, whereas Hengistbury Head 3 was a primary cremation with identical objects to Wilsford G8 (including gold cones, amber beads, a halberd pendant, and another "Stonehenge cup"). The Clandon and Upton Lovell G2e deposits (deposits with lozenges, zig-zags, and other Beaker motifs) were secondary deposits intrusive into primary cremation barrows. Secondary cremations placed near these two deposits suggest that a sequence of definitions and counterdefinitions may have existed at these two locations as well. It is clear that these four barrows were not depositions made under normal circumstances.

In order to identify what caused these particular affirmations, redefinitions, and amalgamations, a good deal more excavation of them and their surrounding barrows would be necessary to understand the context of their particular displays.

Nevertheless, the richness of the displays at the Normanton cemetery, the presence of such a concerted effort to integrate Beaker motifs with Wessex technology, and their context at the interface between practices indicate that the Normanton barrows were likely part of a struggle for the definition of their cemetery. Their location directly above Stonehenge (likely a center for power in the area)—at the frontline of Wessex incursions (judging by figure 6.1 of the Stonehenge landscape)—would have made this struggle critical.

DISCUSSION

As Latour argues, "trials trace the limit of a paradigm . . . what holds tightly and what gives way easily, what is negotiable and what is not" (Latour 1987, 201). By focusing on controversies, and by following each group's representations as they made a case for them, it has been shown that this technique reveals important associations that could explain particular actions and objects. What were clearly negotiable in these different controversies were artifact forms, but even borrowed artifacts appear to have been adapted and used in ways that made statements about their respective traditions. The oblique cruciform, zig-zag, and lozenge motifs traditionally associated with Beaker groups that were inscribed on Wessex-style artifacts (such as exotic necklaces, gold breastplates, and the collared urn in Wilsford G7) in Beaker inhumation graves during these trials suggest that these motifs were highly important to the Beaker tradition. Their association with the angle of eighty-one degrees, the angular distance between the midsummer and midwinter solstices, may also have had something to do with this importance.

The non-negotiable elements in these controversies were clearly the mound forms and burial practices. A case can be made that the crucial difference between the different mound forms, or between Beaker bowl barrows and Wessex bell, disc, or saucer barrows, was the provision of a platform within the barrows for ceremony. The provision of a large berm between the ditch and the mound would have provided a perfect stage for ceremonies—an arena that is lacking in Beaker mounds and cemeteries (Healy and Harding 2007). Indeed, on the few berms that have actually been excavated, several burials and pits with ritual deposits have been found (such as the pits in Collingbourne Kingston G18 and G8 at Snail Down). If these berms provided a local stage for ceremony, it is little wonder that the Wessex barrows stimulated so much controversy in the Early Bronze Age. The promotion of a local stage for ceremony within each cemetery would have undermined the centralized power structure of a society that appears to have depended upon communal attendance at large henges and other centralized ceremonial monuments.

Whether or not this change was stimulated by a concentration of too much power at these places is difficult to establish. A more feasible task would be to trace any changes in the landscape at this time, which might have stimulated or resulted from these changes. The delineation of the landscape into bounded areas (Gingell 1992, 153), the creation of local field systems, and a related intensification of agriculture (Allen 2010) at this time were likely related. Such changes observed in the archaeological record around the time of the first Wessex barrows suggest that communities had become more self-sufficient and sedentary. While Early Bronze Age settlements near the cemeteries are hard to find, this is probably due to their location in the protected valleys below cemeteries (with better access to water) that are now covered by many feet of colluvium. When a settlement was found in the valley beside the Durrington Walls monument in 2006 (largely by accident), it was at a considerable depth that could not have been discovered through field walking (Parker Pearson 2007). Certainly the formation of dozens of substantial barrow cemeteries (with ceremonial functions) during the Wessex period suggests that they were used by local communities that had settled down by this time. Other changes include a shift away from large ceremonial monuments. While a patchwork of Beaker communities continued to exist and practice at Stonehenge and some other henge monuments, many of the other large ceremonial complexes, including many henge sites, were abandoned at this time (Harding 2003, 2010).

If this change was so important to the individuals defining the new Wessex tradition, it can be expected that deposits in their controversial new mounds at the interface with Beaker groups would shed some light upon it too. Indeed, the deposition of the "Stonehenge cup" in the bell barrow Wilsford G8 may have made the statement that ceremonies at Stonehenge were now the prerogative of local communities and could take place at bell barrows or other Wessex mounds instead. Similar "Stonehenge cups" have also been found at Shrewton G5c (a bell barrow at the interface between Wessex and Beaker practices there), and at Hengistbury Head 3 (with a primary cremation), possibly for the same reasons as Wilsford G8. Other symbols of Stonehenge that are found in Wessex barrows include bluestone chips from the bluestones around Stonehenge, used in Amesbury G4 and G11. These were Wessex barrows placed directly beside Stonehenge and possibly represent a brazen statement of difference. The structural similarity between bell, disc, or saucer barrows and henges also indicates an attempt to replicate the henge experience locally (Ashbee 1960; Atkinson 1956). Several Wessex barrows contain stake circles around their berms, and their circular ditches are often reminiscent of monumental henge ditches. The presence of Wilsford G6 at the interface between practices at Normanton is especially significant in this context. This was a saucer-like barrow with an outer bank—a structure that is almost identical to a henge.

The new practice of cremation may also be linked to Stonehenge. Cremation burial was practiced at Stonehenge from around 3000 BC to 2300 BC (based upon three recent radiocarbon dates)—a rare practice for the Neolithic and one that was largely limited, in the south, to Stonehenge (Needham et al. 2010). Cremations were placed mostly in the Aubrey holes around Stonehenge (in twenty-six out of thirty-four pits excavated so far) and may represent a single dynasty over seven centuries (ibid., 36). Further radiocarbon dating may extend this span even later, but the historic association of cremation burial with the monument, even three hundred and fifty years later during the Wessex Culture, would likely have still been strong. If Wessex Culture communities desired to practice ceremonies that were once conducted at Stonehenge at their burial grounds, the burial of cremations may have been an obvious choice.

While the redefinition of Beaker mounds and the adoption of Wessex mounds and practices at the cemeteries studied above may have been hotly contested, it appears that many communities adopted Wessex practices without controversy. This may have been the case at Radley Barrow Hills (although a late Beaker burial from that interface was found with an arrow in his back). This does not mean that less controversial sites did not revise earlier Beaker barrows (with intrusive secondary cremations or structural redefinitions), it just means that an internal or external group did not attempt to counter the insurrection with violence or counterdefinitions. For this reason, while hotly contested sites may provide more explicit information on the essence of practices, all instances of redefinition and innovation at the interface between practices can provide us with information.

This chapter hopefully illustrates how the classification of mounds by form and context provides a much better taxonomic method than classification purely by form. The history of archaeological practice in Early Bronze Age studies is a good example of how purely formal classification cannot help but bias analysis and perpetuate a concept of culture as unified and continuous. The tyranny of artifact typology is most plain when analyses allow a few artifacts to influence our classification of groups but ignore the larger picture of huge changes in burial practice, mound form, and other traits. Hopefully it has been demonstrated that artifacts often change affiliation or are adapted and used in different ways during controversies out of political necessity. For this reason, it is essential that the context of artifacts be taken into account when comparing artifacts and that a better method is found to choose the dimensions of variation than merely accepting artifacts as the categories of difference. Without a critical reevaluation of the typological method in archaeological practice, this concept will probably continue to haunt interpretations and cause further empirical problems. These problems include not only the homogenization of differences, but also a blindness to any interactions that occur between them.

This is important because these interactions often provide the keys to understanding the essence of practices. They enable an empirical approach to be taken to study highly relevant instances of expression rather than having to impose social theories to explain disconnected region-wide data. They also provide a precise time frame for analysis that could never be achieved with the best radiocarbon dating. While analyses must remain local in focus, this does not mean that conclusions are parochial. The analysis of several of these controversies, each a precise analysis of the contextual details at hand, enable more nuances of object use and political maneuvering to be studied than a general study would allow, but they do not preclude the combination of those results to gain a more general picture of the culture in the end.

What are clearly needed for this sort of study, though, are more detailed excavations of these controversies, whether they extend over one, two, or three barrows. Once identified and studied closely, these interactions may help to clear up many of the unusual episodes that have confused Early Bronze Age archaeologists for decades. They may also help us to better understand deposits, practices, and cultural change.

SEVEN

Contestation in the Hopewell

Many instances of controversy can also be found among the Hopewell burial mounds of the Lower Illinois Valley in North America. This next study forms the second practice model for the methodology in this book and best illustrates the great value of controversies to reveal fundamental elements behind representations.

During the Hopewell period (from 50 BC to 250 AD) burial mounds were built along the cliffs of the Lower Illinois Valley in cemeteries of five to ten mounds. Not much is known about the settlements of these people, the majority having been covered by alluvium (Charles 1992, 190; Julieann Van Nest pers. comm.), but it appears that they were semisedentary and may have lived in dispersed hamlets along the Illinois River valley and tributary valleys (Stafford 1985). Alluvium from annual flooding in the river valley was one of the factors that enabled plants and animals to thrive on the valley floor and provided a prodigious surplus for settlements and their construction of mounds. A number of mounds have been excavated in this valley since the 1950s, enabling a total of fifty from eight cemeteries to be examined for this study. Three floodplain mound complexes in the valley were not considered because they appear to have a different function. Every mound or context too damaged by looters or other damaging factors to use as evidence was also not accepted.

To establish a rough chronology of mounds within cemeteries, I have used Douglas Charles' topographical method (Charles 1985). This was established through a survey of 286 Middle and Late Woodland Mounds along the valley. Charles discovered that the earliest mound at each ridge cemetery was nearly always placed in the most prominent or highest position on a ridge, with any later mounds placed in positions of gradually reduced prominence (Charles 1985, 183). According to Charles, "Prominence is defined here in terms of visibility from the floodplain, and includes a component of topographic uniqueness" (Charles et al. 1986, 467). Using topographical maps with fine grading, this method enabled earlier mounds to be distinguished from later mounds in most ridge cemeteries and for cemeteries with an acute gradient to be sequenced fairly precisely (Martin 2002). The length of mound use is difficult to establish precisely and appears to have varied. Surfaces at the Elizabeth mound cemetery were not left exposed long enough for horizons to build up (less than forty years) (Bullington 1988, 221). However, it appears that some were mounded over not long after they were constructed due to the lack of rainfall silting in tombs (Perino 1966, 189).

In 1998 Jane Buikstra et al. proposed the view that these burial mounds operated as microcosmic representations of the world. In their view, mounds expressed a Native American cosmology that exists today in southeastern North American tribes of an upper, middle, and lower world. This, they claim, was manifested in Hopewell burial rituals, which "served to anchor the Middle Woodland World, moving the dead across the lofty platforms representing the upper world, through the flat disk of this world, into the dark, subsurface underworld" (Buikstra et al. 1998, 89).

Although this view helps to elucidate the nature of burial mounds as cosmograms, it ends up conflating all burial mounds together and overlooks too many differences in practice and structure between mounds. This effort to apply a recent regional Amerindian ontology to all prehistoric monuments, like other efforts to apply an analogy or social theory to archaeological remains, also results in overpowering local nuanced explanations that relate to the data at hand.

Instead of ignoring differences between burial mounds and trying to form one general archetype and explanation for them all, the following case study attempts to understand local expressions and the reasons for their differences by actually focusing on those differences. By identifying the various burial practices and mound types that exist in the Lower Illinois Valley and by following any friction that occurred between them—where those different practices interacted—information can be gleaned about what those expressions represented.

STEP 1: RELEVANT DIMENSIONS OF VARIATION

The first study aimed to distinguish the significant dimensions of variation (the contextual factors of Hopewell burial mounds that varied the least) from the insignificant dimensions (those contextual factors that varied the most) in the mounds studied.

In order to determine the significant dimensions of variation, every aspect of each burial mound was described and entered into a full-text site record. Then context records were created for each construction episode within individual mounds and all aspects of these were separated out into micro-context variables within each context record. Records were also created for artifacts that enabled their different contexts to be recorded too. This enabled each micro-context type to be indexed and variations to be quantified. The context types with the least variations were then chosen as significant dimensions of variation. A selection of relevant dimensions that differed the least were:

1. The tomb preparation.
2. The tomb structure.
3. The ramp structure.
4. The type of burial within the tomb.
5. The burial configuration around the tomb.
6. The context of ceramic vessels.

Then, within each dimension/context type, the predominant traits were identified, along with any differences from these traits. The predominant traits actually translated into one group of burial mounds, and the differences from these traits translated into three other groups—groups of mounds categorized through possessing multiple similar contextual factors, rather than singular arbitrary factors such as similar artifacts or structures.

Type 1 Mounds

Within the significant dimensions of variation the predominant traits were:

1. A prepared surface or platform of soil, sand, or clay (the first activity of each mound).
2. A surface tomb of large logs (one to two logs high) cemented with clay from the cliffs.
3. Large ramps surrounding the tomb, often of loaded soil (earthen sods).
4. Only processed human bones in the tomb (evidence of excarnation).
5. A cluster of 1–3 peripheral burials either side of the tomb, if any.
6. Sometimes Hopewell vessels with peripheral burials.

Interestingly, there is a consistency among predominant representations (see appendix H). This means that in representations in which dominant traits are present, most of the other dominant traits occur as well. This helps to confirm that these were the relevant dimensions of variation. The predominant mound type (Type 1) appears early in the Hopewell period according to radiocarbon dates from Elizabeth Mound 6 (120 BC ± 75 and 30 BC ± 70) and Mound 7 (80 BC ± 75 and 10 BC ± 70) (Bullington 1988,

220). This type of mound also appears most in the northern part of the valley.

These mounds contain a large surface tomb with minor human remains, surrounded by a log crib and earthen ramp of sod blocks (Van Nest et al. 2001, 645). The tombs appear to have been the location for several stages of a burial practice. This practice first involved placing multiple bodies in the tomb to be picked clean by ravens or buzzards (Buikstra et al. 1998, 89). The many minor human bones in these tombs (or scattered over their ramps) testify to the processing of many individuals. At Elizabeth Mound 7 it was estimated that over thirty individuals had been processed in the tomb (ibid.). After burial processing, the majority of large bones were removed to an unknown location away from the mound. This has led many to see these tombs as corporate facilities for the processing of community members (Charles 1985). In addition, one to four articulated inhumations were placed at either side of these tombs in clusters, sometimes with elaborate Hopewell vessels or other exotic items. These may have been burials of leaders together with their retainers or close family.

Other Mound Types

However, although this type of mound appears to be predominant, there are many differences from it. I have called these differences "mutations" from the predominant mound type (Type 1), in the Darwinian sense of the word. Before discussing these differences, it should be mentioned that quite a high level of similarity was found between mounds within cemeteries. This suggests that each cemetery may have been used by one community or group of communities practicing a version of dominant or alternative representations, but in their own way, consistently repeating many of the same traits over time, but traits that were not seen elsewhere. These variations account for much of the less significant dimensions of variation observed over the whole valley.

To determine whether mounds were a challenge to the dominant representation or just a different version of it, the next task was to examine differences in traits from the predominant mound type. This involved making a note of any consistent differences within significant context types and ascertaining whether these occurred with any other consistent differences in the same mounds. The outcome was that there appear to be three other mound types in the valley that contrasted with the predominant type. Topographic, stratigraphic, and radiocarbon data suggest that the first two mound types (Types 2 and 3) were contemporary with the dominant Type 1 practice, but both differed radically from it in each relevant dimension of variation. The traits of the first mutation (or Type 2) were:

1. No prepared surface.
2. Subfloor pit tombs (16–18 inches deep) with low log walls and no clay cement.
3. Low or no ramps and no loaded soil (no use of sod layers).
4. Central interments with little or no evidence of processing.
5. Multiple peripheral burials located in rings around the tomb.
6. Sometimes Hopewell vessels with individuals in tombs—*not* with peripheral burials.

Type 2 mounds have also been situated in the early part of the Hopewell because many of these mounds were located on the most prominent or second most prominent positions in ridge-top cemeteries. Although each cemetery with Type 2 mounds emphasizes one or more traits over others, they all contain a high enough number of similarities to be classified together (see appendix H). The most significant difference was the placement of one to three individuals, sometimes with Hopewell vessels or other exotic items, at the center of subfloor tombs and not at the periphery. At the periphery were placed multiple inhumations, also articulated and non-processed, in rings around the tomb ramps (see Mounds 1a and 1b in figure 7.1).

The traits of the second (Type 3) mutation were:

1. No Prepared Surface.
2. Subfloor pit tombs (16–18 inches deep) without log walls.
3. No Ramps.
4. Central interments with little or no evidence of processing.
5. Multiple peripheral burials located in rings around the tomb.
6. Sometimes Hopewell vessels in tombs *or* Baehr vessels at the periphery.

Type 3 mounds contain most of the same differences as Type 2 mounds (see appendix H). These small mounds consisted of one or two central pit tombs containing mostly articulated burials with no evidence of processing, surrounded by circles of multiple peripheral burials. Peripheral burials were sometimes buried with Baehr vessels, a domestic vessel type. Such mounds were originally seen to predate the other mound types. Elizabeth Mounds 1 and 3, exemplars of this mound type, were placed by Jill Bullington at the beginning of the Hopewell period through their prominent position at the distal end of a bluff ridge (Bullington 1988). However, the fact that Elizabeth Mounds 4, 6, and 7 were in the most prominent positions that would support mounds of their size has been overlooked due to the assumption that earlier mounds would have been smaller and less complex anyway (Bullington 1988, 226). Complexity is a very ambiguous term and not really suited to the size, presence, or absence of a few traits that may reflect differences in a world view. According to the position of similar mounds in the valley at the end

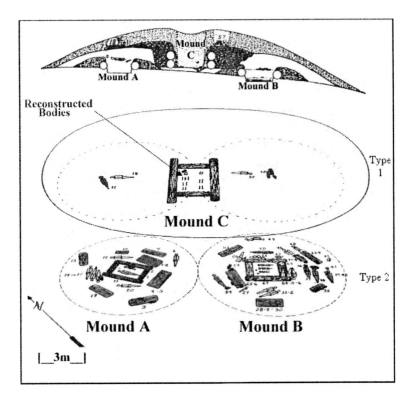

Figure 7.1.   Exploded View of Klunk Mound 1, with Mounds A and B Subsumed by Mound C (from Perino 1968, 18) (Courtesy of Illinois Archaeological Survey)

of cemetery sequences (Gibson Mound 5 and Knoll C) it would make sense that they were constructed toward the end of the Hopewell.

Comparisons of burials by Jane Buikstra (Buikstra 1976, 37) and Joseph Tainter (1980, 311) at the Klunk and Gibson mounds established that there were distinct differences in stature and bone degeneration between central and periphery burials, which most likely reflected a difference in status. This means that the central burials in both Type 2 and 3 mounds and later Type 4 mounds (the only mounds to contain articulated central burials) were most likely leaders. These burials were often associated with elaborate Hopewell vessels or other exotic items. It also means that the multiple individuals placed at the periphery of their tombs were likely to have been community members.

Table 7.1. Type 4 Mounds

Mound No.	Prep.	Tomb Type	Ramps	Tomb Burial	Outer Burials	Hope. pot	Tomb Gender
Klunk 5a	No	Pit	Ramp	Processed	Cluster	Periphery	
Klunk 7	No	Pit	Ramp	Processed	Cluster	Periphery	
Klunk 11a	No	Pit	No Ramp	B/Processed	Cluster	Periphery	M
Klunk 13	No	Pit	Ramp	Burial	None	Tomb roof	M + F
Bedford 4b	Platform	Surface	No Ramp	Burial	Ring Infill		M
L'Orient 1b	Platform	Surf. Log	No Ramp	B/Processed	Clusters		?
Carter 1	?	Pit + Log	No Ramp	B/Processed	Cluster		M
Carter 5	?	Pit	No Ramp	Burial	Clusters		M
Gibson 3	?	Pit + Log	No Ramp	Burial	Clusters		M + C
Gibson 4b	Platform	Surf. Log	Sod Ramp	Burial	Cluster		M + C
Gibson 6	Platform	Pit + Log	Sod Ramp	Burial	None		?
Montezuma 1	?	Surf. Log	Sod Ramp	B/Processed	?		M

The third group of mutant mounds (Type 4) were more local variations, containing amalgamations of Type 1, 2, and 3 traits (table 7.1).
These were positioned in less prominent locations toward the end of
ridges or over Type 3 mounds, indicating that they were also toward the
end of the Hopewell period. However, when two or more of these
mounds occurred in one cemetery (like Klunk Mounds 5a, 7, and 11a),
they often shared the same traits, indicating that these traits were not
random, but formed a coherent local evolution from the predominant
Type 1 mounds.

Context of Mutations

Once rough groupings and chronological sequences have been found,
the first thing to determine is whether these different mutant groups
represented dissention or merely functional differences. In order to determine this, the immediate contexts of mutations were examined for clues.

A study of the Type 2 and 3 mutant mounds revealed that ten of the
nineteen mounds comprised five pairs of mounds. Mounds in these pairs
contained almost identical tombs and/or peripheral burial configurations
to one another. They included Klunk Mounds 1a and 1b, Bedford
Mounds 12a and 11a, L'Orient Mounds 1a and 2, Gibson Mounds 2a and
5a, and Elizabeth Mounds 1 and 3. They were almost always built next to
each other and contained identical associations, indicating that they were
built at a similar time. Latour explains that alternative representations
require demonstrations of support in order to survive (Latour 1987, 31),
and these pairs may reflect such a desire. Without support, a dissenter is
on his own, a threat to no one.

The second study examined the relationship between mutant mounds
and predominant mounds. In the Lower Illinois Valley, many of the
paired mutant mounds were destroyed or submerged by versions of the
predominant Type 1 mounds built directly into the top of them. This
occurred to some Type 3 mounds even before they were mounded
(L'Orient 1a, Gibson 5a and 2a), indicating that the temporal distance
between the two types was virtually non-existent. Elizabeth Mounds 1
and 3 were the only pair of mounds to remain unsuppressed, possibly
because the community that built the Elizabeth Mounds had already
adopted many of their traits in the construction of Mound 7, the last
mound to be built on the ridge at that point. Mound 7 also shows several
signs of destruction and reconstruction indicating that a struggle may
have occurred earlier.

While the idea that these superimpositions were the result of ideological disputes between communities may be difficult to grasp, no other
conclusion holds as much water. Each of these instances comprise one
contrasting mound type excavated into another within a short time
frame, and unless it is believed that two very different representations of

the world can coexist harmoniously in one community at the same time, one has to conclude that they were built by different communities. However, most interpretations of this phenomenon appear to take the view that one community is capable of two different understandings of the world. For instance, Charles et al. claim that secondary mounds were built on top of primary mounds due to a lack of prominent locations (Charles et al. 1986, 467). Yet, the large amount of space between mounds on many ridges (especially at the Klunk and Gibson cemeteries) and the fact that some secondary tombs intruded upon primary mounds before they were even finished, negates the viability of this explanation.

Other interpretations suggest that primary and secondary mounds were built together as one concerted burial program. Jane Bullington argues that the two different types represent different social levels in a group (Bullington 1988, 225), while Charles and Buikstra argue that they represent different functions (i.e., burial versus ceremonial activity) (Buikstra and Charles 1999, 215). However, these suggestions are also problematic. The mounds supposedly representing different social levels or functions were usually built on top of each other where they occurred together, making it difficult to use them at the same time. Other evidence also makes these suggestions difficult to accept.

First, the conclusion that articulated central burials and multiple peripheral burials represented leaders and community members respectively in primary mounds (Buikstra 1976, 38; Tainter 1980, 311) leaves little necessity for another mound type to represent leaders and the community again. Secondly, Type 1 mounds contain a completely contrasting burial practice of burying a few individuals at the periphery and processing multiple individuals in the tomb. The remains of these processed individuals were always removed from the mound, but they were not placed in the Type 2 or 3 mounds, most of which have no evidence of processed remains. This eliminates the possibility that both types were used at the same time by one community for different social levels or functions.

Thirdly, Type 1 mounds only occur together with Type 2 or 3 mounds a few times in the central and southern parts of the Lower Illinois Valley, and only with two Type 3 mounds in the north, at Elizabeth Mound cemetery (Mounds 1 and 3). Mutant burial practices were not part of a general valley-wide practice—they appeared mostly in southern portions of the valley with predominant Type 1 mounds mostly in the north. Finally, the explanation that Type 1 mounds represent a chronologically later version of Type 3 mounds (Bullington 1988, 226) (despite often being built over them before they were mounded) is undermined by the presence of Type 3 tombs excavated into the top of Klunk Type 1 Mounds 5a and 11a. Thus it appears that these different types of mound constitute different contemporary representations of the world shared by different communities that sometimes came into conflict over what constituted a "correct representation."

Violence in the Illinois Hopewell

Finally, a strong indication of the existence of a conflict during these episodes is that the only instances of violence in the valley occur during these interactions between mutant mounds and predominant Type 1 mounds. Fifteen cases of aggression exist at mutant mounds, where tombs were flattened, burnt, smashed, and scattered. Ten of these fifteen mounds were also refaced with a different mound structure, and many contained examples of physical violence to humans, including the burial of decapitated bodies and bodies buried facedown with their hands and feet tied. However, all of these instances have been consistently assumed to be the healthy cultural activities of one group.

Constructions of one representation over another are often observed in archaeology, like Christian churches over pagan sites or Neolithic round barrows over long barrows (Eagles and Field 2004). These are normally considered to be symbolic appropriations or statements of dominance over earlier practices separated by many years (Bradley 1993), despite often being contemporary. As discussed earlier, such assumptions of temporal distance and assumptions of violent actions as cultural may be based on the notion that cultures are monocultural—a belief that precludes the existence of conflicts between representations of the world in one culture at the same time.

STEP 2: FOLLOWING CONTROVERSIES

The next study examined the interactions between different groups at four cemeteries involved in conflicts. By following the proponents of representations during controversies—as they made a case for their representations—many of the associations and relationships behind artifacts and practices were revealed. However, as Latour argues, our "main tenet is that actors themselves make everything, including their own frames, their own theories, their own contexts, their own metaphysics, even their own ontologies" (Latour 2005, 147). Therefore, in order to learn from them it was imperative to follow only the networks of associations laid out in these conflicts rather than impose our own theories. This involved not only describing the structure of representations and the sequence of actions that tied objects together within that structure, but also determining what objectified maneuvers were conducted to make a statement or to solidify or extend the influence of representations.

In addition, Latour makes it clear that each controversy should be dealt with separately since the essence of one group's opinion may differ from another's (Latour 2005). As explained before, an approach that constructs a separate interpretation for each controversy does not preclude a general understanding eventually, as long as this is reached from as many separate conclusions as possible. However, it allows far more differences to be explained than when a single meta-narrative is applied after studying just one of them.

While it took nearly four hundred pages to describe all four controversies (in Martin 2002), due to the limitations of space here I shall venture to describe only the striking interactions that occurred during each of them. This follows Latour's rule for description—to concentrate only upon the actors that make a difference—"If an actor makes no difference, it's not an actor" (Latour 2005, 130).

To illustrate the ability of Latour's methodology to reveal fundamental elements behind representations, I wish to first briefly describe the beginning of a controversy at the Klunk Mound Cemetery (Perino 1968).

Klunk Mound 1

In the exploded view of Klunk Mound 1 (see figure 7.1), Mound 1 emerges as three mounds, each with a full sequence of mound activity. Mounds 1a and 1b are a pair of almost identical Type 2 mounds, each with subfloor tombs containing a male and female and rings of peripheral burials around each tomb. Although the tombs in Mounds 1a and 1b contain some evidence of burial processing, many of these processed burials were placed on the tomb ramps of Mound 1b. This contrasts with the complete removal of processed burials at predominant Type 1 mounds. Several articulated peripheral burials are also excavated into the tomb ramps of both mounds, a practice unheard of in Type 1 mounds.

As if to emphasize their solidarity and dissent, after both tombs and peripheral burials were mounded, five graves were inserted into each of the mounds in rings around their tombs. This seems to emphasize their different practice of placing multiple articulated community members in rings around their tomb peripheries. The circling of tombs with peripheral burials was continued at the Klunk, Gibson, and L'Orient Mound cemeteries wherever Type 2 mounds were built. If central burials contained leaders, and multiple individuals placed at the periphery represented community members (Buikstra 1976, 38; Tainter 1980), then these Type 2 mounds appear to be challenging both the inclusiveness of the Type 1 central tombs and the exclusiveness of the Type 1 periphery.

The reaction to this different configuration is even more revealing. The predominant Type 1 mound intrusive into the top of both Mounds 1a and 1b—Mound 1c—is identical to other Type 1 mounds, except for one feature. In its tomb are a *reconstructed* male and female composed of the bones from many processed individuals. This unusual reconstruction appears to epitomize the Type 1 practice of communal burial processing while using a direct reference to the male and female leaders in the tombs below it. By reconstructing two bodies out of the bones of multiple individuals, leadership may have been represented as comprising many members of the community.

This illustrates Latour's prediction that when a controversy starts, both sides "end up mobilizing the most heterogeneous and distant elements, thus mapping for themselves, for their opponents, and for the observers, what they value most, what they are most dearly attached to" (Latour 1987, 205).

Bedford Mounds

Although the controversy between Type 1 and Type 2 mound representations continues over several mounds at the Klunk Mound cemetery, the Bedford Mound ridge is more acutely graded and therefore somewhat better for sequencing. The value of following this controversy is that it illustrates Latour's understanding of the process of change in representations. This is the discovery that representations often change through interaction between protagonists. As each contender attempts to attract support or reduce the other's polemic during controversies, elements are borrowed from each opponent's representations. By following several interactions between contenders during a controversy we can trace what was negotiable and what was not—to find the core paradigmatic elements and how their representations changed (Latour 1987, 201).

The sequence of excavated Bedford Mounds from the highest through to the lowest prominently positioned mound was obtained through Charles' topographical sequencing method and relates favorably with a radiocarbon date for Mound 4. The first mound, Mound 12, was placed in the most prominent position overlooking the river valley. From there, Mounds 11/10, 9, and 8 were located in gradually diminishing height and prominence along the bluff ridge. Mound 4 was positioned at the least prominent location, toward the bottom of a bluff ridge, and was dated to 230 AD (± 125)—toward the end of the Hopewell period (Perino 1970, 117; Buikstra et al. 1998, 91).

The mounds apparently involved in dissent at the Bedford Mounds were Mounds 12a, 11a, 10, 8a, and 4a. These differ from the predominant Type 1 mounds not only through the presence of burials in their central tombs, but also through the total lack of evidence for burial processing (disarticulated bones) in their central tombs. Unfortunately, peripheral subsoil burials were only found around Mounds 8a and 4a due to the basal soil not being excavated from underneath the other mounds. However, the burials and artifacts placed in tombs and other contexts reveal a further significant dimension of difference.

Bedford Mounds 10/11 and 12

The similarity in measurements and interment practice between Mounds 12a and 11a indicates that these two were built at the same time (Perino 1970, 169; see figure 7.2a–b). For example, the internments in both tombs were wrapped and covered with several inches of soil, bark, and limestone slabs—a practice that is usually conducted for the tomb itself. The only difference between the mounds seems to be the gender of their central burials, a dichotomy that may have been significant in this coordinated statement. Along with other artifacts, Mound 12a contains three males with lamellar blades, an artifact only associated with females in the valley (Leigh et al. 1988, 203). Mound 11a contains three females with a platform pipe, an artifact usually associated with males. This indicates that the placement of females in a Type 2 leadership position at Mound 11a not only represents a challenge to the inclusiveness of the central tomb, but also to the gender of leadership.

Mound 10, also with a central female burial, may have been built in support of this challenge to the gender of leadership. Constructed immediately beside Mound 11a, Mound 10 comprises several Type 2 features, including a small log tomb with grave goods. These include a platform pipe, organic material, and Hopewell vessels—usually associated with male leaders or children outside the tomb in Type 1 peripheral burials. This apparent challenge to the gender of leadership was continued in the rest of the Bedford Mounds with the placement of only females in Type 2 central tombs (Mounds 8a and 4a).

In the same way as Klunk Mounds 1a and 1b were built over by an intrusive Type 1 mound, Bedford Mounds 12a, 11a, and 10 were also built over by Type 1 mounds 12b and 11b (see figure 7.2a–b). Mounds 12b and 11b may have also been built at the same time, judging by the similarity between their tombs. Each mound's tomb had the same dimensions and traits, with equidistant "pockets" excavated in their tomb floors used for the deposition of beads, pearls, chert, and organic items, while processed remains were scattered over the rest of the floor. This unusual way of depositing artifacts appears to be a reaffirmation of the Type 1 mode of deposition—the association of artifacts with the tomb in opposition to the association of artifacts with individuals in the tomb. To one side of Mound 12b was a cluster of peripheral burials in the style of Type 1 mounds.

It is fairly significant that the artifacts associated with the cluster of peripheral burials beside Mound 12b (and over Mound 12a) are actually very similar to those in the Type 2 tombs of Mounds 10, 11a, and 12a. These include a pipe stem associated with a male peripheral burial (similar to pipes with the male tomb burial in Mound 12a and female tomb burial in Mound 11a), a small conch vessel with a peripheral child burial (also found with a male tomb burial in Mound 12a), and a bone spatula

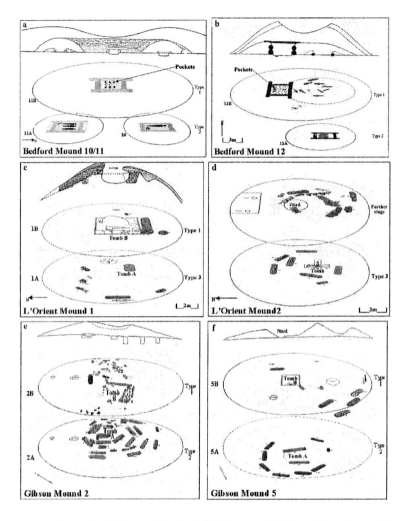

Figure 7.2.   Exploded Views of Bedford, L'Orient, and Gibson Mounds and Manipulations: (a–b) Bedford Mound 10/11 and 12 (from Perino 1970); (c–d) L'Orient Mounds 1 and 2 (from Perino n.d.); (e–f) Gibson Mounds 2 and 5 (from Perino 1970) (Courtesy of the Center for American Archaeology and The Gilcrease Museum)

with a peripheral female burial (similar to one found with a female tomb burial in Mound 10). This also appears to be a direct reconfiguration of these Type 2 mounds' depositional practices.

Soon after the tomb of Mound 11b was inserted between primary Mounds 10 and 11a, both of these mounds were subsumed by the moundfill of 11b—in an apparent act of circumscription. Such an act would have erased the separate identity of these primary mounds. However, this does not appear to be the end of this controversy at these mounds. Sometime later, a separate construction effort was begun. This involved the mounding of earth over both primary mounds, resulting in the outward appearance of two enormous mounds (around seventy feet wide and twenty-two feet high each). Such an effort would have helped reinstate the identities of primary Mounds 10 and 11a, possibly orchestrated by the communities that built the earlier mounds (see top of figure 7.2a).

Bedford Mound 9

Next in the sequence was Mound 9. This is a solitary mound that contains a significant attempt to conciliate the predominant mound type with Bedford Type 2 mounds. This attempt also helps to account for the evolution of the predominant mound type into Type 4. Despite conforming to the predominant mound type in every other way, the central tomb in Mound 9 contains a semi-articulated adolescent, the only predominant Type 1 tomb to contain a postnatal individual. However, this individual is still semiprocessed, with several limbs missing, and is not associated with any artifacts. A cache of grave goods is instead placed at the other end of the tomb, distinctly separate from the body but associated with the tomb instead.

The concession of leaving remains in a Type 1 tomb (albeit without grave goods) is continued in Mound 8b. However, when the final dissenting Bedford tomb (burial 21, Mound 4a) contained a female with bear teeth, an artifact only associated with male leaders and children, a large tomb was built directly over it containing an articulated male with bear teeth. This central burial appears to be a concession to the dissident Type 2 tradition while being an overt reaction to the represented gender of leadership.

Overt distinctions clearly were made between burial practices, despite any concessions. A significant deposit in Mound 9 is an effigy pipe that appears to reference similar deposits in Mounds 12a and 11a. On a log wall at the head of the tomb was found an intentionally broken effigy pipe. This is similar to an intentionally broken effigy pipe placed on a log wall at the head of the tomb in Mound 12a. Both pipes were sprinkled with red ochre. Mound 11a also contained an antler point placed in the same context. However, while the effigy in Mound 12a was of a beaver in a defensive position, the effigy in Mound 9 was of a raven. A raven effigy pipe was also found at the head of an intrusive tomb in Gibson Mound 4b, depicted in the act of pecking the face of a human corpse. The placement of a raven effigy pipe in Mound 9 (a processing facility) in the same context as the beaver effigy in Mound 12a (which lacked processing) appears to be an explicit reference to the practice of burial processing as one of the core paradigmatic bases of the predominant representation.

These explicit references illustrate Latour's statement that "trials trace the limit of a paradigm . . . what holds tightly and what gives way easily, what is negotiable and what is not" (Latour 1987, 201).

L'Orient Mounds

The mounds at the L'Orient Mound Cemetery also contained evidence of conflict, but between Type 3 and Type 1 mounds. Both L'Orient Mounds 1a and 2 contained simple subfloor pit tombs with rounded ends and slanted sides, but no log crib (see figures 7.2c-d). Mound 1a is similar to the dissident Bedford mounds in that its tomb contained three articulated interments with no evidence of processing. Around the neck of one adult was a string of large shell beads made from a conch columella, and near the skull of another was an Archaic Elm Point plummet, grooved for suspension. The L'Orient Mound 2 tomb had two adult males (at right angles to each other), one with a necklace of freshwater pearl beads and the other with shell beads around its ankles.

Surrounding both tombs were wide semicircles of subfloor pits with rounded corners and slanted sides (like the central tombs) containing extended and articulated burials. The peripheral burials around both tombs contained no artifacts.

This radical change in tomb structure from a log crib to just a subfloor pit tomb may represent a further development from earlier challenges. The similarity between central tombs and peripheral pits is evident at Klunk Mound 1a and 1b and Bedford Mounds 10 and 8a in terms of their size and floor level, but appears to be taken a step further at L'Orient Mounds 1a and 2. Together with the lack of a log crib, the similarity in shape between the central burial and peripheral burials—both having rounded ends and slanted sides—suggests that an image of equality between the two was sought. Other mounds with simple primary pit tombs at their center include Bedford Mound 4A, Elizabeth Mound 3, Gibson Mounds 2 and 5, and Lawrence Gay Mounds 1 and 3 in the Mississippi Valley, many of which also have slanted sides. The position of these mounds toward the end of cemetery sequences suggests that this development may have been a late one and explains why these mounds have been classified as Type 3 mounds.

Before L'Orient Mound 1a was even mounded over, Tomb A was destroyed by fire and a large Type 1 log tomb was constructed directly over it (see figure 7.2c). The tomb was one log high, but followed most of the criteria for Type 1 mounds and contained nine flexed and headless processed skeletons without associated artifacts.

Two subfloor graves south of the tomb also contained flexed articulated burials without heads, and a flexed surface burial was placed to the east. These burials likely represented the leadership in this representation—usually placed at the periphery of the tomb in Type 1 mounds.

Below the southern edge of the tomb was a shallow trench, which contained other isolated bones, possibly dragged there from the tomb by birds involved in processing the tomb burials.

This tomb again illustrates the contrast between the Type 1 tradition and the alternative dissident tradition. The large number of processed burials and the "faceless" nature of them—they were decapitated—contrasts distinctly with the three and two articulated interments of Mounds 1a and 2 respectively. The unusual deliberateness evident in the decapitation of all individuals in the tomb as well as those in its two peripheral graves suggests that an explicit statement was being made by a Type 1 group, possibly with the remains of Type 3 dissidents. In a similar way to the intrusive Klunk and Bedford Mounds, the builders of L'Orient Mound 1b appear to have been pushed to forcefully demonstrate the nature of Type 1 burial practice, as is so often the case when ideas are threatened. In this case it appears that the destruction of identity inherent in this mass decapitation extended not only to the members of the community, but also to the leadership, demonstrating some exclusivity of the leadership while illustrating its affinity with the community.

The violence with which this statement was made may have also been a demonstration of oppression and a warning to other challengers. The heads of inhumations were removed long before many of the burials were decomposed, indicating their forcible removal, either before or after death. One of the decapitated peripheral burials also contained a broken projectile point—possibly the cause of this individual's death. Taken all together, the evidence for the destruction of Tomb A, the sudden construction (directly over Tomb A) of Tomb B, and the decapitation of burials in Tomb B indicate a high level of conflict and the possible use of dissenters' bodies for the statement.

After Tomb B was roofed with limestone slabs, it too was destroyed by fire, followed by the scattering of burnt material over the ground surface, indicating that this tomb perhaps met with a similar fate to Tomb A. In a similar way to the action taken at Bedford Mound 10/11 that reinstated the identity of primary Mounds 10 and 11 after having been subsumed by Tomb C, this final action may have been a counteraction by the dissenting community.

Interestingly, L'Orient Mound 2 lacks an intrusive tomb excavated into the top of it. This is unusual for mounds that contain challenging traits and suggests that this mound may have represented a pivotal stage in the controversy when challengers were no longer suppressed at this cemetery. Mounds with similar configurations and no evidence of suppression include late dissenters such as Elizabeth Mound 1 and 3 and Klunk Mound 11 Tomb B, suggesting that it was at this stage in the various controversies that power was ceded from the Type 1 tradition.

Gibson Mounds

A similar controversy to the L'Orient controversy appears to have occurred simultaneously at the Gibson Mounds (see figure 7.2e–f). After Gibson Mound 3, which appears to have been an abstract amalgamation of traits from both traditions, and Gibson Mound 1, for which there is little information, Gibson Mounds 2a and 5a were constructed.

Gibson Mounds 2a and 5a were built on the third and fourth highest natural knolls overlooking the Kampsville tributary valley and the Illinois River, and were almost identical. Both contained two primary subfloor pit tombs with articulated burials encircled by articulated peripheral burials in similar subfloor pits. Except for a domestic Baehr vessel and beads with an infant in 2a, the only artifacts in both mounds were deposited with the tomb burials. These included a galena cube, fragments of mica, and a fragment of a turtle carapace with an articulated male in a Mound 5a pit tomb and a Havana Hopewell vessel with shell, pearl, and copper beads beside an articulated male in a Mound 2a pit tomb.

In a similar way to L'Orient Mounds 1a and 2, the correspondence between these tombs and their peripheral burials may be an attempt to represent an equality between the leadership and the community. Both mounds have subfloor pit tombs of similar shape, length, and depth to peripheral burials. The only distinction is the position and artifact associations of the central interments. The division of the central features into two separate pits may be significant too. Other Type 3 mounds have two or three central interments within their tombs, and L'Orient Mound 2 has two males in separate pits that cross each other. In a similar way to Bedford Mound 8 Tomb A, Gibson Mounds 2a and 5a may represent a proposed division of power into two separate parts. The placement of two adults and a child in one of the central pits in Mound 2a suggests that the two central pits possibly represented two separate families. In this case the division of the concept of leadership into two separate parts may have represented a proposed division of power between two different lineages.

Before the central pits and burials of Mounds 2a and 5a were even covered with moundfill, intrusive log tombs with ramps were built on top of the burials, partially destroying the central pit tombs (see figure 7.2e–f). It appears that these intrusions were part of an immediate clampdown upon the differences in burial practice. Both intrusive tombs were chinked with green clay and contained evidence of processing like other Type 1 tombs.

Peripheral burials were also associated with the intrusive tombs in clusters at the side of the tombs, like at other Type 1 mounds, but some were disarticulated and possibly the remains of burials scattered from the tombs. The only artifacts were deposited with two peripheral burials in 5b, including a Hopewell vessel and a pair of wolf mandibles.

Even before they were covered, both intrusive tombs were also destroyed, with their logs burnt and removed to one side and their processed remains scattered over the ramps. It may be that the community of Mounds 2a and 5a was responsible for the destruction of the intrusive tombs. An indication that violence was involved is the presence of one articulated individual lying facedown in the debris strewn over the ground surface from Tomb 2b. The mound construction was then built, centered over Tomb 2a rather than Tomb 2b, indicating that the dissident community then finished it.

Calibration of Knowledge

The structural differences between Type 1 and dissident Type 3 mounds, fought so hard for during these controversies, would have only been effective in impressing or acting at a distance on others if the connections between the symbolic configurations and their referents were made clear to others. Latour argues that the extension of influence is proportionate to two major factors: first, the active support of dissenters by others who promote their alternative representations. Secondly, the development of metrological devices that allow people to make the connection between the models represented and the real world (Latour 1987, 249; also Richards 1993, 175).

There are several instances of support during these controversies in the pairs of challenges—at Klunk Mounds 1a and 1b, Bedford Mounds 11a and 12a, L'Orient Mounds 1a and 2, and Gibson Mounds 5 and 2. Each of the mounds involved in controversies appears to support another mound, and there is clearly a high level of communication between these communities, indicating that support was given to other challengers along the southern part of the valley, although each has their own separate issues with the predominant practice.

Metrological devices that help communicate the conclusions drawn at centers of calculation (such as burial mounds) with the actual lived world can be any use of artifacts or structures drawn from the lived world and used in centers of calculation (or vice versa). By calibrating symbols used in representations with ordinary objects, the conclusions drawn in centers of calculation can be extended, just as lab conditions are extended to enable facts to work outside of laboratories. However, before Gibson Mound 2 there were few instances of artifacts with peripheral burials (or any other devices) that linked them with the populace. The placement of a Baehr vessel (a common domestic ceramic) with Gibson Mound 2 burial 5, an infant peripheral to the central pits, may represent just such a metrological device enabling a correspondence of association between ritual and real domestic life. By connecting the abstract representation of the populace in peripheral burials with the populace themselves, the idea may have been to fix meaning and ensure the extension of ideational influence from representations in burial rituals. Several mounds that correspond with this Type 3 tradition of creating links with lived existence include Gibson Mound 1a, Mound 3 and Knoll C, and L'Orient Mound 2a, which also have Baehr jars associated with peripheral burials (and usually infants). The coexistence of a Hopewell vessel (in the tomb) and a Baehr vessel (in a peripheral grave) in the same mound indicates that this ceramic dichotomy was not a chronological one, as has been suggested by Lower Illinois Valley archaeologists, but represented a significant ideological contrast.

The construction of mounds in the floodplain around this time (mainly by the Type 1 tradition) may represent another strategy to extend the influence of ideas by bringing the mounds into the domestic realm. Several floodplain mounds contain utilitarian artifacts like knapping tools and abraders (Bullington 1988, 237) and domestic pottery (this time Pike ware under Kamp Mound 9).

However, cemeteries on the valley bluffs tell a different story and appear to have had a different function. Type 3 mounds tend to exist toward the end of cemetery sequences, and the lack of elaboration in the intrusive Type 1 mounds over them, or the later destruction of these Type 1 intrusions and the lack of further censure (at L'Orient Mound 2, Gibson Knoll C, Elizabeth Mounds 1 and 3), suggest that there was a slackening of power and control wielded by the Type 1 tradition over these communities toward the end of the Hopewell.

Late Hopewell Mounds

At the end of the Hopewell period there is actually a marked amalgamation of traits from both traditions, with more localized representations evident at the cemeteries excavated and less conflict. Whether this was a result of constant compromises, or whether there ceased to be the same level of central control, it is difficult to establish. However, developed Type 1 mounds dating to the later part of the Hopewell provide indications. These include Gibson Mound 4 and Klunk Mound 11, mounds placed at the least prominent points of their cemeteries although still involved in controversies. Both are discussed in relation to other mounds that were built at the end of the Hopewell period. These provide useful information regarding the terminal stages of the Hopewell period and pertain to the transition between the Hopewell and the Late Woodland period.

Gibson Mound 4

After Gibson Mounds 2 and 5 were built on the last knolls available on the bluff promontory, Gibson Mound 4 was constructed further back from the bluff edge. This first consisted of a Type 3 pit tomb dug into the ground surface, which was then immediately suppressed before the tomb could be used. This suppression took the form of a large circular earthen platform built over the primary tomb with a large Type 4 tomb built on top of it. The lack of information about the primary tomb unfortunately prevents it from being discussed.

Before Tomb B was constructed, a deep posthole (three feet eight inches deep) was excavated into the platform and chinked with limestone slabs. This may be evidence for a large ritual pole that would have stood on the platform before Tomb B was built and may have been the focus for pre-Tomb B ritual.

Tomb B was built in the center of the platform, over Tomb A and the posthole, consisting of a large two-log-high crib with large ramps. It contained evidence for processing activity, but it also contained the articulated skeletons of an adult male and a child with a large number of artifacts. The male was associated with a hafted copper adze, six copper ear spools, seven projectile points, six bear canines, seven hundred pearl beads, and forty identical platform beads, while the child had three platform pipes. These were similar to artifacts with males at other Type 4 Mounds. At the head of the tomb lay a pipe effigy of a raven pecking the face of a human.

The effigy pipe of a raven pecking a human face is in a similar location to a raven effigy in Bedford Mound 9 and appears to emphasize the processing activity that went on at both of these mounds. Such an explicit representation placed in such a prominent location implies that the constructor of Tomb B was pressed to outline the basis of contestation, just as Latour argues happens when ideas are threatened (Latour 1987, 205).

However, the placement of articulated individuals in the tomb in the same way as other Type 4 tombs implies that a transformation of representation took place at this time, probably as the result of compromises with the challenging tradition. Other Late Hopewell Type 4 Mounds with individual interments are Bedford Mound 4 Tomb B, L'Orient Mound 1 Tomb B, Carter Mound 1, Montezuma Mound 1, and Klunk Mound 11 Tomb A, all of which exist at the end of cemetery sequences and have similar artifact assemblages.

Peripheral to the tomb ramps lay two burials: an articulated child and an articulated female with limestone slabs covering her grave on the ground surface. Both burials lay outside the periphery of the prepared platform, under the edge of the mound. This is identical to some Type 1 peripheral configurations that represented a nuclear family outside of the tomb ramp, except that in this case the male burial was placed in the tomb. The division of the leader's family between the center and the periphery of Mound 4 indicates that while the community was still represented as central in society by being processed in the tomb, the leadership was represented at the center of the microcosm, and probably used as a medium for the expression of leadership in the tomb.

While this expression differed between localities, all of the other Late Hopewell Type 4 central tombs also contained males surrounded by a few burials on the periphery (see table 7.1). While it is not always clear whether any of these constituted the family of the leader, the placement of a Hopewell vessel with the only burial, a woman and child, on the west side of the tomb in Klunk Mound 11 Tomb A is a strong indication that the leadership was represented in both the center and the periphery in this instance, too.

SUMMARY

While a general survey of mounds in the region is useful to identify predominant and alternative mound types, the only way to understand the reasons for the various representations and their development is by following the trajectories of particular controversies and what each community involved saw as important. At the Bedford Mound cemetery, the male/female dichotomy between Mounds 12a and 11a and the continuous placement of solely females in Type 2 central tombs for the duration of the controversy indicates that the gender of leadership was a nonnegotiable issue for the dissident Bedford community. This was the only community that held such a different view in the valley, but it may have helped stimulate an evolution of the predominant Type 1 mound type into Type 4 mounds with male burials at the center.

Other communities in the valley involved in controversy, such as those that built the dissident Gibson, L'Orient, and Elizabeth mounds, stressed the equality between central and peripheral burials through a similarity between their central and peripheral grave structures. Yet all of these central graves contained some indication of being special in some way, indicating that they represented leaders. L'Orient Mound 2 and Gibson Mounds 2a and 5a also split their central tombs into two simple graves indicating some sort of division of leadership.

Nevertheless, several traits were common to all dissenters. Each controversy in the Valley stresses the importance of the position and type of burial within mounds. All dissident communities express both a resistance to being picked clean by birds and removed from the site, and a desire to be buried articulated around the central graves in the position normally reserved for Type 1 leaders. This indicates that the challenge was partly a challenge to the microcosmic representation of community identity and the sociologic behind burial processing. The placement of leaders at the center of the mound, in simple tombs or graves, indicates a challenge to the Type 1 representation of leadership as a peripheral player—since they were placed outside the central tomb. Yet dissenters also challenged Type 1 exclusivity (as Type 1 leaders and their families were usually the only articulated individuals in mounds). The fact that the communities that suppressed these dissident mounds reacted to the position and articulation of leaders in the tomb, often explicitly outlining the nature of their disagreement, indicates that these traits were highly significant. These reactions illustrate Latour's statement that "it is only when there is a dispute, as long as it lasts, and depending on the strength exerted by dissenters, that words such as 'culture,' 'paradigm' or 'society' may receive a precise meaning" (Latour 1987, 201).

At the general level, the examination of fifty mounds (their differences, similarities, distributions, and interactions) offers several possible conclusions as to who the dissidents were. In 2005 I suggested two possible conclusions as to who these different groups were (Martin 2005). The first possibility was that two different groups came together in the valley to take advantage of the rich natural resources there, one from the north and one from the west. The predominant (Type 1) mound has many similar traits to mounds in the Central Illinois Valley, including the placement of tombs on prepared surfaces, the processing of multiple burials in the tomb, and the absence of peripheral burial rings (Bullington 1988, 238–9). The other mound types (Types 2 and 3) have traits similar to mounds west of the Illinois valley (Lawrence Gay Mounds) and in Missouri, where Baehr vessels (also placed in Type 3 mounds in the Lower Illinois Valley) are present (James Brown pers. comm. 2002). In terms of general spatial distribution, Type 1 mounds also occur predominantly in the northern part of the Lower Illinois Valley and may have been in place long before the other group. Type 2 and 3 mounds also exist predominantly in the southern half of the valley (see figure 7.3). However, a recent DNA test of skeletons from the Klunk/Gibson cemeteries has established that there was no significant difference between Type 2 burials and intrusive Type 1 burials (Bolnick and Smith 2007).

While there is a likelihood that the dead used in the intrusive Type 1 tombs to make a statement of dominance were actually the local people from oppressed communities and not individuals from the northern part of the valley, the second possible conclusion may be more likely, given the general similarity between burial structures from the north and the south of the Lower Illinois Valley. This was the possibility that a schism may have formed within the northern group that led to the formation of dissident communities in the south, later spreading ideas to (rather than from) communities in Missouri and along the Mississippi (Martin 2005, 308).

In either case, it appears that at some point Type 1 communities struggled with Type 2 and 3 communities for ideological control, precipitated either by population density and a scarcity of resources (Charles 1992) or the threat to ideology that such prominent differences posed. In our own time the attack on September 11, 2001 brutally illustrated that symbolic structures are the first places likely to be struck by others who differ in worldviews. Similarly, in the Hopewell, the struggle was manifested by

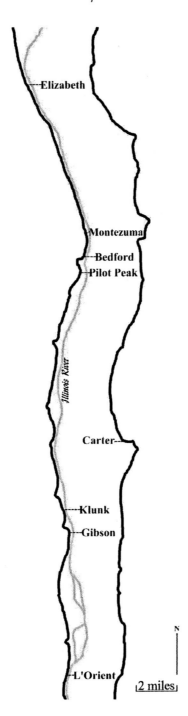

Figure 7.3.   The Lower Illinois Valley with Sites Mentioned in the Text.

the excavation of Type 1 tombs directly into the top of Type 2 and Type 3 mounds and the entire circumscription of those primary mounds by larger encompassing Type 1 mounds. The fact that several of these intrusive tombs (Bedford Mound 11b, Gibson Mound 5b) or other Type 1 tombs (Elizabeth Mounds 6 and 7, Pilot Peak 1, Montezuma mounds 9 and 15) were burnt and destroyed (something that does not occur in the Central Illinois Valley and therefore is not likely to be a cultural trait) indicates that Type 2 communities may have reciprocated through the destruction of the intrusive Type 1 tombs. Mounds involved in contestation are also often accompanied by acts such as the decapitation of all bodies deposited in L'Orient Mound 1b or the placement of bodies facedown with their hands and feet tied behind them (Elizabeth 3, burial 13; Klunk 11, burial 44; Gibson Mound 2; Pilot Peak 3, burial 1). While it is possible that these acts had a more symbolic role, it should not be discounted that in some cases their presence may indicate violence.

Nevertheless, there seems to have been a rapprochement between communities over the duration of these interactions as compromises were made by both groups in the structure of their representations. The eventual fruit of these compromises was the development of Late Hopewell amalgamations of the two traditions. Rather than conforming to a rigid valley-wide model, these mounds can be loosely defined as "Type 4" mounds (differing slightly between cemeteries) (see table 7.1). Many of these Type 4 mounds, having resulted from a local controversy, are best understood by following each controversy that precipitated their evolution. Where these Type 4 mounds occur, they are sometimes the last Hopewell mound type to be built at these cemeteries (Bedford Mound 4a, Gibson Mound 6, and Klunk Mound 13) indicating that such an amalgamation of world views succeeded in diffusing some of the controversies. Otherwise, Type 3 dissident mounds are the last to be built (L'Orient Mound 2 and Elizabeth Mounds 1 and 3) indicating that no such compromise was reached.

DISCUSSION

The graphic nature of these interactions between traditions, involving multiple cases of destruction, suppression, appropriation, and redefinition, indicates that these burial mounds were by no means just the final resting places for the dead. They appear to be the center of ongoing conflicts over truth—an issue, arguably, of the upmost importance to the living. As this case study has hopefully illustrated, by following the controversies between different traditions we can trace their associations, as groups were driven to express what they held dearest. As the history of archaeological interpretation in the Lower Illinois Valley has shown, any attempt to understand burial practices *generally*—through conflating mounds from all cemeteries and traditions to come up with a single archetype and explanation—has resulted in abject confusion or superficiality.

Joseph Tainter was one of the first to attempt a general understanding of society in the Lower Illinois Valley. He formulated his highly influential theory that burial variation reflects differences in social hierarchy from his PhD research on the Klunk and Gibson mounds. With the help of bone variation tables (assuming that less joint degeneration reflects higher status) and estimates of the level of effort involved in burial practices, he came up with twenty-seven different levels of burial treatment that he equated with a complex social hierarchy (Tainter 1978, 1980). Others, through general analyses of the whole valley, have concluded that Hopewell society was more egalitarian, arguing that Tainter's multiple levels of treatment cross-cut categories of age and sex (David Braun 1981), or that society was feudal because adults are rarely associated with artifacts and therefore did not have enough generational stability to be attended well (Richard Kerber 1986). However, the basis of all these explanations is the absence of any consistent patterns or correlations over the whole region, or even over one cemetery—not a very sound basis for an explanation. Such general analyses have resulted in the currently accepted explanation that mounds were "contexts where random variability may occur" (Buikstra et al. 1998, 92).

However, as has been illustrated in this case study, the adoption of a general analysis, even for one Hopewell cemetery, has great difficulty in comprehending variation in both time and representation. While general analyses can be good at identifying the various common types of structures and practices that exist, the reasons for variation or change are unique depending upon particular historical and contextual circumstances, so general analyses cannot comprehend the dynamics behind that change or any anomalies that exist at the interface of changes. Understanding change requires a very different approach, a more focused approach.

In the same way, once a focused approach is adopted, general interpretations of change cannot be imposed upon this data either, whether from anthropological analogies or from other areas, but must emerge from the detailed examination of each place examined. General explanations assume that historical and contextual circumstances are secondary to invisible social or natural forces, forces whose existence is purely the result of modernist perceptions of agency (see chapter 1). A small knowledge of non-modern society is enough to understand that fundamental differences in structure and burial practice would never have been stimulated by something as trivial or general as status. In non-modern societies that see no separation between nature and culture, radical differences in rituals and ceremonial sites represent differences in the representation of culture and its relationship to nature. Such differences in configuration have enormous repercussions for the natural/cultural order. Because of the repercussions that changes in representations present, few major changes ever occur in non-modern cultures. This can be seen in the past, especially in burial practices, as is evidenced by the longevity of burial practices in the British Neolithic.

It is not surprising therefore to find evidence for violent reprisals against Type 2 mounds by Type 1 groups unhappy with major dissent on their doorstep. Violence in the Illinois Hopewell, including the destruction of tombs by fire, the scattering of logs and remains over ramps, the decapitation of bodies and burial of others facedown, has usually been interpreted as part of a cultural milieu of practices. However, the fact that these instances occur primarily in mounds involved in interactions between two very different burial practices, and rarely anywhere else, sheds a very different light on them.

It is also not insignificant that the mounds involved in violent interactions exhibit the largest amount of wealth and effort expenditure in Illinois, and are among the largest for the Eastern Woodlands Hopewell. Each community involved in such a contestation appears to have striven to make their contrasting burial practice the very best representation to date. The Klunk and Gibson cemeteries have some of the most spectacular mounds and deposits in Illinois, and this may be one reason why they are used so often for studies of the Hopewell, to the exclusion of many other well-excavated cemeteries in the Lower Illinois Valley and countless more north of the valley. Like the focus of British archaeologists on the most dramatic burial mounds of Early Bronze Age Wessex—which were often the result of controversies and therefore are anomalous—this focus on the most visible mounds in the Illinois Hopewell has also confused taxonomies due to their involvement in controversies.

What is most interesting about these interactions, however, is the process of change that occurs over the duration of each of these controversies. The politics of borrowing artifacts and traits from opposing groups and using them for their own purposes to illustrate how they are different or to make compromises is fascinating. It illustrates Latour's maxim that through trials between groups some traits are found to be negotiable and others not, resulting in the change in representations on both sides (Latour 1987, 201). While more radiocarbon dates would be helpful to provide a more reliable sequence, it is doubtful that they would give as good a sequence as the topographical one since it appears that most sequences occurred within only a few years at most. Without following the trajectory of these controversies, none of the changes in artifact association, the reasons for traits being adopted, or the non-negotiable traits would ever have been identified. What is needed is a method that can adapt to fast-moving change in associations while understanding long-term change.

Furthermore, the knowledge that several different understandings of the world using the same repertoire of artifacts may exist within one culture or area should stimulate archaeologists to use better databases that can identify different uses of the same artifacts or traits. The possibility that interactions between these different understandings may be the catalysts for the development of new forms or practices makes this need all the more pressing. Databases (such as Modes 1.99) that enable different contexts to be identified, indexed, and compared provide a much better taxonomic tool for identifying the variety of artifact uses.

Finally, Latour's methodology of following interactions between different representations in order to identify the elements and chains of association behind each statement provides an ideal method for archaeologists to examine the definitions of these representations and to follow their development. Through the intricate reconstruction and comparison of sequences of action and reaction, many illuminating details and references can emerge that would be missed by an analysis that concentrates on identifying general archetypes. Such findings should alert archaeologists to the danger of "characterizing" a region, culture, or time period, a practice that neglects differences and any interactions between them and ends up merely perpetuating neo-evolutionary stereotypes. By following variability and how it interacts with and affects others, a richer picture of worldviews and their development can be pieced together that does not preclude a general cultural understanding.   ·

Conclusion

Interpreting ritual and other cultural sites and objects has always been considered a highly subjective activity for archaeologists. As a result, many have rejected such interpretation as futile. Imposing on the past theories constructed from contemporary ethnographic, sociological, or even psychological studies has often been seen as a specious means of interpretation because those borrowed theories are constructed from the contextual details of their particular studies. However, there has never been much choice, with no other (less arbitrary) solution having been identified for organizing the disparate pieces of data found on excavations into coherent interpretations.

The ingenious solution found by historians and sociologists of science to understand the past appears to enable us to get around this problem. It was clear to them that the arbitrary selection and organization of data that occurs when contemporary theories are used to explain past actions cannot be remedied by finding a better theory or analogy. There needs to be a way for information from the past to help form interpretations in the same way that natural elements make an impact upon their explanation in science without being overdetermined by extant scientific theories. The problem with conceiving such a way, however, has been that scientific practice is largely misconceived by the social sciences. From the assumption that universal laws govern the natural and social world, science is seen to operate by finding theories and applying them like hypotheses— backed up by finding evidence to support them or by avoiding falsification. The theoretical and empirical problems with such a conception of scientific practice have long been recognized by social scientists. But instead of proposing a better understanding of science, the postmodernist reaction has been to believe that this approach is how scientists actually operate and therefore that they have little likelihood of finding truth. Yet, without a better understanding of scientific practice, this is the approach that postmodernists have come to use too, with the *proviso* that as a result their own conclusions must ultimately be fanciful too. This conception may be the social sciences' understanding of what scientific method involves, but numerous anthropologies of science have revealed a very different process. It is only by following the actual process of science, translated for the social sciences, that we can begin to interpret the past faithfully.

From years of anthropological work in the sciences, sociologists of science have established that science is not so much the proposition and falsification of theories as the continuous reduction and combination of information into encrypted objects or formulas that then explain that information or predict it. It is this local nature of science that makes it able to be so accurate. As Latour argues, it is really the systematic examination and reduction of information and the ability of objects to "object" to their interpretation that makes science so "objective." In order to remain systematic and to allow objects to "object," it is necessary to always keep analysis to the local level and to acknowledge the reality of the objects under study. If scientific practice is overdetermined by theories, the "objections" from objects cannot be heard.

Once such an analysis was conducted on cultural objects and actions, it was not long before it was realized that culture represented a significant amount of "reality" as well. Objects that had been considered mere symbols of a cultural system of references began to be understood as formulas of a scientific understanding of sorts. But how had this conception of culture been missing for so long? It was clear that without attributing any reality to culture—or in other words, a level of natural information encrypted into culture—sociologists and anthropologists had long applied purely social theories to cultural actions despite their informants claiming that these actions referred to nature. Were they merely ignoring their informants as ignorant of the reasons behind their own actions?

As historians of science researched the origins of this modernist separation between culture and nature, it became clear that the separation was more likely an expedient solution to a political problem in the 1660s than an actual division. The danger of allowing others, apart from a select few, to determine what truth is, was seen as too much of a threat then and is arguably still seen as too much of a threat today. A false dichotomy is believed to be a small price to pay for civil peace and prosperity. However, a faithful description of scientific practice is far less of a threat than it was ever believed to be. There is still an enormous difference in scale and scope between culture and science to distinguish them and to explain the difference in efficacy between them. Yet the correction of our understanding of science has the potential to vastly benefit both science and the social sciences.

Having structured our ontology, spawned modernist and postmodernist theory, and consequently contorted our understanding of scientific and cultural practice, this flawed dichotomy between nature and culture will continue to erode both anthropology and archaeology and many other disciplines too if it is not corrected. Fortunately many in the sciences and social sciences have begun to reevaluate fundamental assumptions in their disciplines that were based upon this dichotomy. The realization that our theories and interpretive practices can no longer be relied upon, since the foundational premise behind them was a flawed ontology, has led many to seek a new philosophy, as well as a new methodology, to explain scientific and cultural practices.

From numerous anthropological studies of Western science, and from indigenous accounts of their own cultural activity, a new philosophy has emerged in the philosophy of science that has the potential to unify the humanities and the sciences. This philosophy has begun to help archaeology too, primarily since it purports to explain the pre-modern as well as Western science and culture. One of the most important aspects of this new philosophy is its profoundly different understanding of cultural objects. No longer can objects be understood as merely irrational symbols formed from purely mental constructs or as functionally useful social currency. As representations of both natural and cultural phenomena, objects in this new philosophy are seen as encryptions of information — as gatherings of heterogeneous associations that are either black-boxed and used without knowledge of the networks of relationships that comprise them, or are part of controversies in which these networks are reevaluated and explicitly represented. The fact that these representations are not merely symbols or cultural capital, but are central to the prediction and organization of natural/social phenomena, has enabled a number of theoretical problems to be solved. The solutions to these problems have also opened up several interesting avenues of political relevance for archaeology.

First, this new understanding of objects helps us to understand the power that objects have over individuals and how they contain the agencies for action — agencies that archaeologists have generally sought in external theories about individual behavior or macro structures. The reason that objects are so powerful comes from how they are created, adapted, and used. Traditionally, objects have been viewed as symbolic props for cultural ideas or functionalist schemes, and therefore the indigenous belief that objects are powerful enough to influence actions has been viewed as misguided at best, or fetishistic at worst. However, when it is understood that indigenous objects are the end point of a vast network of natural and cultural associations and relationships — the same type of network that enables scientific objects to exert powerful forces on us today — we can begin to understand how objects can exert influence.

Just as formulas are created by reducing information about the world into symbols and combining those symbols to represent the contextual relationships between them, so cultural objects are encryptions of natural/cultural information and the relationships between them. Not only does this enable objects to communicate knowledge of the natural and cultural world, but it also enables the natural and cultural world to be controlled and even predicted. As the examples of indigenous science in chapter 3 illustrate, the correct understanding of the world is a matter of life or death for many people. In our own culture, the correct understanding of the world, which determines how to maintain health and live safely, is perhaps one the most powerful influences on one's actions. However, without an acknowledgment of the integration of natural as well as cultural knowledge in indigenous encryptions, the very real power of objects to influence actions will never be grasped.

Such an acknowledgment also has the ability to lend enormous respect to indigenous knowledge systems. Without allowing indigenous knowledge systems any relationship to reality, these systems have commonly been seen as quaint or ridiculous. This means that however much indigenous knowledge is tolerated as a quasi-religious system—by seeing it as one of a multitude of so-called equal cultural systems—unless it is accorded some reality, it will always be essentially treated with the indifference that Western science treats theories that have been disproved. Such a subtle devaluation of their culture has proved disastrous for Native American self-esteem and for many other indigenous populations. But with the understanding that all science is a reduction of local information about the world and that different information combinations produce different conclusions, conclusions in indigenous science are not necessarily false but instead refer to different things at different scales. While Western science may be more accurate in the broader sense due to its scope, this difference between them gives indigenous systems a niche in our Western culture and means that much can be learned from indigenous knowledge.

Second, this new perception of objects is the basis for a new understanding of cultural groups—one that avoids the problems associated with primordialist and instrumentalist models. Objects have always been crucial for identifying affinity with cultural groups. By drawing similarities between object forms, cultural similarities have traditionally been drawn. But using object forms to classify groups, either overtly or unconsciously through the use of typology in its many archaeological manifestations, has had the unfortunate effect of perpetuating a view of culture as monocultural. The search for similarities in the archaeological record and the belief that objects have only one function and attribution means that differences in object use and affinity have been neglected and the opportunity to identify other groups within overarching cultural archetypes has been missed. While processualists and post-processualists overtly rejected the categorization of cultures as a research goal, both have continued, in various ways, to classify cultures or deny cultural groupings based on object form. Moreover, by applying theories to even wider regions, they have embraced the conception of culture as monocultural on an even greater scale.

However, with the understanding that objects are encryptions of information, and that assemblages comprise higher order combinations of those encryptions that define particular worldviews, it is the *use* of objects (or their *context*) that becomes important for classifying different groups. By defining groups according to their context or particular understanding of the world, groups become much more local affairs, although constellations of similar understandings can be charted. The many ethnographic examples of conflict between groups that have similar artifact forms and sites (and who sometimes even live in the same area) illustrate that ostensibly homogenous regions are by no means monocultural but contain an array of differing groups. These groups from the past are finally able to be identified—not just through their different traits, but by their different configurations of similar traits. Rather than attributing these groups to modern categories of gender, ethnicity, age, or class, the particular differences over which groups differ are able to be identified by following the *use* of objects.

The common failure to spot differences between groups illustrates the lack of importance that modernists and postmodernists have accorded objects and their particular configurations. Part of this neglect is due to the lack of natural information believed to be encrypted by objects. Without the realization that objects represent scientific understandings of the world that are a matter of life and death to people, objects are not seen as having importance enough to structure differences between groups. While anthropologies of science have uncovered how objects are powerful enough to structure differences between groups, they have also helped to explain why a large number of objects are shared by differing groups. Instead of "reinventing the wheel" and using unfamiliar objects to set out different understandings, groups in science use the same encryptions in different configurations (Latour and Woolgar 1979, 119). This is a far less costly way than changing all the encryptions, and helps give the appearance of continuity while actually reconfiguring object meaning. This is what Christianity, Rome, and many other successful colonial enterprises (including the Beaker Culture) did best when taking over conquered cultures—aligning their gods and traditions with resident ones while giving the appearance of no change (Cajete 2000, 89).

Third, this new understanding of objects explains the existence of controversies and violence between groups over differing images. Until recently, archaeology has failed to explain or even to recognize controversies or violence over representations. Cultures have commonly been assumed to be monocultural and therefore relatively peaceful (Snead 2008; Arkush 2008). However, unless objects are seen to represent natural as well as cultural phenomena, there is little perception of them as representing actual reality, and it is hard to see groups with differing representations as having any reason to differ. This means that differing groups and their representations in the archaeological record are easily conflated by archaeologists, who lump them together and ignore any conflicts between them. Instead of seeing instances of violence as a fortuitous window into conflicting cultural groups and their understandings of reality, violence is usually assumed to be opportunistic or merely ritualistic and part of a culture's practices. Even today, as overwhelming evidence for violence toward objects can no longer be ignored by archaeologists, this violence is merely explained in terms of strife over status differences (Dye and King 2007).

In our own culture today, the lack of any relation between culture and nature has allowed differing religions and ideologies to generally coexist peacefully in society because of the categorization of culture as purely subjective. It is easy to abide the coexistence of multiple differing representations of the world at the same time and place if they are seen as purely cultural and as not having any relation to reality. However, this perception has the deleterious effect of preventing us from understanding other cultures from the past or at the fringes of the modern world, who take differences in representations very seriously. Thus the general view of culture and religion as subjective has had the unfortunate result of preventing the West from understanding conflicts between religious groups within societies like Turkey or Iraq, between the West and the Middle East, or even within our own countries. Without an understanding that such conflicts are controversies over representations of natural/ cultural information networks, we are prevented from finding meaningful solutions to these conflicts.

In an essay about the Middle East, Latour argues that the solution proposed by philosopher Ulrick Beck that Muslim countries should adopt the Western nature/culture divide—thus rendering their religions as subjective and therefore as innocuous as Western religions—has little chance of being viewed as a peace offering (Latour 2004a). Latour argues that we have already exported our concept of absolute truth—adopted by religious fundamentalists across the world to justify their intransigence. Instead, he argues, it is far more productive to observe how conflict is resolved in non-modern societies that have not adopted such a concept, nor view things in black-and-white terms of nature and culture. Such a non-modern holistic perspective is far more attentive to the *process* of object or ideology construction. This allows similar elements within different networks to be found and networks to consequently be brought together—something that is nearly impossible when objects or ideologies are solidified by categorizing them as "natural" or "cultural."

Archaeology is in a unique position to provide such illustrations of conflict resolution between non-modern cultural and religious groups because the process and results of resolutions are explicitly expressed materially over time. As the two case studies in chapters 6 and 7 have shown, compromises are constantly made between conflicting groups by borrowing elements from each other—elements that eventually transformed burial practices.

Fourth, this new philosophy explains how objects and structures evolve. Unless objects are understood as representing natural as well as cultural phenomena, there is no way to actually explain their evolution except by external influence. If cultural and religious representations are merely seen as cultural, their meaning purely related to their culture's constructs, there is little that can change them unless those constructs change. The only possible way for constructs to change (from this perspective of representations as purely cultural) is through external influence (some social or natural law)—hence the prevalence of economic, ecological, or social theories. But once objects are understood as representations of natural and social phenomena, it allows for change in representations to be understood as changes in conceptions of the natural/social order. This means that not only differences in representations, but also changes in them should be taken very seriously since they may pinpoint pivotal moments in a society's history, not merely accidental or progressive developments.

Of all our modern institutions today, science is one of the few institutions really able to fluidly evolve through its constant accumulation of both natural and cultural information. Religious institutions have remained largely static because they are generally seen to comprise merely cultural information, enabling little impact on them from experience of the world. The history of nineteenth-century cremation in chapter 4 is a case in point. While religions in the past also changed at an extremely slow pace, this was due to the slow speed at which natural information was accumulated and to the paralyzing fear of upsetting the natural/social order. But ideas did change, just as they change at the fringes of modern society today. Without the manacle of absolute truth—adopted by religions to immovably set their theological encryptions of natural/cultural information in stone (Latour 2004a)—compromise and amalgamation is and was a natural progression for religion. As was illustrated in chapters 6 and 7, archaeology has the ability to demonstrate this through illustrating the variability of ceremonial practices over time.

Fifth, Latour's understanding that science and culture are more similar than ever previously thought allows cultural representations to be investigated in a similar way to scientific formulas. The belief that modernist science is radically different in method from indigenous culture has been fueled partly by an ignorance of controversies between differing representations. Apart from the distinction drawn between nature and culture, one of the main distinctions between science and non-science is claimed to be scientists' engagement in controversies over representations and their falsification of others' theories (Popper 1959). Without the understanding that cultural groups are actually formed around differing views of nature/culture, and that their cultural objects express these natural/cultural understandings, the idea that controversies even exist over representations has been hard to imagine. If it were not for empirical evidence of controversies over representations, such as the destruction of Afghan Buddhas or the destruction of Islamic temples by other Islamic groups, such controversies would still be hard to conceive of. It is hard to see anyone getting upset by a purely cultural representation and staking everything they have in order to challenge it, if it is merely seen to be cultural. However, as chapter 3 demonstrates, indigenous science is as much about nature as it is about culture, and thus the cultural representations that emerge from it are as crucial and divisive as scientific theories. The existence of controversies over cultural representations has only begun to be recognized recently, but it can finally be explained in the same terms as modern scientific controversies.

This synchronicity between modernist and indigenous scientific practice (rather than their content) allows archaeological sites and objects to be taken more seriously as representations of nature as well as of culture, and requires us to follow them in a much more careful way. With a rational basis behind cultural representations, it is now completely advantageous to follow actors during controversies over representations, as these controversies now appear as struggles to express the correct representation. By following actors as they attempt to falsify each other's representations and present their own correct representations, the relationships expressed by sites and objects are clearly delineated for the archaeologist. Thus the understanding of indigenous representations as scientific, albeit not constructed using the method we traditionally conceive of as "the scientific method," allows them to be infinitely more accessible than notions of them as purely cultural would allow.

Sixth, Latour's methodology finally enables social archaeology to apply a more genuinely scientific method to the study of culture rather than its current pseudo-scientific method. Instead of assuming that some universal natural or cultural law exists that explains actions and representations—which must be guessed at and evidence found to verify or falsify the guesses (which is the positivist verification model most often used by archaeologists)—in science it is the tests that create the law by determining the contextual interactions of entities and falsifying incorrect explanations of them. Since it is not possible to test the categories of past cultures without a time machine, we need to focus upon instances when the network is already outlined for us. Controversies in the past provide just such instances.

By examining controversies—those instances when the networks of associations are most explicitly arrayed—it is finally possible to build a picture of the agencies and evolution behind objects and structures from the ground up. This methodology avoids the disastrous effects of applying external theories or alternating between micro and macro scales to interpret, and allows analysis to remain purely local (which is how science actually works). Rather than searching for a relevant *universal theory* (that can explain as much data as possible), controversies provide a pool of relevant *local data* (that is limited enough that it can falsify a theory). The later extension of this knowledge by linking it with other local studies in a network is the only defensible way to create a more general view. This restriction of data to a few highly relevant sites and variables through clearly defined criteria, rather than attempting to embrace a random sample or a large dataset, avoids the temptation to arbitrarily select variables and ignore data that does not fit into an applied theory, and it avoids the problem of irrelevant data clouding the analysis. It also allows a more scientific grasp of material by giving objects a chance to "object" (the essence of being objective).

This scientific grasp is most evident once the correct dataset is defined and the process of analyzing controversies begins. Latour's methodology—of following actors as they test opponents' representations—effectively parallels the way scientists follow tests of new elements. In science, new elements are subjected to hundreds of tests, which test their reactions to various other elements. By following each of their reactions, the characters of elements are slowly mapped out and the shapes that then develop define them as entities. Because we are not able to go back in time to conduct these tests ourselves, following controversies is the next best thing to the scientific method for the archaeology of culture. By following controversies—as each group presents their representation in opposition to the other group and tests the character of each other's representations—we can map the character of those representations controversy by controversy and build up a general knowledge of a society.

The understanding that the richest and most exotic examples of a culture (as in the case of the Early Bronze Age and Illinois Hopewell) occur during controversies is also very significant. For instance, the richest deposits of Early Bronze Age Britain, built at the temporal and geographical interface between the Beaker and Wessex Culture, appear to have been constructed during controversies. If this was the case, it means that such structures and deposits must be examined in conjunction with the representations of the group in conflict with them, not merely by themselves or in conjunction with their own group, or similar structures further afield. Only this way will they be understood in the context in which they were created. Unfortunately, the most visible and exotic examples of a culture are often examined in geographic isolation without their context and even used as the exemplars of an entire culture. Yet representations during controversies are often the most anomalous representations of a culture—as is the Bush Barrow deposit—containing borrowed elements from the group in conflict with it. Perhaps even more significant is the influence that these exotic structures have on the other group's structures—such as the structure of Wessex barrows—since it is often the other group's structures that go on to define the later dominant culture. This is the added advantage of studying controversies—it helps to not only define the groups in conflict, but also the evolution of later forms of objects and structures.

Hopefully this book has illustrated the vital importance of understanding how objects emerge and are used, and the far-reaching impact of such an understanding. Although this understanding came from the most unlikely of sources—an understanding of Western science—it was not until anthropology looked at scientific practice that it was finally able to understand how objects could "object" to anthropology's sociological description of them. However, at a time when anthropology and archaeology are at their lowest ebb and poststructuralism is pulling us toward creative destruction, Latour's insights may help to salvage both disciplines through his reevaluation of culture and social scientific methodology.

While this book has attempted to explore the range of impacts of this new understanding, there are likely many more. There are also likely to be other problems with its application. Like any philosophy that takes on such a vast landscape, Latour's runs into unique problems that need to be solved at each turn. Even in the philosophy of science there continue to be questions to be worked out. Questions remain as to how to reduce information from controversies enough that they can be described and presented more effectively. While creating an effective description is still key to explanation, tools need to be created that can give a pictorial description of that information. In the same way that formulas and instruments are crucial to reducing information in science so that information can be digested and illustrated, so too do we need to find ways to reduce descriptions of controversies into effective images. Statistics have traditionally been used to reduce information, but as has been illustrated, the use of statistics is based upon the premise that objects have only one meaning and maintain that meaning, whereas the meanings of objects in controversies are in constant flux. Finding a solution to this dilemma is something that Latour himself is highly involved in. Recently he initiated an extensive collaborative project called "Mapping Controversies" with eight universities (including MIT, Oxford University, and the Ecole de Mines in Paris) to create tools to present the networked information exposed by controversies. This research is ongoing and has produced a number of interesting solutions, but nothing that conveys the transformation of entities. In 2006 I was honored that Latour was curious enough about my adaptation of stylometrics from English literature (Martin 2005, discussed in chapter 5) to want to discuss it with me. Latour's interest in archaeological ways of presenting information, because we are an object-based discipline dealing with the history of objects, illustrates the great value of archaeology in this line of research and a way that we can participate in the ongoing debates of social science.

Appendix A

Structural Similarities between Mounds in Barrow Groups

STRUCTURE

Aldbourne G1, G2, and G3 are identical joined bell barrows (with unusual deposits) except one has an inhumation.

All Cannings G8 and G9 are similar joined bowl barrows of the same size.

Amesbury G71 and G105 are similar bowl/bell barrows.

Amesbury G132 and G133 are identical.

Avebury G13b and 13c are identical joined bowl barrows.

Berwick St. John G9 and G10 have three stake holes around cist.

Codford St. Mary G3, G4, and G5 have scraped up mounds with no ditch.

Collingbourne Kingston G7a, G10a, and G12 are very similar with same height and no deposits in cist.

Collingbourne Kingston G10 and G11 are very similar—same height and lack of deposits.

Collingbourne Kingston G16 and G17 cremation bowls with identical early EBA narrow deep ditches—Wessex I.

Collingbourne Kingston G18 and G8 have retaining pits like Wilsford G38, South Glamorgan, and Down Farm.

Collingbourne Kingston G23 and G23a are identical joined barrows with no interments.

Collingbourne Kingston G25 and G8 very similar (sequence determined by proximity?) with ritual pot breaking.

Durrington G15 and G20 have pyre material in separate cists.

Durrington G47 and G48 same size.

Durrington G34 and G53 similar.

Durrington G63, G64, and G65 triple Beaker barrow on top of a long barrow with much disturbance.

Everleigh G1 and G2 identical in size and deposit.

Idmiston G22 and G23 identical paired bell barrows.

Milton Lilbourne G2, G3, and G4 are identical bells with bowl in between, all built at the same time.

Ogbourne St. Andrew G17 and G17b saucers identical in measurement.

Pewsey G7, G8, and G9 triple discs almost identical in size and deposits (charcoal deposits in G8 and G9).

Roundway G8 and G5a, b are similar.

Shrewton G5a, c, d all have same size ditches, random stake holes, and cairns of chalk upcast.

Wilcot G3a–c and G4 are joined bowl barrows next to each other.

Wilsford G45a and 45b joined disc barrows are identical.

Wilsford G67 possibly deep due to inhumations in G68 replaced with cremations? They seem similar.

Wilsford G64a, G66, G70, G71, and G72 disc barrows here (probably one of the largest concentrations of them).

Wilsford G87a and G87b are almost identical with six inhumations each in similar configurations in pits.

Winterbourne Stoke G14a–c and G15 disc barrows are "adjoining the two last bowl-shaped barrows."

Winterbourne Stoke G32, G33, G38, G39, G47, and G49 all have mortuary structures (two were burnt).

Winterbourne Stoke G49 and G50 have similar ditches.

Winterbourne Stoke G60a–c the only barrows *not* in a line were empty and formed an equilateral triangle.

Winterbourne Stoke G67 and G68 identical discs both with shale rings and beads in urns and encroached upon.

Appendix B

*Correlation of Inhumations and Cremations
with Barrow Types*

	Bowl Barrows	Bell/Disc/Saucer Barrows
Primary EBA Inhumations	156	15
Primary EBA Cremations	22	122
Later Primary E/MBA Cremations	118	
Secondary EBA Inhumations in Cremation Barrows	21	14
Secondary E/MBA Cremations in Inhumation Barrows	54	10

Appendix C

Proximity of Wessex Anomalies to Beaker Barrows

Aldbourne G2 is a joined bell, next to Aldbourne G1.

Aldbourne G4 is a bowl/bell, next to Aldbourne G3.

Amesbury G10 is a twin disc, neighboring Amesbury G4.

Amesbury G15 is a bell, neighboring Wilsford G1.

Amesbury G44 is a twin bell.

Amesbury G85 is a bell.

Avebury G46 is a saucer.

Bulford G47 is a bell, next to undetermined bowl.

Durrington G13 is a saucer.

Durrington G14 is a saucer.

Figheldean G40 is a disc, next to undetermined bowl.

Norton Bavant G12b is a disc.

Pewsey G9 is a disc, neighboring Pewsey G4.

Shrewton G5j is a bell, next to Shrewton G5k.

Shrewton G5L is a bell, next to Shrewton G5k.

Sutton Veny G4a is a bell, next to undetermined bowl.

Wilsford G7 is a bowl/bell, one away from Wilsford G5.

Wilsford G15 is a twin bell, next to undetermined bowl.

Wilsford G58 is a bell, one away from Wilsford G60.

Wilsford G70 is a triple disc, beaker bowl surrounded by a disc.

Wimborne St. Giles G4 is a bell, next to Wimborne St. Giles G2.

Wimborne St. Giles G6 is a triple disc, neighboring Wimborne St. Giles G9.

Wimborne St. Giles G28 is a disc, next to Wimborne St. Giles G15.

Winterbourne Stoke G4 is a twin bell, next to Winterbourne G13 & G6.

Winterbourne Stoke G5 is a twin bell, next to Winterbourne G13 & G6.

Winterbourne Stoke G25 is a bowl/bell, neighboring Winterbourne G24.

Winterbourne Stoke G30 is a bell, next to Amesbury G56.

Winterbourne Stoke G37 is a bell, next to Winterbourne G36.

Winterslow G3 is a Beaker bowl, turned into a bell.

Appendix D

Context of Beaker Barrows

BEAKER BARROWS WITHOUT SECONDARY CREMATIONS

Aldbourne G2 (bell)—next to Wessex barrow (Four Barrows)

Alton G13—no Wessex barrows in cemetery (Knap Hill).

Alvediston G1—no Wessex barrows in cemetery (Middle Down).

Alvediston G1a—no Wessex barrows in cemetery (Middle Down).

Amesbury G8—no Wessex barrows in cemetery (W of Stonehenge Group).

Amesbury G15 (bell)—Wessex barrows in cemetery (W of Stonehenge Group).

Amesbury G39a—no Wessex barrows in cemetery (W of Old Kings Barrows).

Amesbury G40—no Wessex barrows in cemetery (W of Old Kings Barrows).

Amesbury G41—no Wessex barrows in cemetery (Old Kings Barrows).

Amesbury G51—next to Wessex barrow (Cursus Group).

Amesbury G54—next to Wessex barrow (Cursus Group).

Amesbury G56—next to Wessex barrow (Cursus Group).

Amesbury G134—no Wessex barrows in cemetery (Amesbury Archer).

Amesbury G135—no Wessex barrows in cemetery (Bowcombe Bowmen).

Avebury G16a—no Wessex barrows in cemetery (Fox Covert) cremation.

Avebury G48c—no Wessex barrows in cemetery (Windmill Hill).

Berwick St. John G6b—next to Wessex barrow (Barrow Pleck Group).

Berwick St. John G12—no Wessex barrows in cemetery (Tinkley Copse).

Bishops Cannings G34a—no Wessex barrows in cemetery (S of Wandsdyke).

Bishops Cannings G52—no Wessex barrows in cemetery (NE of Shepherd's Shore).

Bishops Cannings G53—no Wessex barrows in cemetery (E of MS Devizes).

Bower Chalke G1—no Wessex barrows in cemetery (Woodminton Down Group).

Bower Chalke G3—no Wessex barrows in cemetery (Woodminton Down Group).

Bower Chalke G6—no Wessex barrows in cemetery (Marley Combe Hill).

Bower Chalke G7—no Wessex barrows in cemetery (Marley Combe Hill).

Boyton G4—no Wessex barrows in cemetery (Conton Down).

Bradford on Avon G1—no Wessex barrows in cemetery (Budbury).

Bratton G8a—no Wessex barrows in cemetery (Bratton Castle).

Bulford G27—next to Wessex barrow (Sling Plantation Group).

Calne Without G2c—no Wessex barrows in cemetery (Oldbury Castle).

Cherhill G6—no Wessex barrows in cemetery (Old Bath Road).

Collingbourne Ducis G9—Wessex barrows in cemetery (Cow Down).

Collingbourne Ducis G16—Wessex barrows in cemetery (Cow Down) cremation.

Collingbourne Kingston G5—Wessex barrows in cemetery (Snail Down).

Durnford G1—no Wessex barrows in cemetery (Little Down Group).

Durrington flat grave—no Wessex barrows in cemetery (Durrington Down).

Durrington G8—no Wessex barrows in cemetery (Durrington Down).

Durrington G25—Wessex barrows in cemetery (north of Cursus) cremations.

Durrington G32—Wessex barrows in cemetery (north of Cursus) cremations.

Durrington G44—no Wessex barrows in cemetery (NW of Down Barn) cremation.

Durrington G50—no Wessex barrows in cemetery (N of E end of Cursus) cremation.

Durrington G64—no Wessex barrows in cemetery (S of Woodhenge).

Durrington G65b—no Wessex barrows in cemetery (Woodhenge Group).

Durrington G67—no Wessex barrows in cemetery (Woodhenge Group).

East Kennet G1c—no Wessex barrows in cemetery (W of Long barrow).

Figheldean G26—no Wessex barrows in cemetery (Alton Parva).

Figheldean G40 (disc)—Wessex barrows in cemetery (Farm Brigmerston Firs).

Fittleton 9b—next to Wessex barrow (WSW Haxton Down).

Fittleton 9c—next to Wessex barrow (WSW Haxton Down).

Fovant G1—no Wessex barrows in cemetery (Fovant Down).

Heytesbury G3—no Wessex barrows in cemetery (Heytesbury).

Heytesbury G4a—no Wessex barrows in cemetery (Heytesbury).

Heytesbury G4c—no Wessex barrows in cemetery but cremations (W of Knook Barrow).

Heytesbury G4e—no Wessex barrows in cemetery (W of Knook Barrow).

Heytesbury G4f—no Wessex barrows in cemetery (W of Knook Barrow).

Idmiston 25b—no Wessex barrows in cemetery (Whitesheet Hill) cremation.

Kilminton G4—no Wessex barrows in cemetery (Long Knoll) cremations.

Kilminton G6—no Wessex barrows in cemetery (Long Knoll) cremations.

Mere G6a—no Wessex barrows in cemetery (Mere Down) cremation.

Monkton Farleigh G2—no Wessex barrows in cemetery (Jugs Grave).

Norton Bavant G12b (disc)—no Wessex barrows in cemetery.

Pewsey G8 or 9 (disc)—next to Wessex barrow (Down Farm Group).

Preshute 1a—no Wessex barrows in cemetery (Manton Barrow).

Roundway G8—no Wessex barrows in cemetery (Roundway Hill).

Roundway G9—no Wessex barrows in cemetery (Roundway Hill).

Shrewton G24—Wessex barrows in cemetery (Rolleston Field Group).

Shrewton G27—next to Wessex barrow (Rolleston Field Group).

South Newton G1—no Wessex barrows in cemetery (Newton Barrow).

Sutton Veny G11a—no Wessex barrows in cemetery (E of Henge).

Sutton Veny G11b—no Wessex barrows in cemetery (E of Henge).

Upavon G1—no Wessex barrows in cemetery (in Upavon Barracks).

Upton Lovell G2a—Wessex barrows in cemetery (NE of Great Barrow).

Upton Lovell G2c—no Wessex barrows in cemetery (Upton Lovell Down).

Upton Scudmore G1a—no Wessex barrows in cemetery (S of Village) cremation.

Warminster G7—no Wessex barrows in cemetery (Oxendean Down).

Warminster G8—no Wessex barrows in cemetery (Oxendean Down).

Warminster G13—no Wessex barrows in cemetery (SW of Battlesbury).

West Overton G1—next to Wessex barrow (Overton Hill Group).

Wilsford G2b—next to Wessex barrow (Normanton).

Wilsford G5—next to Wessex barrow (Normanton).

Wilsford G7 (bowl/bell)—next to Wessex barrow (Normanton).

Wilsford G19—next to Wessex barrow (Normanton).

Wilsford G29—next to Wessex barrow (Normanton).

Wilsford G50a—next to Wessex barrow (Lake Group).

Wilsford G50c—no Wessex barrows in cemetery although neighboring (E of Lake Group).

Wilsford G58 (bell)—Wessex barrows in cemetery (Wilsford Down).

Wilsford G62—next to Wessex barrow (Wilsford Down).

Wilsford G67—next to Wessex barrow (Wilsford Down).

Wilsford G87a—no Wessex barrows in cemetery (Lake House) cremation.

Wilsford G87b—no Wessex barrows in cemetery (Lake House) cremation.

Wilsford G87d—no Wessex barrows in cemetery (Lake House) cremation.

Wimbourne St. Giles G1—Wessex barrows in cemetery (Oakley Down).

Wimbourne St. Giles G4 (bell)—Wessex barrows in cemetery (Oakley Down).

Wimbourne St. Giles G15—Wessex barrows in cemetery (Oakley Down).

Wimbourne St. Giles G18—Wessex barrows in cemetery (Oakley Down).

Wimbourne St. Giles G28 (disc)—Wessex barrows in cemetery (Oakley Down).

Winterbourne G7—no Wessex barrows in cemetery (W of Horse Barrow).

Winterbourne Monkton G3—next to Wessex barrow (Windmill Hill).

Winterbourne Monkton G9—next to Wessex barrow (Monkton Hill).

Winterbourne Stoke G6—next to Wessex barrow (Winterbourne Stoke Group).

Winterbourne Stoke G9—Wessex barrows in cemetery (Winterbourne Stoke Group).

Winterbourne Stoke G20—next to Wessex barrow (Winterbourne Stoke Group).

Winterbourne Stoke G35a—next to Wessex barrow (Small Cursus).

Winterbourne Stoke G35b—next to Wessex barrow (Small Cursus).

Winterbourne Stoke G35c—next to Wessex barrow (W of Small Cursus).

Winterbourne Stoke G36—next to Wessex barrow (W of Small Cursus).

Winterbourne Stoke G37 (bell)—next to Wessex barrow (W of Small Cursus).

Winterbourne Stoke G57—no Wessex barrows in cemetery (Winterbourne East Group) cremations.

Winterslow G20—no Wessex barrows in cemetery (Easton Down).

Woodford G13—next to Wessex barrow (W of Hooklands Plantation).

Unlocated Beaker Graves

Avebury G23c.

Avebury G23d.

Avebury G46—(bowl/saucer).

Avebury G48c—no Wessex barrows in cemetery (Windmill Hill E Slope) cremations.

Avebury G48d—no Wessex barrows in cemetery (Windmill Hill E Slope) cremations.

Avebury G49—(between Avebury and Winterbourne Monkton).

Bulford G71a—no Wessex barrows in cemetery (At Bulford unlocated).

Bulford G72a—no Wessex barrows in cemetery (At Bulford unlocated).

Bulford G72b.

Bulford G72c.

BEAKER MOUNDS WITH
SECONDARY CREMATIONS

Amesbury G22—no Wessex barrows in cemetery (Plantation SE Stonehenge) cremation.

Amesbury G71— next to Wessex barrow (Earl's Farm Down Group).

Avebury G25—next to Wessex barrow (Overton Hill).

Avebury G35—next to Wessex barrow (Avebury Down).

Bishops Cannnnings G15—next to Wessex barrow (north Down).

Bishops Cannings G81—Wessex barrows in cemetery (SW Beckhampton Firs).

Cholderton G2a—no Wessex barrows in cemetery (Cow Down).

Codford St. Mary G2—no Wessex barrows in cemetery (Lamb Down) cremation.

Codford St. Mary G3—no Wessex barrows in cemetery (Lamb Down) cremation.

Collingbourne Ducis G11—next to Wessex barrow (Cow Down Group).

Collingbourne Ducis G12—next to Wessex barrow (Cow Down Group).

Durrington G35—Wessex barrows in cemetery (Durrington Down).

Durrington G36—Wessex barrows in cemetery (Durrington Down).

Durrington G68—no Wessex barrows in cemetery (Woodhenge Group).

Figheldean G16—no Wessex barrows in cemetery (N Brigmerston Firs) cremation.

Figheldean G25—no Wessex barrows in cemetery (Barrow Clump) cremation.

Idmiston G25d—no Wessex barrows in cemetery (Horse Barrow Group) cremation.

Idmiston G25e—no Wessex barrows in cemetery (Horse Barrow Group) cremation.

Knook G5b—no Wessex barrows in cemetery (Knook Castle).

Milston G51—next to Wessex barrow (Silk Hill).

Ogbourne St. Andrew G6—next to Wessex barrow (Rockley Plantation).

Pewsey G4—next to Wessex barrow (Down Farm Group).

Shrewton G5a—next to Wessex barrow (Net Down Group).

Shrewton G5e—next to Wessex barrow (Net Down Group).

Shrewton G5k—next to Wessex barrow (Net Down Group).

Shrewton G23—next to Wessex barrow (Net Down Group).

Sutton Mandeville G1—no Wessex barrows in cemetery (Buxbury Hill Barrow).

Sutton Veny G4a (bell)—Wessex barrows in cemetery (W of Knoll Barrow).

Upavon G1a—no Wessex barrows in cemetery (Upavon Down).

West Overton G6b—next to Wessex barrow (Overton Hill Group).

West Overton G19—Wessex barrows in cemetery (Hartshill Cottage).

Wilsford G39—next to Wessex barrow (The Lake Group).

Wilsford G40—next to Wessex barrow (The Lake Group).

Wilsford G51—Wessex barrows in cemetery (Wilsford Down) cremation.

Wilsford G52—Wessex barrows in cemetery (Wilsford Down) cremation.

Wilsford G60—next to Wessex barrow (Wilsford Group).

Wilsford G68—next to Wessex barrow (Wilsford Group).

Wilsford G70 (disc)—next to Wessex barrow (Wilsford Group).

Wilsford G87f —Wessex barrows in cemetery (Lake Down).

Wimbourne St. Giles G2—next to Wessex barrow (Oakley Down Group).

Wimbourne St. Giles G9—next to Wessex barrow (Oakley Down Group).

Winterbourne Stoke G5 (bell)—next to Wessex barrow (Oakley Down Group).

Winterbourne Stoke G8—Wessex barrows in cemetery (Winterbourne Stoke Group) cremation.

Winterbourne Stoke G10—Wessex barrows in cemetery (Winterbourne Stoke Group).

Winterbourne Stoke G13—next to Wessex barrow (Winterbourne Stoke Group).

Winterbourne Stoke G24—Wessex barrows in cemetery (N of Winterbourne Stoke Group) cremation.

Winterbourne Stoke G43—no Wessex barrows in cemetery (Green-
land Farm) cremation.

Winterbourne Stoke G54—Wessex barrows in cemetery (N of Winterbourne Stoke Group).

Winterbourne Stoke G56—no Wessex barrows in cemetery (Winterbourne Stoke East Group) cremation.

Winterslow G3 (bell)—next to Wessex barrow (N of The Pheasant).

Woodford G12—no Wessex barrows in cemetery (Hookland Plantation).

Unlocated

Avebury G6 Unlocated.
Avebury G46 Unlocated.

SUMMARY OF CONTEXTS

No Wessex or cremation barrows in cemetery: 61
Just cremations beside Beaker barrows: 22
Wessex barrows in cemetery: 28
Next to Wessex barrow: 53
Unlocated: 8
Barrows with questionable data: 39
Inhumation barrows in total: 172

Appendix E

Comparison of Size between Last Beaker and Wessex Barrows

SECONDARY CREMATIONS AT INTERFACE

Aldbourne G2 (bell)—next to bell (G1 and G3) joined and identical in size and structure.

Amesbury G71 (bell/bowl)—next to bell (G70) identical in size and structure.

Avebury G46 (bowl/saucer)—next to saucer (Wint Monk G4), not similar.

Avebury G25 (bowl)—next to bell (G26) identical in size.

Avebury G35 (bowl)—neighboring bell (G36) 69 ft. vs. 75 ft. and 6 ft. vs. 3 ft. high.

Bishops Cannings G15 (disc/saucer)—neighboring disc (G11) destroyed.

Collingbourne Ducis G11 (bowl)—next to disc (G13) 111 ft. vs. 106 ft.

Collingbourne Ducis G12 (bowl)—next to disc (G13) no similarity but similar to G7 cremation bowl.

Pewsey G4 (bowl)—next to bowl (G5) 60 ft. vs. 65 ft. similar in size.

Shrewton G5a (bowl/bell)—next to bell (G5c) identical in size and structure.

Shrewton G5e (bowl/bell)—next to bell (G5c) identical in size and structure.

Shrewton G5k (bowl/bell)—next to bell (G5c) identical in size and structure

West Overton G6b (bowl)—next to Twin bell (G4) 44 ft. vs. 66 ft. little similarity.

Wilsford G39 (bowl)—next to G42 (bell) not similar.

Wilsford G40 (bowl)—next to G42 (bell) very similar 102 ft. vs. 105 ft.

Wilsford G60 (bowl)—one away from G58 (bell) not similar 75 ft. vs. 90 ft.

Wilsford G68 (bowl)—next to pond (G63) similar and disc (G66) not similar.

Winterbourne Stoke G5 (bell)—next to twin bell (G4) identical in size and structure.

Winterbourne Stoke G13 (bowl)—next to disc (G14) and pond (G12) no similarity.

N Winterbourne Stoke G24 (bowl)—next to bell (G25) small vs. 84 ft. little similarity.

Winterslow G3 (bell)—next to Idmiston G23 (bell) similar in size 144 ft. by 176 ft. (huge).

BEAKERS WITHOUT SECONDARY CREMATIONS
AT INTERFACE

Amesbury G51 (bowl)—neighboring bell (G47) 66 ft. vs. 60 ft. similar.

Amesbury G54 (bowl)—next to bell (G55) 78 ft. vs. 90 ft. some similarity.

Amesbury G56 (bowl)—next to bell (Wint. Stoke G30) 72 ft. vs. 53 ft. little similarity.

Bulford G27 (bowl)—next to disc (G23) 144 ft. vs. 104 ft. little similarity.

Pewsey G8 or 9 (disc)—next to disc (G7) 20 ft. vs. 17 paces some similarity.

Shrewton G27 (bowl)—next to bell (G28) 30ft. vs. 100 ft. no similarity.

West Overton G1 (bowl)—neighboring bell (G2) 75 ft. vs. 70 ft. similar.

Wilsford G2a (bowl)—next to disc (G2) unsure about similarities.

Wilsford G5 (bowl)—next to disc (G4) 128 ft. vs. 120 ft. similar size.

Wilsford G7 (bowl/bell)—next to bell (G8) 100 ft. vs. 75 ft. little similarity.

Appendix F

Context of Secondary Cremations

SECONDARY CREMATIONS IN BEAKER BARROWS AT INTERFACE

Amesbury G22 — bowl barrow with cremation and bronze dagger next to it.

Amesbury G61 — a disc barrow on top of Beaker flat grave w/ smashed inhumations next to twin bell.

Amesbury G71 — bell barrow (G70) with cremation next to it.

Avebury G25 — next to G26 (bell).

Avebury G35 — 2 bells neighboring (500 yds. away but no others near).

x Avebury G46 — bowl/saucer barrow near saucer barrow (Wint. Monkton G4) with urn and bones.

Bishops Cannings G15 — neighboring disc (G11).

Codford St. Mary G2 — next to bowl (G4) with cremation collared urn and bronze pin.

x Codford St. Mary G — next to bowl (G4) with cremation.

Collingbourne Ducis G11 — next to disc G13 and bowl G10.

Collingbourne Ducis G12 — next to disc G13 and bowl G15 with cremation.

Durrington G35 — neighboring G28 and G29 (saucer) and G33 and G34 (bowls w/ cremations).

x Durrington G36 — neighboring G28 and G29 (saucer) and G33 and G34 (bowls w/ cremations).

Figheldean G16 — next to G9, G9a, b, c (bowls with cremations).

Milston G51 — next to disc G8.

Idmiston G25d — next to G25c (bowl with enlarged food vessel).

x Idmiston G25e — next to G25c (bowl with enlarged food vessel).

Ogbourne St. Andrew G6 — neighboring G9 (bell) and next to G7 (bowl with cremation urn).

Pewsey G4 — next to bell G3.

Shrewton G5a — next to G5c (bell) or same size and structure.

Shrewton G5e — neighboring G5c (bell).

Shrewton G5k — next to G5j (bell) and G5L (bell).

Shrewton G23 — neighboring G23a (bowl with outer bank with cremation).

Sutton Veny G4a (bell itself)—but not near any cremations or bells (possibly G4).

West Overton G6b—neighboring twin bell barrow (G4).

Wilsford G39—next to G42 (bell).

Wilsford G40—next to G42 (bell).

Wilsford G51—neighboring G52 and G53 (bowls with cremations).

Wilsford G60—one away from G58 (bell).

Wilsford G68—next to pond G63 and one away from G66 (disc).

Wimbourne St. Giles G2—next to G4 (bell) and other cremation bowls (G3, G5).

Wimbourne St. Giles G9—next to G7, G8, G13 (discs).

Winterbourne Stoke G5 (bell)—next to G4 (bell).

Winterbourne Stoke G8—near to pond G12 and G11 bowl with cremation.

Winterbourne Stoke G13—next to G14 (disc) and G12 (pond).

Winterbourne Stoke G24—next to G25 (bowl/bell).

Winterbourne Stoke G43 (bowl/bell)—next to cremation bowl G44.

Winterbourne Stoke G56 (bowl)—next to cremation bowls (G55a, G58a).

Winterslow G3 (bell)—next to Idmiston G23 (bell).

Cremations and bells at interface: 39
Bells at interface: 25
Near bowls with cremations: 9

SECONDARY CREMATIONS IN PRIMARY CREMATION BARROW

Aldbourne G1—cremation in primary cremation mound.

Avebury G43—cremation above primary cremation.

Bishops Cannings G30—cremation above primary cremation in bowl between two bell barrows.

Collingbourne Ducis G15—cremations at four levels above primary cremation encircled by flints.

Collingbourne Ducis G21—cremations in food vessels above primary cremation.

Collingbourne Kingston G6—secondary deposit in food vessel above primary cremation.

Collingbourne Kingston G18—secondary cremations in both twin primary cremation mounds.

Collingbourne Kingston G25—token secondary cremations in primary cremation mound.

Durrington G29—secondary cremation in primary cremation mound.

Market Lavington G2—cremation in primary cremation mound.

Ogbourne St. Andrew G7—cremations in cremation (?) mound with later inhumation with arrowhead.

Pewsey G5—cremation in primary cremation mound (unusual cone shaped barrow).

Shrewton G5g—cremation in primary cremation mound.

Warminster G5—cremation in collared urn in cremation mound.

West Overton G4—cremation in cremation mound (in a twin bell barrow with bowl in between).

West Overton G8—cremation (LBA?) in primary cremation mound.

Wilcot G5—cremations in primary cremation mound.

Wilsford G75—cremation in primary cremation mound.

Wimbourne St. Giles G17—cremation in primary cremation mound.

SECONDARY CREMATION IN EMPTY BARROW

Aldbourne G19—disturbed 6 ft. by 3 ft. grave with cremation in collared urn placed in its place.

Avebury G9—primary not found.

Avebury G24—primary not found.

Berwick St. John G9—empty grave with secondary cremation to SW (LBA cremations to NE).

Bromham G1—primary not found.

Bulford G47 bell—primary not found but secondary cremation urns with Beaker inhumation above.

Collingbourne Kingston G10a—empty primary deep cist with cremation on surface.

Durnford G2—primary internment not found.

Edinton G2—primary not found with intrusive cremation with grooved dagger and two flat daggers.

Froxfield G3a—primary not found.

Laverstock and Ford G14—primary not found.

Laverstock and Ford G15—primary not found.

Laverstock and Ford G16—primary not found.

Ogbourne St. Andrew G11—6 ft.–7 ft. long primary pit empty.

Wilsford G38—4 ft. by 1.5 ft. primary interment empty with many cremations.

CREMATIONS WITH INHUMATIONS

Figheldean G40—food vessel with inhumation.

SECONDARY DEPOSITS IN CREMATION BARROW

Upton Lovell G2e—deposit in primary cremation mound (Golden Barrow).

SECONDARY CREMATIONS IN CREMATION BARROW
AT INTERFACE

Avebury G24—two bell barrows (unexcavated) next to bowls.
Berwick St. John G9—next to cremation bowl.
Bromham G1—bowl G2 with cremation and incense cup next to it.
Bulford G47 (bell)—next to discs (G44 and G43) unexcavated.
Collingbourne Kingston G10a—one away from G8 (bell) and G13 (bell).

Appendix G

Secondary Inhumations in Cremation Mounds

Aldbourne G4?

Amesbury G44—head to N.

Amesbury G61—on right side crouched outside central mound under extension.

Amesbury G85—head to NW crouched with dagger.

Berwick St. John G10—head to NW on left side on causeway.

Bratton G1?

Bulford G47—crouched covered with flints.

Codford St. Peter G1—crouched male lying face down.

Collingbourne Ducis G3?

Durnford G2 ?—on left side in a sloping position covered with large flints (Saxon?).

Durrington G13—child inhumation?

Durrington G14—cremation removed to bury inhumation with four lignite beads around neck.

Durrington G35—secondary cremation disturbed by inhumation with antlers.

Durrington G36—secondary cremation disturbed by inhumation with antlers.

Laverstock and Ford G16—on left side on causeway crouched.

Ogbourne St. Andrew G7—with leaf arrowhead.

Shrewton G5j—head to SW On right side crouched with necklace of beads.

Shrewton G5l—head to NE crouched.

Upton Scudmore G1—head to E in wooden box/tree trunk with bronze dagger.

Wilsford G15—head to N.

Wilsford G36f—face down crouched covered by extension.

Wilsford G52—head to SE and NE with Beaker shards.

Winterbourne Stoke G25?

Winterbourne Stoke G4?

Winterbourne Stoke G43?

Appendix H

Characteristics of Type 1, Type 2, and Type 3 Mounds

Type 1 Mounds

Mound No.	Prep.	Tomb Type	Ramps	Tomb Burial	Outer Burials	Hope. Pottery
Elizabeth 4	Soil	Surface	Ramp	Processed	Cluster	
Elizabeth 6	Soil	Surface Log	Ramp	Processed	Clusters	Periphery
Elizabeth 7	Soil	Surface Log	Sod Ramp	Processed	Burial Ring	Periphery
Montezuma 5	?	Surface Log	Ramp	Processed	?	
Montezuma 9	?	Surface Log	Ramp	Processed	?	
Montezuma 11	?	Surface Log	Ramp	Processed	Cluster	Periphery
Montezuma 12	?	Surface Log	Ramp	Processed	?	
Montezuma 15	?	Surface Log	Ramp	Processed	?	
Pilot Peak 1	?	Surface Log	Ramp	Processed	?	
Klunk 1c	Soil	Surface Log	Sod Ramp	Processed	Clusters	
Klunk 2a	Soil	Surface Log	Sod Ramp	B/Processed	Clusters	Periphery
Klunk 6b	Soil	Surface Log	Sod Ramp	Processed	Clusters	Periphery
Bedford 9	Soil	Surface Log	Sod Ramp	B/Processed	?	
Bedford 12b	Sand	Sub-surf Log	Ramp	Processed	Cluster	
Bedford 11b	Sand	Sub-surf Log	Ramp	Processed	?	
Bedford 8b	?	Surface Log	Sod Ramp	Processed	Cluster	
Gibson 5b	?	Surface Log	Ramp	Processed	Clusters	Periphery
Gibson 2b	?	Surface log	Ramp	Processed	?	

Type 2 Mounds

Mound No.	Prep.	Tomb Type	Ramps	Tomb Burial	Outer Burials	Hope. Pottery
Klunk 1a	No	Pit + Log	Low Ramp	B/Processed	Burial Ring	C. Tomb
Klunk 1b	No	Pit + Log	Low Ramp	B/Processed	Burial Ring	C. Tomb
Klunk 2b	No	Surface Log	Low Ramp	Processed	Burial Ring	
Pilot Peak 3	?	Surface Log	?	Burial	?	C. Tomb
Bedford 12a	?	Surface Log	Low Ramp	Burial	?	
Bedford 11a	?	Surface Log	Low Ramp	Burial	?	
Bedford 10	?	Pit + Log	No Ramp	Burial	?	C. Tomb
Bedford 8a	?	Pit + Log	No Ramp	Burial	Burial Ring	C. Tomb

Type 3 Mounds

Mound No.	Prep.	Tomb Type	Ramps	Tomb Burial	Outer Burials	Baehr Pottery
Bedford 4a	No	Pit	No Ramp	Burial	Interrupted	
L'Orient 1a	No	Pit	No Ramp	Burial	Burial Ring	
L'Orient 2a	Platf	Pit	No Ramp	Burial	Burial Ring	Periphery
Gibson 5a	No	Pit	No Ramp	B/Processed	Burial Ring	
Gibson 2a	No	Pit	No Ramp	B/Processed	Burial Ring	Periphery
Gibson 4a	No	Pit	No Ramp	None	Interrupted	
Klunk 5b	No	Pit	No Ramp	Burial	None	
Klunk 11b	No	Pit	No Ramp	Burial	Burial Ring	Periphery
Elizabeth 3	No	Pit	No Ramp	Burial	Burial Ring	
Elizabeth 1	No	?	No Ramp	?	Burial Ring	
Gibson Knoll C	No	?	No Ramp	?	Burial Ring	Periphery

References

Adams, W., and E. Adams. 1991. *Archaeological Typology and Practical Reality: A Dialectical Approach to Artifact Classification and Sorting.* Cambridge: Cambridge University Press.

Agrawal, A. 1995. "Dismantling the Divide between Indigenous and Scientific Knowledge." *Development and Change* 26:413–39.

Aikenhead, G., B. Calabrese, and P. Chinn. 2006. "Forum: Toward a Politics of Place-based Science Education." *Cultural Studies of Science Education* 1:403–16.

Aikenhead, G., and M. Ogawa. 2007. "Indigenous Knowledge and Science Revisited." *Cultural Studies of Science Education* 2(3):539–620.

Alberti, B., and Y. Marshall. 2009. "Animating Archaeology: Local Theories and Conceptually Open-ended Methodologies." *Cambridge Archaeological Journal* 19(3):345–57.

Allen, M. 2010. "*Did the Farming Economy Generate the Wessex Culture Wealth; Changes in Environment and Agriculture?*" Paper presented at the annual conference for the British Prehistoric Society, *Wessex Culture "Revolution" or Late Beaker "Evolution"? Defining Changes in the Early 2nd Millennium BC,* Bournemouth, UK, April 16–18.

Annable, F., and D. Simpson. 1964. *Guide Catalogue of the Neolithic and Bronze Age Collections in Devizes Museum.* Devizes: Devizes Museum.

Appadurai, A. 1986. "Introduction: Commodities and the Politics of Value." In *The Social Life of Things: Commodities in Cultural Perspective,* edited by Arjun Appadurai, 3–63. Cambridge: Cambridge University Press.

ApSimon, A. M. 1954. "Dagger Graves in the 'Wessex' Bronze Age." *Annual Report of the University of London Institute of Archaeology* 10:37–62.

Argyle, M. 1992. *The Social Psychology of Everyday Life.* London: Routledge.

Arkes, Hadley. 1986. *First Things: An Inquiry into the First Principles of Morals and Justice.* Princeton: Princeton University Press.

Arkush, E. 2008. "Warfare and Violence in the Americas: Book Review Essay." *American Antiquity* 73(3):560–65.

Ashbee, P. 1960. *The Bronze Age Round Barrow in Britain.* London: Phoenix.

Ashmore, W. 2002. "'Decisions and Dispositions': Socializing Spatial Archaeology." *American Anthropologist* 104(4):1172–83.

Atkinson, J. C. 1956. *Stonehenge.* London: Hamish Hamilton.

Aya, Rod. 1996. "The Devil in Social Anthropology, or, The Empiricist Exorcist; or, The Case against Cultural Relativism." In *The Social Philosophy of Ernest Gellner,* edited by John A. Hall and Ian Jarvie, 553–62. Amsterdam: Rodopi.

Bachelard, G. 1967. *La Formation de L'esprit Scientifique [Education of the Scientific Mind].* Paris: Vrin.

Badham, P. 2005. "Soul." In *Encyclopedia of Cremation,* edited by D. Davies and L. Mates, 376–77. London: Ashgate.

Barclay, A. 1999. "Chapter 4: Final Neolithic/ Early Bronze Age." In *Excavations at Barrow Hills, Radley, Oxfordshire. Volume 1: The Neolithic and Bronze Age Monument Complex,* edited by A. Barclay and C. Halpin, 35–148. Oxford: Oxford University School of Archaeology.

Barclay, G. 2002. Introduction, in Special Section. *Antiquity* 76: 777–83.

Barnes, B. 1974. *Scientific Knowledge and Sociological Theory.* London: Routledge and Kegan Paul.

———. 1982. *T. S. Kuhn and Social Science.* London: Macmillan.

Barrett, J., R. Bradley, and M. Green. 1991. *Landscape, Monuments and Society: The Prehistory of Cranborne Chase*. Cambridge: Cambridge University Press.

Barrett, J. C. 1994. *Fragments from Antiquity*. Oxford: Blackwell.

———. 2000. "A Thesis on Agency." In *Agency in Archaeology*, edited by M. Dobres and J. Robb, 61–8. London: Routledge.

Barrett, J. C., and I. Ko. 2009. "A Phenomenology of Landscape. A Crisis in British Landscape Archaeology?" *Journal of Social Archaeology* 9:275–94.

Barrett, K., and M. Bowden. 2010. *Stonehenge World Heritage Site Landscape Project, Normanton Down Archaeological Survey Report*. Swindon: English Heritage.

Barth, F. 1969. "Introduction." In *Ethnic Groups and Boundaries*, edited by F. Barth, 9–39. Boston: Little, Brown.

———. 1971. "Tribes and Intertribal Relations in the Fly Headwaters." *Oceania* 41:171–91.

———. 1975. *Ritual and Knowledge among the Baktaman of New Guinea*. New Haven, CT: Yale University Press.

Barthes, R. 1988. *The Semiotic Challenge*. Translated by R. Howard. New York: Hill & Wang.

Basso, K. 1996. "Wisdom Sits in Places: Notes on a Western Apache Landscape." In *Senses of Place*, edited by S. Feld and K. Basso, 53–90. Santa Fe, NM: School of American Research Press.

Battiste, M., and J. Henderson. 2000. *Protecting Indigenous Knowledge and Heritage*. Saskatoon, Canada: Purich.

Beck, R., D. Bolender, J. Brown, and T. Earle. 2007. "Eventful Archaeology: The Place of Space in Structural Transformation." *Current Anthropology* 48(6):833–60.

Beecher, H. 1955. "The Powerful Placebo." *Journal of the American Medical Association* 159(17):1602–6.

Bendixen, M. 2006. "Humans in Innovative Work—a Semiotic Discussion." Paper presented at the conference *EASST 2006*, University of Lausanne, Switzerland. Accessed July 12, 2012.http://www.innovationspsykologi.dk/upl/8821/Humansininnovativework.pdf.

Benedetti F., M. Amanzio, S. Vighetti, and G. Asteggiano. 2006. "The Biochemical and Neuroendocrine Bases of the Hyperalgesic Nocebo Effect." *The Journal of Neuroscience* 26:12014–22.

Benedict, R. 1934. *Patterns of Culture*. Boston: Houghton Mifflin.

Bentley, G. 1987. "Ethnicity and Practice." *Comparative Studies in Society and History* 29:24–55.

Binford, L. 1982. "Meaning, Inference and the Material Record." In *Ranking, Resource and Exchange*, edited by C. Renfrew and S. Shennan, 160–63. Cambridge: Cambridge University Press.

———. 1983. *In Pursuit of the Past*. London: Thames and Hudson.

Blackwell, B., S. Bloomfield, and C. Buncher. 1972. "Demonstration to Medical Students of Placebo Responses and Non-drug Factors." *The Lancet* 299(7763):1279–82.

Bloch, M. 1971. *Placing the Dead: Tombs, Ancestral Villages and Kinship Organization in Madagascar*. London: Seminar Press.

———. 1977. "The Past and the Present in the Present." *Man* 13:278–92.

———. 1982. "Death, Women and Power." In *Death and the Regeneration of Life*, edited by Maurice Bloch and Jonathan Parry, 211–30. Cambridge: Cambridge University Press.

Bloor, D. (1976) 1991. *Knowledge and Social Imagery* (2nd ed.). Chicago: University of Chicago Press.

———. 1999. "Anti-Latour." *Studies in History and Philosophy of Science* 30(1):81–112.

Boas, F. 1897. "The Social Organization and the Secret Societies of the Kwakiutl Indians." *Report of the U.S. National Museum for 1895*, 311–738. Washington.

Boast, R. 1997. "A Small Company of Actors: A Critique of Style." *Journal of Material Culture* 2(2):173–98.

Boivin, N. 2008. *Material Cultures, Material Minds: The Role of Things in Human Thought, Society and Evolution*. Cambridge: Cambridge University Press.

Bolnick, D., and D. Smith. 2007. "Migration and Social Structure among the Hopewell: Evidence from Ancient DNA." *American Antiquity* 72:627–44.

Bonta, M., and J. Protevi. 2004. *Deleuze and Geophilosophy: A Guide and Glossary*. Edinburgh: Edinburgh University Press.

Boudon, R. 2004. *The Poverty of Relativism*. Oxford: Bardwell Press.

Bourdieu, P. 1977. *Outline of a Theory of Practice*. Cambridge: Cambridge University Press.

———. 1984. *Distinction: A Social Critique of the Judgment of Taste*. London: Routledge.

———. 1990. *The Logic of Practice*. Cambridge: Polity Press.

Bradley, R. 1984. *The Social Foundations of Prehistoric Britain*. London: Longman.

———. 1993. *Altering the Earth: The Origins of Monuments in Britain and Continental Europe*. Edinburgh: Society of Antiquaries of Scotland.

———. 2007. *The Prehistory of Britain and Ireland*. Cambridge: Cambridge University Press.

Bradley, R., and M. Edmonds. 1993. *Interpreting the Axe Trade: Production and Exchange in Neolithic Britain*. Cambridge: Cambridge University Press.

Bradley, R., and E. Fraser. 2011. "Round Barrows and the Boundary between the Living and the Dead." In *Places in Between: The Archaeology of Social, Cultural and Geographical Borders and Borderlands*, edited by D. Mullin, 40–47. Oxford: Oxbow Books.

Brake, M. 1985. *Comparative Youth Culture: The Sociology of Youth Culture and Youth Subcultures in America, Britain and Canada*. London: Routledge and Kegan Paul.

Branthwaite, A., and P. Cooper. 1981. "Analgesic Effects of Branding in Treatment of Headaches." *British Medical Journal* 282:1576–8.

Braun, D. 1981. "A Critique of Some Recent North American Mortuary Studies." *American Antiquity* 46:398–416.

Bray, T. 2009. "An Archaeological Perspective on the Andean Concept of Camaquen: Thinking Through Late Pre-Columbian." *Cambridge Archaeological Journal* 19(3):357–66.

Brown, J. 1997. "The Archaeology of Ancient Religion in the Eastern Woodlands." *The Annual Review of Anthropology* 26:465–85.

Brown, L., and W. Walker. 2008. "Prologue: Archaeology, Animism and Non-Human Agents." *Journal of Archaeological Method and Theory* 15(4):297–9.

Brown, M. 2008. "Cultural Relativism." *Current Anthropology* 49(3):363–84.

Brück, J. 2006. "Fragmentation, Personhood and the Social Construction of Technology in Middle and Bronze Age Britain." *Cambridge Archaeological Journal* 16(2):297–315.

Buikstra, J. 1976. *Hopewell in the Lower Illinois Valley: A Regional Study of Human Biological Variability and Prehistoric Mortuary Behavior*. Evanston, IL: Northwestern Archaeological Program Scientific Papers.

Buikstra, J., and D. Charles. 1999. "Centering the Ancestors: Cemeteries, Mounds, and Sacred Landscapes of the Ancient North American Midcontinent." In *Archaeologies of Landscape: Contemporary Perspectives*, edited by W. Ashmore and A. Knapp, 201–28. Oxford: Blackwell.

Buikstra, J., D. Charles, and G. Rakita. 1998. *Staging Ritual: Hopewell Ceremonialism at the Mound House Site, Greene County, Illinois*. Kampsville: Center for American Archaeology.

Bullington, J. 1988. "Middle Woodland Mound Structure: Social Implications and Regional Context." In *The Archaic and Woodland Cemeteries at the Elizabeth Site in the Lower Illinois Valley*, edited by D. Charles, S. Leigh, and J. Buikstra, 218–41. Kampsville: Center for American Archaeology.

Burgess, C. 1980. *The Age of Stonehenge*. London: Dent.

Cajete, G. 2000. *Native Science: Natural Laws of Interdependence*. Santa Fe, NM: Clear Light.

———. 2004. "Philosophy of Native Science." In *American Indian Thought: Philosophical Essays*, edited by A. Waters, 45–57. Malden: Blackwell.

Callon, M. (ed.) 1998. *The Laws of the Markets*. Oxford: Blackwell.

Carter, L. 2004. "Thinking Differently about Cultural Diversity: Using Postcolonial Theory to (Re)Read Science Education." *Science Education* 88:819–36.

Case, H. 2003. "Beaker Presence at Wilsford G7." *Wiltshire Archaeological and Natural History Magazine* 96:161–94.

Chalmers, A. 1999. *What Is This Thing Called Science?* Maidenhead: Open University Press.

Chamberlin, M. 2006. "Symbolic Conflict and the Spatiality of Traditions in Small-scale Societies." *Cambridge Archaeological Journal* 16:39–51.

Chapman, R. 1981. "The Emergence of Formal Disposal Areas and the 'Problem' of Megalithic Tombs in Europe." In *The Archaeology of Death*, edited by R. Chapman, I. Kinnes, and K. Randsborg, 1–24. Cambridge: Cambridge University Press.

Charles, D. 1985. "Corporate Symbols: An Interpretive Prehistory of Indian Burial Mounds in West-Central Illinois." PhD diss., Northwestern University.

———. 1992. "Woodland Demographic and Social Dynamics in the American Midwest: Analysis of a Burial Mound Survey." *World Archaeology* 24:175–97.

Charles, D., J. Buikstra, and L. Konigsberg. 1986. "Behavioral Implications of Terminal Archaic and Early Woodland Mortuary Practices in the Lower Illinois Valley." In *Early Woodland Archaeology*, edited by K. Farnsworth and T. Emerson, 458–74. Kampsville: Center for American Archaeology Press.

Childe, G. 1945. "Directional Changes in Funerary Practices during 50,000 Years." *Man* 45:13–19.

———. 1949. *Social Worlds of Knowledge*. Oxford: Oxford University Press.

———. 1956. *Piecing Together the Past: The Interpretation of Archaeological Data*. London: Routledge and Kegan Paul.

———. 1956. *Piecing Together the Past: The Interpretation of Archaeological Data*. London: Routledge and Kegan Paul.

Christie, M. 1991. "Aboriginal Science for the Ecologically Sustainable Future: Australian Science." *Teachers Journal* 37:26–31.

Clark, J. G. 1966. "The Invasion Hypothesis in British Archaeology." *Antiquity* 40:172–89.

Clarke, D. L. 1970. *Beaker Pottery of Great Britain and Ireland*. Cambridge: Cambridge University Press.

Colapietro, V. 1989. *Peirce's Approach to the Self: A Semiotic Perspective on Human Subjectivity*. Albany: State University of New York Press.

Coles, J., and J. Taylor. 1971. "The Wessex Culture: A Minimal View." *Antiquity* 45:6–14.

Collins, H. 1985. *Changing Order: Replication and Induction in Scientific Practice*. London: Sage Press.

Collins, H., and T. Pinch. 1998. *The Golem: What You Should Know About Science.* Cambridge: Cambridge University Press.

Collins, H., and T. Pinch. 2005. *Dr. Golem: How to Think about Medicine*. Chicago: University of Chicago Press.

Colt-Hoare, R. 1810. *The History of Ancient Wiltshire, Vol. 1*. London: William Miller.

———. 1822. *The History of Ancient Wiltshire, Vol. 2*. London: William Miller.

Connell, R. 1984. *Which Way Is Up? Essays on Class, Sex and Culture*. Sydney: Allen and Unwin.

Conneller, C. 2004. "Becoming Deer: Corporeal Transformations at Star Carr." *Archaeological Dialogues* 11(1):37–56.

Cook, J. 1999. *Morality and Cultural Differences*. New York: Oxford University Press.

Corsiglia, J., and Snively, G. 1997. "Knowing Home: Nisga'a Traditional Knowledge and Wisdom Improve Environmental Decision-Making." *Alternatives Journal* 32:22–27.

Cosgrove, D. 1984. *Social Formation and Symbolic Landscape*. London: Croom Helm.

Crawford, O. 1921. *Man and His Past*. Oxford: Oxford University Press.

Damasio, A. 2003. *Looking for Spinoza: Joy, Sorrow and the Feeling Brain*. London: William Heinemann.

Dartigues, A. 2005. "Resurrection of the Dead." In *Encyclopedia of Christian Theology Vol. 3*, edited by Jean-Yves Lacoste, 1381. New York: Routledge.

Darvill, T. 1997. "Ever Increasing Circles: The Sacred Geographies of Stonehenge and Its Landscape." In *Science and Stonehenge*, edited by B. Cunliffe and C. Renfrew, 167–202. Oxford: Oxford University Press.

———. 2006. *Stonehenge: The Biography of a Landscape*. Stroud: Tempus.

Davies, D. 2005. "Rites of Passage." In *Encyclopedia of Cremation*, edited by D. Davies and L. Mates, 359–62. London: Ashgate.

Davies, W. 2005. "Argentina." In *Encyclopedia of Cremation*, edited by D. Davies and L. Mates, 28–33. London: Ashgate.

Deleuze, G., and F. Guattari. 1980. *A Thousand Plateaus: Capitalism and Schizophrenia*. Translated by B. Massumi. Minneapolis: University of Minnesota Press.

Deuel, T. 1952. "The Hopewellian Community." In *Hopewellian Communities in Illinois, Scientific Papers Vol. 5*, edited by T. Deuel. Springfield: Illinois State Museum.

Demarest, A. 2007. "Ethics and Ethnocentricity in Interpretation and Critique: Challenges to the Anthropology of Corporeality and Death." In *The Taking and Displaying of Human Body Parts as Trophies by Amerindians*, edited by R. Chacon and D. Dye, 591–617. New York: Springer.

Descola, P. 1993. *In the Society of Nature*. Cambridge: Cambridge University Press.

Dobres, M., and J. Robb. 2000. "Agency in Archaeology: Paradigm or Platitude?" In *Agency in Archaeology*, edited by M. A. Dobres and J. E. Robb, 3–17. London: Routledge.

Dolwick, J. 2009. "'The Social' and Beyond: Introducing Actor-Network Theory." *Journal of Maritime Archaeology* 4(1):21–49.

Donald, L. 1985. "On the Possibility of Social Class in Societies Based on Extractive Subsistence." In *Status, Structure and Stratification: Current Archaeological Reconstructions*, edited by M. Thompson and F. Garcia, 237–244. Calgary: University of Calgary Archaeological Association.

Dornan, J. 2002. "Agency and Archaeology: Past, Present and Future Directions." *Journal of Archaeological Method and Theory* 9(4):303–29.

———. 2004. "Beyond Belief: Religious Experience, Ritual, and Cultural Neuro-Phenomenology in the Interpretation of Past Religious Systems." *Cambridge Archaeological Journal* 14:25–36.

Durkheim, E. 1972. *Selected Writings*. Translated by A. Giddens. Cambridge: Cambridge University Press.

Dye, D., and A. King. 2007. "Desecrating the Sacred Ancestor Temples: Chiefly Conflict and Violence in the American Southeast." In *North American Indigenous Warfare and Ritual*, edited by R. Chacon and R. Mendoza, 160–81. Tucson: University of Arizona Press.

Eagles, B., and D. Field. 2004. "William Cunnington and the Long Barrows of the River Wylye." In *Monuments and Material Culture*, edited by R. Cleal and J. Pollard, 47–69. Salisbury: Hobnob Press.

Edmonds, M. 1999. *Ancestral Geographies of the Neolithic: Landscape, Monuments and Memory*. London: Routledge.

Eriksen, T. 1992. *Us and Them in Modern Societies: Ethnicity and Nationalism in Trinidad, Mauritius and Beyond*. Oslo: Scandinavian University Press.

Ewick, P., and S. Silbey. 1998. *The Common Place of Law: Stories from Everyday Life*. Chicago: University of Chicago Press.

Festinger, L., H. Riecken, and S. Schachter. 1956. *When Prophecy Fails*. Minneapolis: University of Minnesota Press.

Feuer, L. 1974. *Einstein and the Generations of Science*. New York: Basic Books.

Feyerabend, P. 1975 *Against Method: Outline of an Anarchistic Theory of Knowledge*. London: New Left.

Fleming, A. 2006. "Post-processual Landscape Archaeology: A Critique." *Cambridge Archaeological Journal* 16(3):267–80.

Ford, J. 1954. "On the Concept of Types." *American Anthropologist* 56:42–57.

Foucault, M. 1977. *Discipline and Punish: The Birth of the Prison*. London: Allen Lane.

———. 1980. *Power/Knowledge: Selected Interviews and Other Writings 1972–1977*. London: Harvester.

Franklin, S. 1997. "Dolly: A New Form of Transgenic Breedwealth." *Environmental Values* 6(4):427–37.

Frazier, I. 2000. *On the Rez*. New York: Picador.

Gale, J., I. Hewitt, and M. Russell. 2008. *High Lea Farm, Hinton Martell, Dorset: A Third Interim Report on Fieldwork Undertaken During 2006–7*. Dorchester: The Dorset Natural History and Archaeological Society.

Garwood, P. 2007. "Before the Hills in Order Stood: Chronology, Time and History in the Interpretation of Early Bronze Age Round Barrows." In *Beyond the Grave: New Perspectives on Round Barrows*, edited by Jonathan Last, 30–52. Oxford: Oxbow Books.

Gell, A. 1998. *Art and Agency: An Anthropological Theory*. Oxford: Oxford University Press.

Gellner, E. 1985. *Relativism and the Social Sciences*. Cambridge: Cambridge University Press.

Gerloff, S. 1975. *The Early Bronze Age Daggers in Great Britain, and a Reconsideration of the Wessex Culture*. Prahistorische Bronzefunde 1(2), Munich: C. H. Beck.

Gero, J. 2000. "Troubled Travels in Agency and Feminism." In *Agency and Archaeology*, edited by M. Dobres and J. Robb, 34–9. London: Routledge.

Gero, J. M., and M. Conkey, eds. 1991. *Engendering Archaeology: Women and Prehistory*. New York: Basil Blackwell.

Giddens, A. 1984. *The Constitution of Society: Outline of the Theory of Structuration*. Cambridge: Polity.

———. 2006. *Sociology*, 5th ed. Cambridge: Polity.

Gilchrist, R. 1994. *Gender and Material Culture: The Archaeology of Religious Women*. London: Routledge.

Gillings, M., and J. Pollard. 1999. "Non-portable Stone Artefacts and Contexts of Meaning: The Tale of Grey Whether." *World Archaeology* 31(2):179–93.

Gingell, C. 1992. *The Marlborough Downs: A Later Bronze Age Landscape and Its Origins*. Devizes: Wiltshire Archaeological and Natural History Society.

Glass, P. 1988. "Trobriand Symbolic Geography." *Man* 23(1):56–76.

Goldacre, B. 2008. *Bad Science*. London: HarperCollins.

Goldstein, L. 1981. "One-Dimensional Archaeology and Multi-Dimensional People: Spatial Organization and Mortuary Analysis." In *The Archaeology of Death*, edited by R. Chapman, I. Kinnes, and K. Randsborg, 53–70. Cambridge: Cambridge University Press.

Golinski, J. 1998. *Making Natural Knowledge: Constructivism and the History of Science*. Cambridge: Cambridge University Press.

Gosden, C. 1994. *Social Being and Time*. Oxford: Blackwell.

Gosden, C., and Y. Marshall. 1999. "The Cultural Biography of Objects." *World Archaeology* 31:169–178.

Gough, A., and N. Gough. 2003. "Decolonising Environmental Education Research: Stories of Queer(y)ing and Destabilizing." Paper presented at the University of Bath, UK. Accessed November 01, 2012.

Gracely, R., R. Dubner, W. Deeter, and P. Wolskee. 1985. "Clinicians' Expectations Influence Placebo Analgesia." *The Lancet* 335:43.

Green, C., and S. Rollo-Smith. 1984. "The Excavation of Eighteen Round Barrows Near Shrewton, Wiltshire." *Proceedings of the Prehistoric Society* 50:255–318.

Grinsell, L. 1957. "Archaeological Gazetteer." *VCH Wiltshire* I(i). London: Oxford University Press.

Gross, P., and N. Levitt. 1994. *Higher Superstition: The Academic Left and Its Quarrels with Science*. Baltimore: Johns Hopkins University Press.

Haber, A. 2009. "Animism, Relatedness, Life: Post-Western Perspectives." *Cambridge Archaeological Journal* 19(3):418–30.

Hacking, L. 1983. *Representing and Intervening: Introductory Topics in the Philosophy of Natural Science*. Cambridge: Cambridge University Press.

Hahn, R., and A. Kleinman. 1983. "Belief as Pathogen, Belief as Medicine: 'Voodoo Death' and the 'Placebo Phenomenon' in Anthropological Perspective." *Medical Anthropology Quarterly* 4:16–19.

Hall, R. 1997. *The Archaeology of the Soul*. Chicago: University of Illinois Press.

Haraway, D. 1985. "A Cyborg Manifesto: Science, Technology, and Socialist-Feminism in the Late Twentieth Century." *Socialist Review* 80:65–108.

———. 1997. *Modest-Witness@Second-Millennium: FemaleMan -Meets- OncoMouse*. New York: Routledge.

Harding, J. 2003. *Henge Monuments of the British Isles*. Stroud: Tempus.

———. 2010. "Henges and Ceremonialism in Late Third Millennium Wessex." Paper presented at the annual conference for the British Prehistoric Society, *Wessex Culture "Revolution" or Late Beaker "Evolution"? Defining Changes in the Early 2nd Millennium BC*, Bournemouth, UK, April 16–18.

Harman, G. 2009. *Prince of Networks: Bruno Latour and Metaphysics*. Melbourne: Re.press.

Harrington, A. 1999. "Introduction." In *The Placebo Effect: An Interdisciplinary Approach*, edited by A. Harrington, 1–11. Cambridge: Harvard University Press.

Healy, F., and J. Harding. 2007. "A Thousand and One Things to Do with a Round Barrow." In *Beyond the Grave: New Perspectives on Barrows*, edited by J. Last, 53–72. Oxford: Oxbow Books.

Hebdige, D. 1979. *Subculture: The Meaning of Style*. London: Methuen.

Heckenberger, M. 2005. *The Ecology of Power: Culture, Place, and Personhood in the Southern Amazon, A.D. 1000–2000*. London, Routledge.

Heidegger, M. 1927. *Being and Time*, 1962 edition. Oxford: Blackwell.

Hill, J., and R. Evans. 1972. "A Model for Classification and Typology." In *Models in Archaeology*, edited by D. Clarke, 231–71. London: Methuen.

Hill, T., and R. Hill. 1994. "Across the Generations." In *Creation's Journey: Native American Identity and Belief*, edited by T. Hill and R. Hill, 175–77. Washington: Smithsonian Institution.

Hodder, I. 1982. *Symbols in Action: Ethnoarchaeological Studies of Material Culture*. Cambridge: Cambridge University Press.

———. 1986. *Reading the Past: Current Approaches to Interpretation in Archaeology*, 1st ed. Cambridge: Cambridge University Press.

———. 1991. *Reading the Past: Current Approaches to Interpretation in Archaeology*, 2nd ed. Cambridge: Cambridge University Press.

———. 1994. "Architecture and Meaning: The Example of Neolithic Houses and Tombs." In *Architecture and Order: Approaches to Social Space*, edited by M. Parker-Pearson and C. Richards, 73–86. London: Routledge.

———. 2012. *Entangled: An Archaeology of the Relationships between Humans and Things*. Oxford: Wiley-Blackwell.

Holbraad, M. 2009. "Ontology, Ethnography, Archaeology: An Afterword on the Ontography of Things." *Cambridge Archaeological Journal* 19(3):431–41.

Horning, A. 2004. *Cultural Overview of City Point, Petersburg National Battlefield, Hopewell, Virginia*. Report for the National Park Service, Petersburg National Battlefield. Williamsburg: Colonial Williamsburg Foundation.

Horton, R. 1967. "African Traditional Thought and Western Science." *Africa* 37:50–71, 155–87.

Hoyrup, J. 2008. "Geometry in the Near and Middle East." In *Encyclopaedia of the History of Science, Technology, and Medicine in Non-Western Cultures*, edited by H. Selin, 845–50. Dordrecht, The Netherlands: Kluwer Academic Publishers.

Hunter, P. 1980. "The National System of Scientific Measurement." *Science* 210:869–74.

Husserl, E. (1931) 1960. *Cartesian Meditations*. Translated by D. Cairns. Dordrecht: Kluwer.

Inglis, D., and J. Bone. 2006. "Boundary Maintenance, Border Crossing and the Nature/Culture Divide." *European Journal of Social Theory* 9(2):272–87.

Ingold, T. 1998. "Totemism, Animism, and the Depiction of Animals." In *Animal, Anima, Animus*, edited by M. Seppala, J. Vanhala, and L. Weintraub, 181–207. Pori: Frame/Pori Art Museum.

Jackson, J., and D. Thomas. 2008. "The End/s of Anthropology: Meeting-Theme." Accessed January 5, 2009. http://www.aaanet.org/meetings/presenters/Meeting-Theme.cfm.

Jarvie, I. 1984. *Rationality and Relativism: In Search of a Philosophy and History of Anthropology*. London: Routledge and Kegan Paul.

———. 1993. "Relativism Yet Again." *Philosophy of the Social Sciences* 23:537–47.

Johnson, J. [alias Latour, B.] 1988. "Mixing Humans and Nonhumans Together: The Sociology of a Door-closer." *Social Problems* 35:298–310.

Johnson, M. 2011. "On the Nature of Empiricism in Archaeology." *Journal of the Royal Anthropological Institute* 17:764–87.

Johnson, M., ed. 1992. *Lore: Capturing Traditional Environmental Knowledge*. Ottawa, Ontario: Dene Cultural Institute.

Jones, A. 2002. *Archaeological Theory and Scientific Practice*. Cambridge: Cambridge University Press.

———. 2007. *Memory and Material Culture*. Cambridge: Cambridge University Press.

———. 2012. *Prehistoric Materialities: Becoming Material in Prehistoric Britain and Ireland*. Oxford: Oxford University Press.

Jones, A. M. 2011. "Regionality in Prehistory: Some Thoughts from the Periphery." In *Beyond the Core: Reflections on Regionality in Prehistory*, edited by A. M. Jones and G. Kirkham, 1–4. Oxford: Oxbow Books.

Jones, S. 1996. "Discourses of Identity in the Interpretation of the Past." In *Cultural Identity and Archaeology: The Construction of European Communities*, edited by P. Graves-Brown, S. Jones, and C. Gamble. London: Routledge.

———. 1997. *The Archaeology of Ethnicity: Constructing Identities in the Past and Present*. London: Routledge.

Joy, J. 2009. "Reinvigorating Object Biography: Reproducing the Drama of Object Lives." *World Archaeology* 41(4):540–56.

Joyce, A. 2000. "The Founding of Monte Albán: Sacred Propositions and Social Practices." In *Agency in Archaeology*, edited by M. Dobres and J. Robb, 71–91. London: Routledge.

Joyce, R., and C. Claassen. 1997. "Women in the Ancient Americas: Archaeologists, Gender and the Making of Prehistory." In *Women in Prehistory: North America and Mesoamerica*, edited by C. Claasen and R. Joyce, 1–14. Philadelphia: University of Pennsylvania Press.

Jupp, P. 2005a. "Catholic Church." In *Encyclopedia of Cremation*, edited by D. Davies and L. Mates, 113–16. London: Ashgate.

———. 2005b. "Cremation Society of Great Britain." In *Encyclopedia of Cremation*, edited by D. Davies and L. Mates, 135–43. London: Ashgate.

———. 2005c. "Resurrection." In *Encyclopedia of Cremation*, edited by D. Davies and L. Mates, 353–358. London: Ashgate.

Kawagley, A., D. Norris-Tull, and R. Norris-Tull. 1998. "The Indigenous Worldview of Yupiaq Culture: Its Scientific Nature and Relevance to the Practice and Teaching of Science." *Journal of Research in Science Teaching* 35:133–44.

Kazmier, L. 2005. "Thompson, Sir Henry." In *Encyclopedia of Cremation*, edited by D. Davies and L. Mates, 398. London: Ashgate.

Keoke, E., and K. Porterfield. 2003. *American Indian Contributions to the World: 15,000 Years of Inventions and Innovations*. New York: Checkmark Books.

Kerber, R. 1986. *Political Evolution in the Lower Illinois Valley.* PhD diss., Northwestern University.

Kilpinen, E. 2010. "Problems in Applying Peirce in Social Sciences." In *Ideas in Action: Proceedings of the Applying Peirce Conference,* edited by M. Bergman, S. Paavola, A-V. Pietarinen, and H. Rydenfelt, 86–104. Helsinki: Nordic Pragmatism Network.

Kirk, T. 1993. "Space, Subjectivity, Power and Hegemony: Megaliths and Long Mounds in Early Neolithic Brittany." In *Interpretative Archaeology,* edited by C. Tilley, 181–223. Oxford: Berg.

Knappett, C. 2005. *Thinking through Material Culture: An Interdisciplinary Perspective.* Philadelphia: University of Pennsylvania Press.

Knappett, C., and L. Malafouris, eds. 2008. *Material Agency: Towards a Non-Anthropocentric Approach.* New York: Springer.

Kopytoff, I. 1986. "The Cultural Biography of Things: Commoditization as Process." In *The Social Life of Things: Commodities in Cultural Perspective,* edited by A. Appadurai, 64–91. Cambridge: Cambridge University Press.

Kossack, G. 1974. "Prunkgraber: Bemerkungen zu Eigenschaften und Aussagewert." In *Studien zur Vor- und Fruhgeschichtlichen Archaologie,* edited by G . Kossack and G. Ulbert, 3–33. Munich: Beck.

Kosso, P. 1991. "Method in Archaeology: Middle-Range Theory as Hermeneutics." *American Antiquity* 56(4):621–27.

Kuhn, T. 1962. *The Structure of Scientific Revolutions.* Chicago: University of Chicago Press.

Kuznar, L. 2008. *Reclaiming a Scientific Anthropology,* 2nd ed. Lanham, MD: AltaMira Press.

Labinger, J., and H. Collins, eds. 2001. *The One Culture? A Conversation about Science.* Chicago: University of Chicago Press.

Lakatos, I. 1970. "Falsification and the Methodology of Scientific Research Programmes." In *Criticism and the Growth of Knowledge,* edited by I. Lakatos and A. Musgrave, 91–195. Cambridge: Cambridge University Press.

Lancaster, C. 1974. "Ethnic Identity, History and 'Tribe' in the Middle Zambezi Valley." *American Ethnologist* 1(4):707–30.

Lancaster, I. 1996. "Phrasal Repetends in Literary Stylistics: Shakespeare's Hamlet III.1." In *Research in Humanities Computing 4: Selected Papers from the 1992 ALLC-ACH Conference,* edited by S. Hockey and N. Ide, 34–68. Oxford: Oxford University Press.

Last, J. 1998. "Books of Life: Biography and Memory in a Bronze Age Barrow." *Oxford Journal of Archaeology* 17(1):43–53.

———. 2007. "Covering Old Ground: Barrows as Closures." In *Beyond the Grave: New Perspectives on Barrows,* edited by J. Last, 156–75. Oxford: Oxbow Books.

Latour, B. 1987. *Science in Action.* Cambridge, MA: Harvard University Press.

———. 1992. "Where Are the Missing Masses? Sociology of a Few Mundane Artefacts." In *Shaping Technology, Building Society: Studies in Sociotechnical Change,* edited by W. Bijker and J. Law, 225–58. Cambridge, MA: MIT Press.

———. 1993. *We Have Never Been Modern.* Cambridge, MA: Harvard University Press.

———. 1996. "On Actor-Network Theory—A Few Clarifications." *Soziale Welt* 47(4):367–81.

———. 1998a. "How to Be Iconophilic in Art, Science and Religion?" In *Picturing Science—Producing Art,* edited by C. Jones and P. Galison, 418–40. London: Routledge.

———. 1998b. "On Recalling ANT." *The Sociological Review* 46(5):15–25.

———. 1999. *Pandora's Hope: Essays on the Reality of Science Studies.* Cambridge, MA: Harvard University Press.

———. 2001a. "Progress or Entanglement? Two Models for the Long Term Evolution of Human Civilization." In *Challenges of Civilization in the 21st Century,* edited by H. Tien and C. Lo, 311–34. Taiwan: Institute for National Policy Research.

———. 2001b. "'Thou Shalt Not Take the Lord's Name in Vain'—Being a Sort of Sermon on the Hesitations of Religious Speech." *Res* 39:215–34.

———. 2002a. "Gabriel Tarde and the End of the Social." In *The Social in Question: New Bearings in History and the Social Sciences*, edited by P. Joyce, 117–32. London: Routledge.

———. 2002b. "Iconoclash? Or Is There a World Beyond the Image Wars?" In *Iconoclash: Beyond the Image Wars in Science, Religion and Art*, edited by B. Latour and P. Weibel, 16–38. Boston: MIT Press.

———. 2004a. "Whose Cosmos, Which Cosmopolitics? Comments on the Peace Terms of Ulrich Beck." *Common Knowledge* 10:450–62.

———. 2004b. "Why Has Critique Run Out of Stream? From Matters of Fact to Matters of Concern." *Critical Inquiry* 30(2):225–48.

———. 2004c. *Politics of Nature: How to Bring the Sciences into Democracy.* Cambridge: Harvard University Press.

———. 2005. *Re-assembling the Social: An Introduction to Actor Network Theory.* Oxford: Oxford University Press.

———. 2007. "The Recall of Modernity: Anthropological Approaches." *Cultural Studies Review* 13(1):11–30.

———. 2009a. *The Making of Law: An Ethnography of the Conseil D'Etat*, Oxford: Oxford University Press.

———. 2009b. "Perspectivism: 'Type' or 'Bomb'?" *Anthropology Today* 25(2):1–2.

Latour, B., and S. Woolgar. 1979. *Laboratory Life: The Social Construction of Scientific Facts.* Los Angeles: Sage Publications.

———. 1986. *Laboratory Life: The Construction of Scientific Facts*, 2nd ed. Princeton: Princeton University Press.

Latour, B., G. Harman, and P. Erdelyi. 2011. *The Prince and the Wolf: Latour and Harman at the LSE.* Alresford: Zero Books.

Latour, B., and P. Weibel. 2002. *Iconoclash.* Cambridge, MA: MIT Press.

Latour, B., and A. Yaneva. 2008. "Give Me a Gun and I Will Make All Buildings Move: An ANT's View of Architecture." In *Explorations in Architecture: Teaching, Design, Research*, edited by R. Geiser, 80–89. Basel: Birkhäuser.

Law, J. 2004. *After Method: Mess in Social Science Research.* London: Routledge.

Lawson, A. 2007. *Chalkland: An Archaeology of Stonehenge and Its Region.* Salisbury: Hobnob Press.

Leigh, S., D. Charles, and D. Albertson. 1988. "Middle Woodland Component." In *The Archaic and Woodland Cemeteries at the Elizabeth Site in the Lower Illinois Valley*, edited by D. Charles, S. Leigh, and J. Buikstra, 41–84. Kampsville: Center for American Archaeology.

Leone, M., P. Mullins, M. Creveling, L. Hurst, and B. Jackson-Nash. 1995. "Can an African-American Historical Archaeology Be an Alternative Voice?" In *Interpreting Archaeology: Finding Meaning in the Past*, edited by I. Hodder, M. Shanks, A. Alexandri, V. Buchli, and J. Carman, 110–24. London: Routledge.

Leroi-Gourhan, A. 1964. *Le Geste et la Parole I & II.* Paris: Albin Michel.

Levi-Strauss, C. 1962. *The Savage Mind.* London: Weidenfeld and Nicolson.

Levy, J. 1992. *Orayui Revisited: Social Stratification in an Egalitarian Society.* Santa Fe, NM: School of American Research Press.

Lewis-Williams, J. 2002. *The Mind in the Cave: Consciousness and the Origins of Art.* London: Thames and Hudson.

Li, X. 2006. *Ethics, Human Rights, and Culture: Beyond Relativism and Universalism.* New York: Palgrave Macmillan.

Lillios, K. 2008. "Engaging Memories of European Prehistory." In *European Prehistory*, edited by A. Jones, 228–252. Oxford: Blackwell.

Little Bear, L. 2000. "Foreword." In *Native Science: Natural Laws of Interdependance*, by G. Cajete, ix-xii. Santa Fe: Clear Light Publishers.

Longworth, I. 1961. "The Origins and Development of the Primary Series in the Collared Urn Tradition in England and Wales." *Proceedings of the Prehistoric Society* 27:63–306.

Losey, R. 2010. "Animism as a Means of Exploring Archaeological Fishing Structures on Willapa Bay, Washington, USA." *Cambridge Archaeological Journal* 20:17–32.

Love, E. 2005. "Resurrection of the Body." In *Encyclopedia of Cremation*, edited by D. Davies and L. Mates, 358–59. London: Ashgate.

Luntz, F. 2003. "The Environment: Cleaner, Safer, Healthier America." In *Straight Talk*, edited by F. Luntz, 131–45. Washington: The Luntz Research Company.

Mann, R. 2005. "Intruding on the Past: The Reuse of Ancient Earthen Mounds by Native Americans." *Southeastern Archaeology* 24(1):1–10.

Martin, A. 2002. "Rethinking the Illinois Hopewell: A Constructive Comparison with Approaches from British Archaeology and Bruno Latour." PhD diss., University of Cambridge.

———. 2005. "Agents in Inter-Action: Bruno Latour and Agency." *Journal of Archaeological Method and Theory* 12(4):283–311.

———. 2011. "The Alien Within: The Forgotten Subcultures of Early Bronze Age Wessex." In *Beyond the Core: Reflections on Regionality in Prehistory*, edited by A. Jones and G. Kirkham, 63–73. Oxford: Oxbow Books.

Mates, L. 2005. "Politics." In *Encyclopedia of Cremation*, edited by D. Davies and L. Mates, 338–42. London: Ashgate.

Matthews, K. 1995. "Archaeological Data, Subculture and Social Dynamics." *Antiquity* 69:586–94.

Meillassoux, C. 1972. "From Reproduction to Production: A Marxist Approach to Economic Anthropology." *Economy and Society* 1:93–105.

Meller, H. 2004. "Die Himmelsscheibe Von Nebra." In *Der Geschmiedete Himmel–Die Weite Welt im Herzen Europas Vor 3600 Jahren*, edited by H. Meller, 27–31. Stuttgart: Landesmuseum Fur Vorgeschichte.

Meskell, L. 1999. *Archaeologies of Social Life: Age, Sex, Class, etc. in Ancient Egypt.* Oxford: Blackwell.

Meynen, T. 1992. "The Bringing Forth of Dialogue: Latour versus Maturana." In *New Perspectives on Cybernetics: Self-organisation, Autonomy and Connectionism*, edited by G. van de Vijver, 157–74. Dordrecht: Kluwer.

Milner, G. 1999. "Warfare in Prehistoric and Early Historic Eastern North America." *Journal of Archaeological Research* 7:105–51.

———. 2007. "Warfare, Population, and Food Production in Prehistoric Eastern North America." In *Warfare and Violence among the Indigenous Peoples of North America*, edited by R. Chacon and R. Mendoza, 182–20. Tucson: University of Arizona Press.

Mizoguchi, K. 1995. "Re-aligning Mortuary Archaeology: A Study of British Late Neolithic and Early Bronze Age Mortuary 'Human' Practices." PhD diss., University of Cambridge.

Moerman, D. 1983. "General Medical Effectiveness and Human Biology: Placebo Effects in the Treatment of Ulcer Disease." *Medical Anthropology Quarterly* 14(3):13–16.

Montgomery, S. 2000. *Science in Translation: Movements of Knowledge through Cultures and Time*. Chicago: University of Chicago Press.

Mueller M., E. Bjørkedal, and S. Kamping. 2012. "Manipulation of Expectancy and Anxiety in Placebo Research and Their Effects on Opioid-Induced Analgesia." *The Journal of Neuroscience* 32(41):14051–52.

Needham, R. 1967. "Percussion and Transition." *Man* 2:606–14.

Needham, J., and C. Ronan. 1985. *The Shorter Science and Civilisation in China: An Abridgement of Joseph Needham's Original Text: Vol. 2.* Cambridge: Cambridge University Press.

Needham, S., A. Lawson, and A. Woodward. 2009. "Rethinking Bush Barrow." *British Archaeology* 104(1). Accessed June 1, 2012. http://www.britarch.ac.uk/ba/ba104/feat1.shtml.

Needham, S., and A. Martin. 2010. "Conclusion to Wessex Culture Conference." Paper presented at the annual conference for the British Prehistoric Society, *Wessex Culture "Revolution" or Late Beaker "Evolution"?: Defining Changes in the Early 2nd Millennium BC*, Bournemouth, UK, April 16–18.

Needham, S., M. Parker Pearson, M. Richards, M. Jay, and A. Tyler. 2010. "A First 'Wessex 1' Date From Wessex." *Antiquity* 84:363–73.

Nordmann, A. 2009. "The Hypothesis of Reality and the Reality of Hypotheses." In *The Significance of the Hypothetical in the Natural Sciences*, edited by M. Heidelberger and G. Schiemann, 313–39. Berlin: deGryter.

Normark, J. 2010. "Involutions of Materiality: Operationalizing a Neomaterialist Perspective through the Causeways at Ichmul and Yo'okop." *Journal of Archaeological Method and Theory* 17:132–73.

Novarino, M. 2005. "Freemasonry in Italy." In *Encyclopedia of Cremation*, edited by D. Davies and L. Mates, 207–10. London: Ashgate.

Ochsendorf, J., and D. Billington. 1999. "Self-Anchored Suspension Bridges." *Journal of Bridge Engineering, American Society of Civil Engineers* 4(3):151–56.

Ogawa, M. 1995. "Science Education in a Multiscience Perspective." *Science Education* 79:583–93.

Olsen, B. 2003. "Material Culture after Text: Remembering Things." *Norwegian Archaeological Review* 36(2):87–104.

———. 2010. *In Defense of Things: Archaeology and the Ontology of Objects*. Lanham, MD: AltaMira Press.

Ozanne, P. 1972. "The Excavation of a Round Barrow on Rollestone Down, Winterbourne Stoke, Wiltshire." *Wiltshire Archaeological and Natural History Magazine* 67:43–60.

Parker Pearson, M. 1982. "Mortuary Practices, Society and Ideology: An Ethnoarchaeological Study." In *Symbolic and Structural Archaeology*, edited by I. Hodder, 99–113. Cambridge: Cambridge University Press.

———. 2007. "The Stonehenge Riverside Project: Excavations at the East Entrance of Durrington Walls." In *From Stonehenge to the Baltic: Living with Cultural Diversity in the Third Millennium BC*, edited by M. Larsson and M. Parker-Pearson, 125–44. Oxford: BAR International Reports Series 1692.

Parker Pearson, M., and Ramilisonina. 1998. "Stonehenge for the Ancestors: The Stones Pass on the Message." *Antiquity* 72:308–26.

Peat, D. 2002. *Blackfoot Physics: A Journey into the Native American Universe*. Boston: Wieserbooks.

Pearson, M., and M. Shanks. 2001. *Theatre/Archaeology*. London: Routledge.

Peirce, C. 1934. *The Collected Papers of Charles Sanders Peirce Vol. V: Pragmatism and Pragmaticism*, edited by C. Hartshorne and P. Weiss. Cambridge, MA: Harvard University Press.

———. 1992. "Man's Glassy Essence." In *The Essential Peirce: Selected Philosophical Writings, Volume 1 (1867–1893)*, edited by N. Houser and C. Kloesel, 334–51. Bloomington: Indiana University Press.

———. 1998. "The Three Normative Sciences: Harvard Lecture on Pragmatism 5." In *The Essential Peirce: Selected Philosophical Writings, Volume 2 (1893–1913)*, edited by the Peirce Edition Project, 196–207. Bloomington: Indiana University Press.

Perino, G. 1966. "Excavation Report of the Montezuma Mounds Site in West-central Illinois." Unpublished manuscript on file, Kampsville, Center for American Archaeology.

———. 1968. "The Pete Klunk Mound Group, Calhoun County, Illinois: The Archaic and Hopewell Occupations." In *Hopewell and Woodland Site Archaeology in Illinois*. Illinois Archaeological Survey Bulletin 6, 9–124.

———. 1970. "Excavation Report of the Gibson and Bedford Mounds Site in West-central Illinois." Unpublished manuscript on file, Kampsville, Center for American Archaeology.

———. n.d. "Excavation Report of the L'Orient Mounds Site in West-central Illinois." Unpublished manuscript on file, Kampsville, Center for American Archaeology.

Piaget, J. 1985. *The Equilibration of Cognitive Structures: The Central Problem of Intellectual Development*. Chicago: University of Chicago Press.

Pickering, A. 1995. *The Mangle of Practice: Time, Agency, and Science*. Chicago: University of Chicago Press.

Pierce, M. 2011. "Have Rumours of the 'Death of Theory' Been Exaggerated?" In *The Death of Archaeological Theory?* edited by J. Bintliff and M. Pierce, 80–89. Oxford: Oxbow Books.

Piggott, S. 1938. "The Early Bronze Age of Wessex." *Proceedings of the Prehistoric Society* 4:52–106.

Piggott, S. 1973. "The Wessex Culture of the Early Bronze Age." In *VCH Wiltshire Vol. 2*, 352–75. London: Oxford University Press.

Pollard, J. 2002. "The Nature of Archaeological Deposits and Finds Assemblages." In *Prehistoric Britain: The Ceramic Basis*, edited by A. Woodward and J. Hill, 22–32. Oxford: Oxbow Books.

Popper, K. (1934) 1959. *The Logic of Scientific Discovery*. English translation. London: Hutchinson.

Porr, M., and R. Bell. 2012. "'Rock-art,' 'Animism' and Two-way Thinking: Towards a Complementary Epistemology in the Understanding of Material Culture and 'Rock-art' of Hunting and Gathering People." *Journal of Archaeological Method and Theory* 19(1):161–205.

Preucel, R. 2006. *Archaeological Semiotics*. Malden: Blackwell.

Renfrew, C. 2004. "Towards a Theory of Material Engagement." In *Rethinking Materiality*, edited by E. Demarrais, C. Gosden, and C. Renfrew, 23–32. Cambridge: McDonald Archaeological Institute.

Restivo, S. 2011. "Bruno Latour." In *The Wiley-Blackwell Companion to Major Social Theorists Vol. 2*, edited by G. Ritzer and J. Stepinsky, 520–40. Oxford: Blackwell.

Richards, C. 1991. "Scara Brae: Revisiting a Neolithic Village in Orkney." In *Scottish Archaeology: New Perceptions*, edited by W. Hanson and E. Slater, 24–43. Aberdeen: Aberdeen University Press.

———. 1993. "Monumental Choreography: Architecture and Spatial Representation in Late Neolithic Orkney." In *Interpretative Archaeology*, edited by C. Tilley, 143–80. Oxford: Berg.

Richards, C., and M. Parker Pearson. 1994. *Architecture and Order: Approaches to Social Space*. London: Routledge.

Richards, C., and J. Thomas. 1984. "Ritual Activity and Structured Deposition in Later Neolithic Wessex." In *Neolithic Studies: A Review of Some Current Research*, edited by R. Bradley and J. Gardiner, 189–218. Oxford: BAR British Series 133.

Rouse, J. 2002. *How Scientific Practices Matter: Reclaiming Philosophical Naturalism*. Chicago: University of Chicago Press.

Rudman, J. 2010. "The State of Non-Traditional Authorship Attribution Studies—2010: Some Problems and Solutions." Paper presented at the Digital Humanities meeting, King's College, London. Accessed November 6, 2012. http://dh2010.cch.kcl.ac.uk/academic-programme/abstracts/papers/pdf/ab-596.pdf.

Rudwick, M. 1985. *The Great Devonian Controversy: The Shaping of Scientific Knowledge among Gentlemanly Specialists*. Chicago: University of Chicago Press.

Sahlins, M. 1976. *Culture and Practical Reason*. Chicago: University of Chicago Press.

Sahtouris, E., and J. Lovelock. 2000. *Earthdance: Living Systems in Evolution*. Lincoln, NE: iUniverse.

Salk, J. 1979. "Introduction by Jonas Salk." In *Laboratory Life: The Social Construction of Scientific Facts*, by B. Latour and S. Woolgar, 11–13. London: Sage Publications.

Sanders, D. 1979. "Navajo Indian Medicine and Medicine Men." In *Ways of Health: Holistic Approaches to Ancient and Contemporary Medicine*, edited by D. Sobel. New York: Harcourt Brace Jovanovich.

Saussure, F. 1974. *Course in General Linguistics*. Translated by W. Baskin. London: Fontana/Collins.

Savage, J. 2001. *England's Dreaming: Anarchy, Sex Pistols, Punk Rock, and Beyond*. London: Macmillan.

Schaffer, S. 1991. "The Eighteenth Brumaire of Bruno Latour." *Studies in the History and Philosophy of Science* 22(1):174–92.

Schiffer, M. 1972. "Archaeological Context and Systemic Context." *American Antiquity* 37(2): 156–65.

Schinkel, W. 2007. "Sociological Discourse of the Relational: The Cases of Bourdieu and Latour." *The Sociological Review* 55(4):707–29.

Schutz, A. 1953. "The Problem of Rationality in the Social World." *Economica* 10:130–49.

Secord, J. 1986. *Controversy in Victorian Geology: The Cambrian-Silurian Dispute.* Princeton: Princeton University Press.

Seeman, M. 2007. "Predatory War and Hopewell Trophies." In *The Taking and Displaying of Human Body Parts as Trophies by Amerindians,* edited by R. Chacon and D. Dye, 167–89. New York: Springer Science.

Selin, H. 2008 "Introduction." In *Encyclopaedia of the History of Science, Technology, and Medicine in Non-Western Cultures,* 2nd ed., edited by H. Selin, xv–xx. Dordrecht, The Netherlands: Kluwer Academic Publishers.

Service, E. 1972. *Primitive Social Organization: An Evolutionary Perspective,* 2nd ed. New York: Random House.

Shanks, M., and C. Tilley. 1982. "Ideology, Symbolic Power and Ritual Communication: A Reinterpretation of Neolithic Mortuary Practices." In *Symbolic and Structural Archaeology,* edited by I. Hodder, 129–54. Cambridge: Cambridge University Press.

———. 1987a. *Social Theory and Archaeology.* Cambridge: Polity Press.

———. 1987b. *Reconstructing Archaeology: Theory and Practice.* Cambridge: Cambridge University Press.

Shapin, S. 1998. "Placing the View from Nowhere: Historical and Sociological Problems in the Location of Science." *Transactions of the Institute of British Geographers* 23:5–12.

Shapin, S., and S. Schaffer. 1985. *Leviathan and the Air-pump: Hobbes, Boyle, and the Experimental Life.* Princeton, NJ: Princeton University Press.

Sismondo, S. 2004. *Introduction to Science and Technology Studies.* Oxford: Blackwell.

Smith, A. 2001. "The Limitations of Doxa." *Journal of Social Archaeology* 1(2):155–71.

Snead, J. 2008. "War and Place: Landscapes of Conflict and Destruction in Prehistory." *Journal of Conflict Archaeology* 4:137–57.

Snively, G., and J. Corsiglia. 2000. "Discovering Indigenous Science: Implications for Science Education." *Science Education* 85:6–34.

———. 2005. "Response to Carter's Postmodern, Postcolonial Analysis of Snively and Corsiglia's (2000) Article 'Discovering Science.'" *Science Education* 89:907–12.

Söderberg, J. 2011. "ANT and Hegelian Marxism." *Journal of Peer Production* 0. Accessed September 7, 2012. http://peerproduction.net/issues/issue-0/debate-ant-and-power/ant-hegelian-marxism/.

Sokal, A. 1996. "A Physicist Experiments with Cultural Studies." *Lingua Franca* 6(4):62–64.

———. 1997. "Les mystifications philosophiques du professeur Latour." *Le Monde,* January 31.

Spinuzzi, C. 2008. *Network: Theorizing Knowledge Work in Telecommunications.* Cambridge: Cambridge University Press.

Stafford, B. 1985. "Summary." In *Smiling Dan: Structure and Function at a Middle Woodland Settlement in the Illinois Valley,* edited by B. Stafford and M. Sant, 447–55. Kampsville: Center for American Archaeology.

Star, S. 1995. *Ecologies of Knowledge: Work and Politics in Science and Technology,* SUNY series in Science, Technology and Society. Albany: State University of New York Press.

Star, S., and J. Griesemer. 1989. "Institutional Ecology, 'Translations' and Boundary Objects: Amateurs and Professionals in Berkeley's Museum of Vertebrate Zoology, 1907–39." *Social Studies of Science* 19:387–420.

Stengers, I. 1995. "Le Médecin et Le Charlatan." In *Médecins et Sorciers*, edited by T. Nathan and I. Stengers, 115–61. Paris: Le Plessis-Robinson, Synthélabo.

———. 1996. Cosmopolitiques–Tome 1: La Guerre des Sciences. Paris: La Découverte.

Stone, T. 2003. "Social Identity and Ethnic Interaction in the Western Pueblos of the American Southwest." *The Journal of Archaeological Method and Theory* 10(1):31–67.

Strathern, M. 1992. *Reproducing the Future: Anthropology, Kinship and the New Reproductive Technologies*. Manchester: Manchester University Press.

Strum, S., and B. Latour. 1987. "Redefining the Social Link: From Baboons to Humans." *Social Science Information* 26:783–802.

Tainter, J. 1978. "Mortuary Practices and the Study of Prehistoric Social Systems." In *Advances in Archaeological Method and Theory (Vol. 1)*, edited by M. Schiffer, 105–41. New York: Academic Press.

———. 1980. "Behavior and Status in a Middle Woodland Mortuary Population from the Illinois Valley." *American Antiquity* 45:308–13.

Tarde, G. 1999. *Les Lois Sociales*. Paris: Les empêcheurs de penser en rond / Institut Synthelabo.

Tarlow, S. 1997. "The Dread of Something after Death, Violation and Desecration on the Isle of Man in the Tenth Century." In *Material Harm: Archaeological Studies of War and Violence*, edited by J. Carman, 133–42. Glasgow: Cruithne Press.

Taylor, W. 1948. *A Study of Archaeology*. Memoirs of the American Anthropological Association 69. Menasha, WI: American Anthropological Association.

Thévenot, L., and L. Boltanski. 2006. *On Justification: The Economies of Worth*. Princeton: Princeton University Press.

Thom, A., J. Ker, and T. Burrows. 1988. "The Bush Barrow Gold Lozenge: Is It a Solar and Lunar Calendar for Stonehenge?" *Antiquity* 62:492–502.

Thomas, J. 1991. *Rethinking the Neolithic*. Cambridge: Cambridge University Press.

———. 1996. *Time, Culture and Identity*. London: Routledge.

———. 1999. *Understanding the Neolithic*. London: Routledge.

———. 2004. *Archaeology and Modernity*. London: Routledge.

Thorpe, I., and C. Richards. 1984. "The Decline of Ritual Authority and the Introduction of Beakers into Britain." In *Neolithic Studies*, edited by R. Bradley and J. Gardiner, 61–66. Oxford: British Archaeological Reports 133.

Tilley, C. 1994. *A Phenomenology of Landscape*. Oxford: Berg.

———. 1996. *An Ethnography of the Neolithic*. Cambridge: Cambridge University Press.

———. 1999. *Metaphor and Material Culture*. Oxford: Blackwell.

———. 2004. *The Materiality of Stone: Explorations in Landscape Phenomenology*. Oxford: Berg.

Titiev, M. 1988. *Old Oraibi*. Albuquerque: University of New Mexico Press.

Tringham, R. 1994. "Engendered Places in Prehistory." In *Gender, Place and Culture* 1(2):169–203.

Tuan, Y. 1979. *Landscapes of Fear*. Minneapolis: University of Minnesota Press.

Turnbull, D. 2000a. "Rationality and the Disunity of the Sciences." In *Mathematics across Cultures*, edited by H. Selin, 37–54. Dordrecht, The Netherlands: Kluwer Academic Publishers.

Turnbull, D. 2000b. *Masons, Tricksters, and Cartographers: Comparative Studies in the Sociology of Scientific and Indigenous Knowledge*. Amsterdam: Harwood Academic Publishers.

Turner, N. 1991. "Burning Mountain Sides for Better Crops: Aboriginal Landscape Burning in British Columbia." *Archaeology in Montana* 32:57–74.

Turner, V. 1967. *The Forest of Symbols: Aspects of Ndembu Ritual*. Ithaca, NY: Cornell University Press.

———. 1969. *The Ritual Process: Structure and Anti-Structure*. London: Routledge.

Van Nest, J., D. Charles, J. Buikstra, and D. Asch. 2001. "Sod Blocks in Illinois Hopewell Mounds." *American Antiquity* 66:633–50.

Veblen, T. 1899. *Theory of the Leisure Class: An Economic Study in the Evolution of Institutions*. New York: Macmillan.

Vickers, B. 2011. "Shakespeare and Authorship Studies in the Twenty-First Century." *Shakespeare Quarterly* 62(1):106–42.

Viveiros de Castro, E. 1998. "Cosmological Deixis and the Amerindian Perspectivism." *Journal of the Royal Anthropological Institute* 4(3):469–88.

Voss, B. 2000. "Feminisms, Queer Theories, and the Archaeological Study of Past Sexualities." *World Archaeology* 32(2):180–92.

———. 2008. *The Archaeology of Ethnogenesis: Race and Sexuality in Colonial San Francisco.* Berkeley: University of California Press.

Watson-Verran, H., and D. Turnbull. 2005. "Science and Other Indigenous Knowledge Systems." In *Knowledge: Critical Concepts,* edited by N. Stehr and R. Grundmann, 345–69. London: Routledge.

Weatherford, J. 1988. *Indian Givers: How the Indians of the Americas Transformed the World.* New York: Crown Publishers.

———. 1991. *Native Roots: How the Indians Enriched America.* New York: Crown Publishers.

Webmoor, T. 2007. "What About 'One More Turn after the Social' in Archaeological Reasoning? Taking Things Seriously." *World Archaeology* 39(4):547–62.

White, S. 2005a. "Price, Dr. William." In *Encyclopedia of Cremation,* edited by D. Davies and L. Mates, 349–51. London: Ashgate.

———. 2005b. "Stephen, James Fitzjames." In *Encyclopedia of Cremation,* edited by D. Davies and L. Mates, 387–89. London: Ashgate.

———. 2005c. "The Ashes." In *Encyclopedia of Cremation,* edited by D. Davies and L. Mates, 397–98. London: Ashgate.

Whiteley, P. 1988. *Deliberate Acts: Changing Hopi Culture through the Oraibi Split.* Tucson: University of Arizona Press.

Whitley, J. 2002. "Too Many Ancestors." *Antiquity* 76:119–26.

Whittle, A. 2003. *The Archaeology of People: Dimensions of Neolithic Life.* London: Routledge.

Whittle, A., and M. Wysocki. 1998. "Parc le Breos Cwm Transepted Long Cairn, Gower, West Glamorgan: Date, Contents and Context." *Proceedings of the Prehistoric Society* 64:177.

Wiessner, P. 1990. "Is There a Unity to Style?" In *The Uses of Style in Archaeology,* edited by M. Conkey and C. Hastorf, 105–12. Cambridge: Cambridge University Press.

Williams, H. 1904. *A History of Science Vol. 1: The Beginnings of Science.* London: Harper and Brothers.

Williams, N., and G. Baines, eds. 1993. *Traditional Ecological Knowledge: Wisdom for Sustainable Development.* Canberra: Center for Resource and Environmental Studies, Australian National University.

Winner, L. 1993. "Upon Opening the Black Box and Finding It Empty: Social Constructivism and the Philosophy of Technology." *Science, Technology, & Human Values* 18(3):362–78.

Witmore, C. 2004. "On Multiple Fields. Between the Material World and Media: Two Cases from the Peloponnesus, Greece." *Archaeological Dialogues* 11(2):133–64.

———. 2006. "Archaeology and Modernity or Archaeology and a Modernist Amnesia?" *Norwegian Archaeological Review* 39(1):49–52.

Woodward, A. 2000. *British Barrows: A Matter of Life and Death.* Stroud: Tempus.

———. 2002. "Beads and Beakers: Heirlooms and Relics in the British Early Bronze Age." *Antiquity* 76:1040–47.

Woodward, A., and P. Woodward. 1996. "The Topography of Some Barrow Cemeteries in Bronze Age Wessex." *Proceedings of the Prehistoric Society* 62:275–92.

Wylie, A. 1985. "The Reaction against Analogy." In *Advances in Archaeological Method and Theory,* edited by M. Schiffer, 63–111. New York: Academic Press.

———. 2002. *Thinking from Things: Essays in the Philosophy of Archaeology.* Berkeley: University of California Press.

Index

About the Author

Andrew M. Martin is an independent scholar in Boston. He completed his doctoral and postdoctoral research at Cambridge University. Martin was also a research fellow at Bournemouth University and has lectured at several universities in the UK. He directed a major project to document and digitize the Neolithic and Bronze Age collections at the Wiltshire Museum and has been the principal investigator for the Wessex Barrow Project.